God's Country, Uncle Sam's Land

God's Country, Uncle Sam's Land

FAITH AND CONFLICT IN THE AMERICAN WEST

Todd M. Kerstetter

UNIVERSITY OF ILLINOIS PRESS

URBANA AND CHICAGO

Library of Congress Cataloging-in-Publication Data

Kerstetter, Todd M., 1963–
God's country, Uncle Sam's land : faith and conflict in
the American West / Todd M. Kerstetter.
p.   cm.
Includes bibliographical references (p.   ) and index.
ISBN-13: 978-0-252-03038-3 (alk. paper)
ISBN-10: 0-252-03038-9 (alk. paper)
1. West (U.S.)—Church history. 2. West (U.S.)—Religion. 3. West
(U.S.)—History. 4. Mormon Church—Utah—History. 5. Teton
Indians—South Dakota—Religion. 6. Branch Davidians. I. Title.
BR545.K47   2006
277.8'08—dc22   2005017270

★

CONTENTS

★

ACKNOWLEDGMENTS

MANY PEOPLE DESERVE THANKS for supporting this project's completion. The staff at the University of Nebraska's Love Library provided considerable help, as did staff at the Nebraska State Historical Society, the Utah State Historical Society, the Historical Department of the Church of Jesus Christ of Latter-day Saints, the Center for Western History at Augustana College, the Mary Coutts Burnett Library at Texas Christian University, and the Beinecke Rare Book and Manuscript Library at Yale University.

Several history department faculties kept me going through the long production and revision process. Thanks to my colleagues at the University of Nebraska at Kearney and at TCU. Thanks to my mentors at the University of Nebraska at Lincoln, especially those who served on my dissertation committee: Parks Coble, Dane Kennedy, Ken Winkle, and the lone geographer in the group, David Wishart. I owe special thanks to John Wunder, who directed my graduate studies and taught me more than I can acknowledge about teaching, history, and being a kind and decent human.

One of my greatest joys came from studying the Lakota language with Jim Gibson and the now late Anne Keller. Some fruits of their labors can be seen in chapter 3. I wish I had worked a little faster on this so Anne might have seen it. Toksa akhe, Unci.

Some of this research has been published in *American Journalism* and the *Western Historical Quarterly*. I am grateful for the interest and support of those journals and am particularly indebted to their editorial personnel for helping me improve my writing. Several anonymous readers at each provided helpful critiques, which have helped this work, too.

Elizabeth Dulany has my gratitude for enthusiastically supporting this project and for the wisdom of sending the manuscript to Jan Shipps and Ferenc Szasz for evaluation. This work could not have had two better minds applied to it, and I am grateful for their input, which improved the manuscript significantly. Margaret Connell Szasz put some tough questions to me that helped me sharpen my approach. Bruce Bethell did an excellent job editing the copy and improving my writing.

Finally, I appreciate the moral, financial, and other support given by my brother and sister-in-law, Chad and Patsy Kerstetter, by my parents, Ned and Joyce Kerstetter, and by Holly McFarland. To all of you, many thanks. I couldn't have done it without you.

❖ ❖ ❖

Portions of this book have appeared previously, in somewhat different form, in the following:

Todd M. Kerstetter, "'Mobocratic Feeling': Religious Outsiders, the Popular Press, and the American West," *American Journalism* 20 (Winter 2003): 57–72.

Todd M. Kerstetter, "Spin Doctors at Santee: What the Dakota Press Said—and Didn't Say—about the Ghost Dance and Wounded Knee," *Western Historical Quarterly* 28 (Spring 1997): 45–67. Copyright by the Western History Association. Reprinted by permission.

Todd M. Kerstetter, "'That's Just the American Way': The Branch Davidian Tragedy and the American West," *Western Historical Quarterly* 35 (Winter 2004): 453–71. Copyright by the Western History Association. Reprinted by permission.

★

Introduction: Guns, God, and Government in the West

We mind our own business and would to God that the world would mind theirs and let us alone.

—Brigham Young, June 29, 1857

The dance was our religion, but the government sent soldiers to kill us on account of it.

—Anonymous Lakota, early 1891

Then you don't understand my doctrine. You don't want to hear the word of my God.

—David Koresh, March 2, 1993

THREE POWERFUL FORCES in American history—liberty, faith, and the West's mythology—have intersected with unique results in the American West. Writers have covered each force extensively, but the three together have been explored lightly at best. Historians have overlooked faith in particular. When first considering this triad, most Americans probably envision stereotypes of each: the West as a place nurturing liberty and rugged individuality; religion as a keystone of society and one of the prized freedoms or unfettered pursuits guaranteed by the U.S. Constitution; and the federal government as guarantor of the free exercise of religion and, in this case, a key developer of the West. In fact, widely diverse religious groups have found homes in the West, and the elements of the triad typically enjoy a neat symbiosis or peaceful coexistence. Three episodes, however, constitute glaring and tragic exceptions. A reporter characterized one case as a collision of guns, God, and government, a shorthand description that fits all three. Beyond that, each group in some way understood the West to be God's country. Nonetheless, as part of the United States, it was also Uncle Sam's land. The difference between those ideas' meanings points to a cultural battleground in the West.

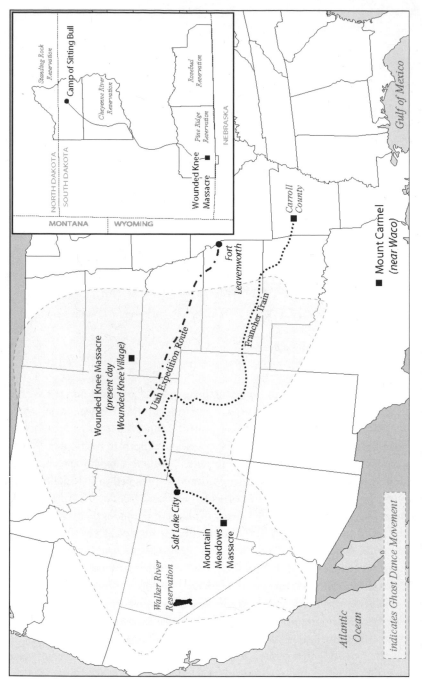

Map showing locations of principal events discussed in this book

At certain points from 1857 to 1993, each of three religious groups—Mormons in Utah, Lakota Ghost Dancers in South Dakota, and Branch Davidians in Texas—strained the national fabric. They confronted bedrock issues such as family, property, and prophecy and challenged existing religious and cultural practices so substantially that mainstream America demanded action. In all three cases the federal government responded, twice with the U.S. Army and once with heavily armed agents. U.S. soldiers occupied Utah Territory and enforced martial law. U.S. soldiers in South Dakota shot hundreds of fleeing religious refugees, including unarmed women and children. Federal agents besieged a Texas religious commune, destroying its compound and nearly obliterating its membership in a mysterious conflagration. These events raise important questions about U.S. history. How open and tolerant is the American West? How freely has religion been practiced? What role did the federal government play in establishing social and cultural norms? What role did religion play in shaping the West? What happens when a group deviates too far from mainstream values? This book addresses those questions through three stories in which the promise of the West was broken.

The American West holds an esteemed place in U.S. history, and many have argued that it played an important role in creating an identity for the nation and its people. In his paper "The Significance of the Frontier in American History," Frederick Jackson Turner made the quintessential argument for the frontier, continually receding westward until 1890, as shaping a unique American character and experience.[1] Although Turner's frontier should not be confused with the West, the two are closely linked, and many frontier characteristics have been associated with the West. In the century since Turner's essay appeared, scholars have continued to study the West, its mythology, and its impact on the nation. Henry Nash Smith argues that the West has been a "formative influence on the American mind." Exploring this influence by studying representations of the West in popular culture, he finds a notion of American empire based on a populous society inhabiting North America's interior.[2] Following a similar approach, the historian Robert V. Hine claims that the West has provided the United States with a "national epic." "Like a mother," the federal government created the West. After the West survived its birth and adolescence, "the nation turned to its matured offspring for the symbols that would hold its other parts together." Those symbols included heroes—such as Leatherstocking, Buffalo Bill, Calamity Jane, Deadwood-Dick, and Joaquin Murieta—who realized difficult goals while basking in moral righteousness. These heroes faced an era of open options with a clear sense of right and wrong and a deep trust in their individual "inner truth and certitude."[3] This raises a

significant question: what happens when an individual or group deeply trust-
ing its inner truth and certitude encounters another individual or group with
an equally deep trust in a conflicting inner truth?

One way to approach that problem would be to characterize those who
follow a religiously based truth using Edwin Scott Gaustad's term: *dissenters.*
Gaustad calls religious dissent a "manifestation of the unfettered human
spirit." He describes religious dissenters as "autonomous," "inner-directed"
people "displaying all of the pompous arrogance or heroic sacrifice of which
a free spirit is capable." Aside from pompous arrogance, these often-admired
characteristics could be ascribed to classic heroes of the West; such dissenters
could exert positive forces for change. Of course, they could also threaten civilization, but in analyzing U.S. western expansion, Gaustad sounds positively
Turnerian. He discusses "tension between barbarism and culture, between
nature and civilization," along the advancing nineteenth-century frontier.
That frontier tension, he argues, gave western settlers independence, hardi-
hood, self-reliance, and individualism and shaped religion as well as people.
At the same time, the frontier could be considered synonymous with Satan's
dominion. Frontier innovation worried the eastern religious establishment,
which sought to impose control. Dissenters, notably the kind who threatened
civilization, could present real problems in the West, the land of opportunity,
the contested borderland between civilization and Satan's dominion.[4]

Enter the federal government. The western historians Patricia Limerick
and Richard White portray the federal government as a crucial sponsor of
western development and a subsidizer of the myth. The U.S. government ac-
quired the West, explored it, surveyed it, and distributed parts to individual
owners. It administered territories and held other parts in trust for the nation. It regulated how federally held land could be used by private interests
such as miners and ranchers. It subsidized the establishment of transporta-
tion networks and reclamation projects to make private and corporate farming and grazing feasible on an otherwise inhospitable terrain.[5] These examples provide just a sample of federal influence in the West.

Donald Worster, too, eloquently tackles this theme and its implications
for the western myth in *Rivers of Empire.* While allowing that parts of the West
live up to its myth, Worster categorizes most of the West as "a land of authority and restraint, of class and exploitation, and ultimately of imperial
power." The individual could do only so much to tame the West and make it
a productive contributor to the nation. The arid climate demanded irrigation
projects beyond the financial and technological capabilities of individuals.
When frustrated residents cried out for help subduing the land, federal au-

thorities answered their pleas with massive reclamation projects designed by government bureaucracies and funded by government coffers. The reclamation projects then spawned new state bureaucracies to maintain them and to provide ongoing state management of the western environment. The state became an agency of conquest and, in partnership with private capitalists, created a "hydraulic society" that demanded order and regimentation on the part of the masses to make the investment pay off, to make the arid West bloom and prosper.[6]

Other historians—Gerald Nash, for instance—have pointed to the way federal policy transformed the West socially, culturally, and economically in the twentieth century. Prior to World War II the West sleepily served its role as a material-rich colony of the East. By the war's end, however, a massive infusion of federal funds into the region's defense industries created a diversified economic juggernaut that brought job-seeking immigrants, energized the West's people, and made the region the nation's economic pacesetter, a role it still retains. Despite the federal government's role in building the West and the region's dependence on federal largesse, western individuals and state governments have continually snapped at the hand that fed them. They complain about federal regulatory meddling and demand that the government get off their backs. Like junkies, however, they bridle at the thought of losing their fix from the federal pocketbook.[7] Historians, then, have covered the government's political, economic, social, and to an extent cultural role in creating the West in its own republican image, but they have largely neglected the religious implications of this creative effort.

Even as the U.S. government influenced the West, the West was influencing the U.S. government, too. Promoting and administering the region turned it into a boot camp (or kindergarten, as White puts it) where the government learned administrative lessons for the growth of the federal bureaucracy. As a developing region added to an existing state, the West lacked infrastructure. The federal government provided a civil service, an army, and economic regulation. Administering the West boosted the development of the Bureau of Indian Affairs, the Land Office, and the U.S. Geological Survey, to name a few, which became essentially western bureaucracies. Because state and local institutions were new and relatively weak, the federal agencies thrived and assumed more power and influence than they had in other regions. In response to demands for its services, the government expanded and learned about bureaucratic administration as it went. As White writes, "Anglo Americans thought of the federal government as a necessary agency of order in the West that did not seem necessary in the East."[8] Acting in this capacity was not a strictly secular task. Bureaucratic machinery established an order freighted with mainstream social and cultural values, including those rooted in faith.

This leads to the historian William Deverell's suggestion that the West provides a prism for studying power throughout American history.[9] Western history narratives portray the region as a crucible in which the nation forged its identity. Some of the West's (Deverell might prefer "Wests'") stories tell of "people get[ting] squashed by the weight of a capitalist nation-state . . . as land- and gold-hungry Anglo Americans become the shock troops of a nation flexing its imperial muscle."[10] In this sense, the West can become a laboratory for studying the federal government's sponsorship of values. Deverell points to governmental promotion of industrial capitalism, including the "quieting and tamping—hushing and crushing—of conflict."[11] One could add to that list the federal government's sponsorship of cultural values, including religious ones.

The West, sparsely settled by westward-reaching U.S. citizens, lacked many of the social and legal controls available in areas of the country whose settlement histories stretched further back, such as the East. According to the myth, westward-moving settlers would spread values and controls of the dominant U.S. culture with them. In an eighteenth-century poem Timothy Dwight recorded his version of this American dream:

> All hail, though western world! by heaven design'd
> Th' example bright, to renovate mankind
> Soon shall thy sons across the mainland roam;
> And claim, on far Pacific shores, their home;
> Their rule, religion, manners, arts, convey,
> And spread their freedom to the Asian sea.[12]

This early, confident expression of manifest destiny shows the expectation that with divine guidance and inspiration, the United States would spread its brand of civilization—including the power of law over the individual; property rights; and the establishment of formal, institutional religion as opposed to natural intuitive theology—across North America.[13] Nevertheless, despite the myth's promise of individual opportunity and freedom, the West would not welcome all.

Spreading these values would take time, and until mature society took hold in the West, "civilization's" gradual advance left local authorities looking for help from the federal government. This came in forms ranging from economic-development assistance to military aid from the U.S. Army. Thomas Hart Benton, for one, called for the federal government to build a road across the continent to facilitate travel, commerce, and control. The road to the Pacific could speed delivery of troops to the West and would promote political unity by connecting the East with the West. Commerce, of course, would also play an important role in that linkage.[14]

The military, too, would help spread and enforce the nation's values. In 1871, for example, Secretary of War William Belknap reported to President Ulysses S. Grant that in the previous year the army had received 100 requests for troops from civil authorities. The army responded to requests ranging from arresting fugitive Canadian bandits and controlling striking coal miners in Wyoming to dealing with recalcitrant Mormon leaders in Utah. The U.S. Army of the nineteenth-century played a little-known role regularly reinforcing frontier law-enforcement officials. The frequency of that role diminished markedly after 1896, by which time local and federal law-enforcement organizations had spread throughout the West.[15]

One might also argue that the West reflected an image of a mature United States because much of it was settled by Americans and assimilated into the nation after the Civil War, which resolved a long-standing identity crisis. It might be said that the nation had a different, clearer image of itself after the Civil War, and this mature nation created western states in its own image and made them part of the whole. David M. Emmons argues along this line when he says that the federal government constructed the West much as it reconstructed the South. Emmons posits that it took many generations to conquer the region, a process that still continues. He calls the federal government the "prime contractor" in this construction, for it sent social engineers and agent contractors to shape the land and its people. In a claim more pertinent to my work, he argues that the government subjected "dissenting forces" to its "reconstructive powers." These powers sprang from the same "culturally imperialistic energies that both helped bring on and were strengthened by the Civil War." As early as 1850 the future president James Buchanan pondered the effects such forces might have on the nation and wrote, "God forbid that fanaticism should ever apply a torch to this, the grandest and most glorious temple which has ever been erected to political freedom on the face of the earth."[16]

During the 1850s the pace of changes wrought by the government quickened. In addition, these developments began reflecting aspirations of the newly formed Republican Party, notably its free-labor ideology. Western lands and their resources had to be accessible to all. To ensure this, the government employed agents of conquest, including the U.S. Army and national corporations such as railroads. These organizations brought a fierce and fast conquest accompanied by a "more hierarchical, less anarchic" social structure than existed in the East and "left little to the spontaneity of individual settlers." During this time "industrial capitalism and a unified national state" not only worked big changes on American society but actually built a West with a unique character (as they continue to do).[17]

As it built this West, the nation created a set of myths to justify its work. Often the myths played an important role in creating the region's—and nation's—identity. The mythic West is an agrarian paradise dominated by simplicity, virtue, and happiness that supposedly reflects, as Walt Whitman wrote, "the real genuine America." As Emmons put it, this mythic West is a land settled by "Protestant, hard-working, independent people, aware of their historical mission to combat savagery and replace it with their own brand of civilization." Related myths paint the West as a land of escape, a "guarantor of national moral and economic health," and as a God-given land of second chances.[18] The West emerged as an Edenic garden to be cultivated so that it would produce a recognizable fruit: American civilization.

The myth not only swayed elites and academicians but found wide currency in popular culture. Entertainers such as Buffalo Bill Cody and Captain Jack Crawford promoted the myth in their shows. Across the nation and in Europe, Crawford used his poetry, plays, and lectures to define the West as a land of freedom, plenty, and rugged self-reliance. Adults also encountered the myth in everyday media, such as church sermons, dime novels, newspaper and magazine editorials, and other popular literature. The mythic West even appeared in children's schoolbooks.[19]

The power elite and print media counted on reinforcement from Protestant zealots in establishing a dominant Protestant culture in the United States during the first half of the nineteenth century. Martin E. Marty argues convincingly that Protestants dominated early America and "set the terms for the religious dimensions of empire." The creation of the United States and its acquisition of western territories coincided with a revolution in Protestantism's attitude toward a worldwide mission. The West needed to be not just conquered but also converted. Westerners were to become Americans as well as Protestants, or at least Christians. State and religion reinforced each other, one providing the machinery for expansion and the other providing justification and national unity of purpose. Evangelical Christianity and democratic republican political institutions joined forces for the good of humankind, the nation, and the Kingdom of God.[20]

More important, the state bought into the myth of the West and promoted it as a national ideology with strong Protestant overtones. Nineteenth-century schoolbooks, publications used by the state's educational arm to promote standards of behavior and belief, presented the frontier to budding Americans as "Xanadu, a mind-expanding experience as well as a semi-magical place symbolizing opportunity, civilization over savagery, predestination, material progress and freedom, and Arcadia."[21] But this was no secular myth, as the inclusion of predestination indicates. The religious link becomes obvious when we learn that many authors of nineteenth-century schoolbooks were either ministers or educated in a New England steeped with a missionary spirit. Although they presented the West as a land of opportunity where poor individuals could rise from rags to riches, they cast their presentations in the American way—namely, within the bounds of the dominant capitalist, Judeo-Christian value system, an identification that remains true today.[22]

Nineteenth-century U.S. Mormon and Indian policies illustrate this point. In his book *Dissent in American Religion,* Gaustad discusses both groups in a chapter titled "The Misfits: Sinners against Society." From the 1850s through the 1890s the "Mormon Question" nagged the nation. What should be done about the theocratic, polygamous community that had established itself in Utah? The question went straight to the bedrock of liberty and democracy in the United States. Those opposed to Mormon ways believed that civilized life depends on a relationship between governmental structure and Christian morality. Mormons saw beauty in the Constitution's protection of religious liberty and local difference, which would allow them to thrive despite their belief in a distinctive, divinely revealed moral order. The conflict between Mormons and their opponents—which included a U.S. Army occupation of Utah, federal legislation, and U.S. Supreme Court decisions in which the Court protected the constitutional vision of American Protestants—shows a debate over the nation's religious nature that endured until the end of the century. The same could be said of U.S. Indian policy. During the nineteenth century's final three decades, the so-called peace policy produced widespread suppression of Indian cultures by a tag team of church and state. Even as churches lost administrative control during the 1870s, Protestant reformers played significant roles in shaping government policy. The three-pronged policy included land allotment to destroy communal holdings and replace it with private ownership. It also included programs to suppress Indian family life, community organization, and religion and to replace the tribal values structuring those institutions with mainstream American Protestant ones.[23]

These turbulent relationships between the U.S. mainstream, including the federal government, and each of these two groups of outsiders (Mormons and American Indians) occurred at a historiographic watershed. Historians who have written about America and the United States through about 1870 have been much more willing to address religion's role and to include it in the interpretive mainstream than have those who have written about the United States since 1870; the latter have found religion "more anomalous than normal and more innocuous than powerful," according to the historian Jon Butler in an article titled "Jack-in-the-Box Faith: The Religion Problem in Modern American History." That is, the historians who have addressed the United States' entry into modernity have documented the decline of religion defined as "conceptions of life and moral behavior rooted in supernatural and transcendent beliefs" and the ascent of secularity defined as "the absence of religious conceptions in the customary conduct of public and personal life." This assumed secularization contributed to historians' tendencies to treat religion in modern America as if it were a jack-in-the box—it pops up unexpectedly and with little explanation or context.[24]

Such an approach fails to do justice to the topic. To remedy the situation, Butler suggests that more historians ask, "Did religion make a difference in modern America? If so, how and why?" While religion may have become less visible, it has not become less influential. Twentieth-century Americans believed in God and the supernatural at rates far higher than those for Europeans, for instance. American church, synagogue, and mosque affiliation increased from 40–45 percent during the 1880s and 1890s to 60–65 percent during the 1970s and 1980s. Twentieth-century Americans remained religious people and joined religious institutions at rates higher than those at any other time since seventeenth-century Puritan Massachusetts. Furthermore, election data from 1952 through 1996 indicate that religion served as the second most important factor dividing American voters after race, which was twice as important. Religion ranked ahead of both class and gender. In the 2004 election both major-party candidates spoke explicitly about faith, and a televangelist told a convention audience in Fort Worth, Texas, that God's judgment would fall upon those who failed to register to vote or who voted for the "wrong agenda"—supporting same-sex marriage and abortion.[25]

The subjects of my study raise pointed questions about interpretations of Western history and religious freedom in the West and the United States more broadly. Some historians accept the myth of the West, portraying it as a region notable for its religious diversity and tolerance. Carl Guarneri, for instance, argues that "no one group dominated the others" in the West, which he says has become "the seedbed of new religions," especially in the twentieth century. Ferenc M. Szasz and Margaret Connell Szasz also stand in this group, arguing that "with a few notable exceptions, tolerance and openness characterized the world of western faiths." In an excellent survey of religion in the modern West (a rare commodity in a neglected field), Ferenc Szasz puts a finer point on interpreting religion's role, contending that "although the modern American West participated in all national religious trends, westerners generally bent these trends along their own trajectories." Those trajectories "never produced any religious mainstream" in the West, and aside from a few exceptions, "the celebrated individualism of western life has remained preeminent." Although the West might not have produced a religious mainstream, the exceptions show powerful mainstream forces at work.[26]

Others argue that the frontier provided a fertile environment for Protestant sects but proved inhospitable to other denominations—to the point that the nineteenth-century frontier has been called a "Protestant phenomenon." Furthermore, although the West saw some adaptations within established practice, it "probably pushed heaviest in the assertion of conservatism and preservation of old religious values." To be sure, non-Protestants participated in western expansion and inhabited the West, but when their behavior exceeded the bounds of Protestant taste, they experienced what Robert Hine has called "the inability of frontier society to tolerate differences."[27] When that happened, trouble often followed.

In this book I examine that trouble. In chapter 1 I survey the wide variety of religious groups that have found at least some degree of peace and success in the West. Although some of these groups ran into minor problems, for the most part they support Ferenc Szasz's arguments about religion in the West. The chapter closes with an introduction to the book's three case studies from the perspective of intermediaries, people who tried to defuse conflicts before they turned disastrous. The volatile nature of these conflicts outstripped the abilities of these negotiators. In chapter 2 I survey nineteenth-century Mormon history, emphasizing the plural-marriage issue but with most attention focused on the Utah Expedition and subsequent U.S. legislative and judicial attempts to "civilize" Mormons. In chapter 3 I examine the Wounded Knee tragedy as a violent spasm related to the Ghost Dance movement that can be understood only against the backdrop of U.S. policies aimed at "civilizing" American Indians. In chapter 4 I analyze the Branch Davidian disaster, which occurred much later than did the previous cases but which produced remarkably similar rhetoric. The three core chapters (2–4) focus extensively on the rhetoric used by the relevant factions, namely, what I call mainstream America and exceptional religious groups. Each complex episode involved many factors, but religion drove them all. In chapter 5 I provide concluding reflections on the parallels among the episodes and on the meanings these stories bear for the West and the larger United States.

Despite the West's well-deserved reputation for individuality and opportunity, the region had little room for certain types of dissenters. Despite its
well-deserved reputation for separation of church and state, the United States
operated under a social and legal system heavily influenced by Protestant
ideals. As it incorporated the West, a region rich with resources and ripe with
opportunity, the United States confronted communities with rival notions of
family, social organization, and manifest destiny based on divine revelation,
communities that made no pretense of separating church and state. Mormons,
Lakota Ghost Dancers, and Branch Davidians fit into these categories. According to the dictates of their religious beliefs, they envisioned a different version of the West's mythic promises, one unacceptable to the greater state. Manifest destiny had run out of space.[28] According to mainstream America, they
lived as barbarians in the garden. Jon Butler asked, "Did religion make a difference in modern America?" One might add a corollary question, "Did religion make a difference in the American West?" Telling these stories may help
answer both.

★

1   God's Country

THE PEOPLING OF NORTH AMERICA may have been an inherently religious
venture. Judging by this chapter's epigraphs, Providence guided the process,
perhaps with a purpose. Variations on the first remark appear in Native
American creation stories that say the Creator placed certain people in certain places. Before trying to answer the questions asked at the end of the introduction, it would be worthwhile to test a broader canvas and ask whether
religion made a difference in American history. It certainly did, but the details defy a simple interpretation.

Patricia Nelson Limerick's four-word summary of the principal elements
of the "New Western History," the four Cs of continuity, convergence, conquest, and complexity, provides useful guidance in tackling this question.
Many of the themes found shaping the nation's earliest religious history continue to the present. The events in which religion made a difference resulted
from the convergence of peoples, and when those events involved conflict,
they frequently stemmed from some element of conquest, be it by European
colonial powers or the United States after its creation and evolution into a
colonizing power in its own right. Finally, as seems true for any discussion
of religion, complexity dominates.[1] Three themes present themselves in any
survey of religion's role in American history. First, non-Indians generally attempted to force their religion on Indians as a part of conquest; whether or

not the Indians accepted the proposition, the attempt sometimes bred Indian revitalization movements. Second, access to new space opened by conquest may have encouraged religious refugees or innovators fleeing the constrictions of mainstream society to try their new ideas or practice established ideas in an area they took to be free of persecution. Some of those passed quickly into obscurity, but others survived or even thrived. The final theme stems from the Catholic-Protestant split within Christianity, which periodically led the Protestant-dominated United States to suspect that Catholic loyalty to the pope would undermine republican institutions.

Revitalization movements appeared several times over the centuries following European arrival in the portion of North America that would become the United States. English settlers had a spiritual agenda in their relations with Native Americans. Members of the Virginia Company, for example, tried to convert members of the Powhatan Confederacy. For more than a decade they eroded Powhatan culture. Finally, in 1620–21, the political leader Opechancanough allied with a prophet, military leader, and adviser, Nemattenew, to lead a revitalization movement. Nemattenew professed to be immortal and therefore invulnerable to English bullets. In addition, he claimed to have ointments and special powers that could make other Indians impervious to English attacks. Together the two Powhatans touched off the Second Anglo-Powhatan War in 1622; over the following twenty years of hostilities, the Powhatans struggled in vain to drive the English from Virginia.[2]

Like the English, Spaniards spread their brand of Christianity—Catholicism—as they expanded into the Americas. After heated criticism of the bloody conquests of native peoples in what is now Mexico, the Spanish crown sought to carry out further native subjugation in a more Christian and humane manner. This policy guided Spanish expansion into New Mexico by the late sixteenth century and early seventeenth century, with Franciscan missionaries working hand in glove with the Spanish military as both expanded their influence. Spanish missions included not only priests to proselytize the natives but also soldiers for protection from and coercion of those not convinced of the merits of Spanish or Catholic ways. Some Pueblo Indians, facing starvation or attack from neighboring tribes, professed Christian beliefs to secure Spanish protection but continued to practice their own religion covertly. For nearly a century Spanish Catholicism appeared to be gaining a foothold among the Pueblos.

Starvation and the Spaniards' inability to protect them from raids by neighboring Athapaskans led to increasing discontent among the Pueblos during the 1660s and 1670s. When Spanish civil and clerical authorities undertook a policy of complete intolerance for Pueblo traditions, including bans on meetings in kivas and the destruction of underground ceremonial chambers, resentment among Pueblos pushed them to the breaking point. An influential medicine man, Popé, spread word that three key Pueblo deities had told him to revolt against Spanish rule and the Spanish god. After the revolt Popé would lead the return to Pueblo life as it existed before Spanish arrival. Popé played a leading role in organizing the Pueblo Revolt of 1680, which removed the Spaniards from Pueblo life for more than a decade.[3]

Less than a century later European encroachment into the Great Lakes region contributed to similar results. Among the Delawares lived a man who experienced visions directing him to lead his people back to the glorious days before European contact. Known among whites as the Delaware Prophet, he urged his followers to purify themselves, abstain from sex, give up using firearms, and return as nearly as possible to the way they lived before Europeans arrived. The Delaware Prophet told his followers that if they did these things and listened to subsequent divine revelations as he received and revealed them, they could drive the white people from the region. Pontiac, an Ottawa chief, harnessed the sentiment stirred by the Delaware Prophet to recruit supporters for a pan-Indian alliance he was organizing to expel British invaders from the Great Lakes area. The movement failed, however, and Indian revitalization movements and pan-Indian anti-European alliances faded for a generation or so.[4]

In the early nineteenth century American expansion contributed to new religious movements among indigenous peoples as the site of cultural collision moved west of the Appalachians. In the Ohio River valley Shawnees experienced cultural stresses and changes from contact with European Americans. Early in the nineteenth century the Shawnees saw their land base shrink and game supplies dwindle as American settlers, backed by the U.S. military, invaded Kentucky and the Northwest. In 1805 an alcoholic Shawnee named Lalawethika fell for several hours into a trancelike state, appearing dead to his relatives and neighbors. On waking Lalawethika told of dying and visiting the spirit world, where he glimpsed a paradise for his people. He changed his name to Tenskwatawa, meaning "Open Door," and became a religious leader among the Shawnees, advocating a resurgence of traditional values and mores. Tenskwatawa preached that to attain paradise, the Shawnees must not only abandon polygamy but also shun the whites' ways. They were to forsake alcohol; stop accumulating property; cast off American clothing; and for the most part cease using American technology, such as metal (guns could be used for self-defense, but the Shawnees were to kill game with stone-tipped spears and arrows). Ultimately, all intercourse between Shawnees and Americans would cease.

Tenskwatawa left his village and led followers (including his older brother Tecumseh, who converted to his sibling's way after Tenskwatawa experienced additional visions) to found a village at Greenville, in western Ohio. Waves of religious converts descending on the new village soon outstripped its capacity to feed them. Hostile reactions by neighboring tribes and U.S. officials led Tecumseh and Tenskwatawa to accept an invitation from other Indians to relocate in what is now western Indiana. The Shawnees moved west with a number of converts to a spot near the confluence of the Tippecanoe and Wabash rivers, where they established Prophetstown.

As Tenskwatawa spread word of his visions, Tecumseh talked to other receptive Indian nations of his plan for a pantribal military and political alliance to preserve Indian control of lands in the face of U.S. expansion. Tenskwatawa joined in the recruitment. While continuing to preach religious revitalization, he also told arrivals at Prophetstown that a political and military union would be necessary and advised them to begin hoarding arms and ammunition.

As governor of Indiana, William Henry Harrison became concerned about the growing strength of this new Indian confederacy. He denounced Tenskwatawa's religious messages and urged potential converts to question the prophet's religious authority. In 1811 Harrison led a force including federal troops, Indiana militia, and Kentucky volunteers against the confederacy and claimed victory in the battle of Tippecanoe. Although a comparison of casualties suffered by each side suggests a draw, Tenskwatawa's inability to protect his followers from American bullets demolished his credibility as a prophet and ended his days as a religious leader.[5]

People already living in the West sometimes found religious practices restricted when they stepped beyond what the mainstream considered "reasonable" behavior. In August 1881 the federal government dispatched two companies of cavalry to arrest Nokay Delklinne, an Apache medicine man who advocated a "fanatic idea" not unlike the Ghost Dance religion that later swept the Great Plains. For two months Nokay Delklinne had been holding dances that he promised would resurrect two chiefs of whom the Apaches had been fond and repopulate the region with resurrected Apaches who would drive out whites. According to one account, when the dead did not materialize, the medicine man told his followers that the dead would not return for fear of white people. Once the whites left, the dead Apaches would return. According to this story, he said that the whites would be out of their country by the time the corn ripened. In any event, the army ordered Nokay Delklinne arrested. The local Indian agent, less particular than the army and apparently more fearful of the medicine man, asked that Nokay Delklinne be arrested, killed, or both. Nokay Delklinne surrendered peacefully and was headed to the army's camp when Apache scouts turned on their army employers and, aided by others apparently from Nokay Delklinne's camp, attacked the soldiers. Someone shot Nokay Delklinne, mortally wounding him, and the soldiers withdrew when fighting subsided with darkness.[6]

The Puritans provided the colonial period a classic (perhaps "all-American" might be more fitting) example of the second theme, refugees or innovators fleeing the confines of mainstream society to live their version of a righteous life without hindrance. These English Protestants brought to their era's American frontier many ideas, values, and institutions that left an indelible stamp on colonial American society. Under John Winthrop's leadership, the Puritans set about building a righteous, authoritarian community with government limited to those determined to be filled with God's grace. The Puritans had no interest in diversity and banished dissenters such as Roger Williams and Anne Hutchinson, who moved on to new frontiers.[7]

Religion constituted a particularly important element in the intellectual atmosphere that produced the American Revolution and created the United States of America, whose citizens, shortly after their nation's birth, Tocqueville described as the most Christian on earth. Because Thomas Jefferson was both a founding father and an expansionist, his ideas deserve attention here. Leonard Levy argues that on matters of religious liberty Jefferson displayed a remarkable congruity of thought and action not present in his record on civil liberties overall. In building and maintaining a wall separating church from state, for instance, Jefferson lived by the philosophies he espoused.[8] Perhaps his clearest enunciation on religious liberty appears in "An Act for Establishing Religious Freedom," which he wrote in 1786. There Jefferson condemns state compulsion to worship and lists several negative side effects of forced worship. The proposed act then mandates that "all men shall be free to profess, and by argument to maintain, their opinions in matters of religion, and that the same shall in no wise diminish, enlarge, or affect their civil capacities."[9] Jefferson, then, vigorously defended the free practice of religion.

When it came to the republic, however, Jefferson believed that the United States had been ordained by God to set an example for the world. He displayed what Levy calls a "messianic nationalism" when it came to fulfilling that example. When defending the republic from threats in the press or exercising extraconstitutional powers as president, Jefferson succumbed to political pres-

sures and compromised his libertarian values and strict reading of the Constitution.[10] How would Jefferson have responded to a divinely inspired religion
that threatened his messianic nationalism and the republic, especially in areas
such as the West, where the republic crept onto new territory? A possible answer rests in his faith in the yeoman farmer. Jefferson's vision for the West included its eventual settlement by yeoman farmers who would provide moral
guidance for the American republic. "The small land holders," Jefferson wrote,
"are the most precious part of a state." He viewed the small landholder's economic and moral independence to be indispensable in exercising the fran-
chise.[11] How Jefferson would have handled competing visions that threatened
the yeoman farmer culture remains a matter for speculation. Three subsequent
presidents, however, would have to face that question in all too real situations.

Other founding fathers had more conventional relationships with faith,
which may have moved them to revolt. Ruth Bloch argues that millennial
movements in the colonies helped spur patriots to action. Certainly they had
constitutional and institutional grievances, she notes, but they acted on those
grievances in an atmosphere of millennialism that allowed them to envision
themselves acting to perfect the world, transforming it into "a paradise for
the righteous," and to support the Revolution fervently.[12]

Coincidentally, the denominations most taken with millennialism—
Congregationalists, Presbyterians, and Baptists—were those that most rigorously backed the Revolution and tended to apply millennial thought to
shaping the new republic. Nathan O. Hatch argues that New England ministers, partly to ensure order for their own well-being, sought to portray politics as a battleground between good and evil. In that worldview, church and
government would work together to spread principles of liberty, just government, and pure Christianity as embodied in American churches. These
ideas would find their way into the U.S. government via New England's Fed-
eralists and in the progeny of New Englanders who settled the Midwest.[13]

During the nation's first century this northern and midwestern constituency would form the Republican Party, elect a president with virtually no
support from the South, and successfully fight a war that would entrench its
view of the United States as a particular kind of moral republic. Specifically,
these people believed that God had chosen the United States of America as
the nation to lead the world toward the millennium. Christianity and republican government, they believed, would work in symbiosis to prepare for
the Second Coming. This notion led New England Christians to subordinate
their denominational differences to faith in the state's redemptive power and
to subscribe to belief in a Christian republic. The Christian republic would

protect religious liberty—Christian liberty, at least—and thus help prepare for the millennium.[14] This constituency's values guided American actions in the 1850s as the nation prepared for cataclysmic conflict and was exercised after the Civil War as the United States matured under Republican Party rule.

What would become a traditional intersection of mainline Protestant Christianity with federal action germinated during the early national period, even with the nation's constitutional protection of religious practice. Although the founders recognized natural laws and liberties as expressed in the Declaration of Independence, they had no intention of creating a secular nation. James Madison, perhaps the leading political theorist behind the U.S. Constitution, addressed his "Memorial and Remonstrance against Religious Assessments" to the Virginia Assembly in 1785: "Before any man can be considered as a member of Civil Society, he must be considered as a subject of the Governor of the Universe." Although Madison argues against governmental establishment of religion, later in the same document he writes that non-Christians live "under the dominion of false Religions."[15] The United States would be a nation under a Christian God; religion and the republican state would be separate, but they would reinforce each other.

The ideologies of liberty and democracy also created an atmosphere conducive to an explosion of popular religious movements that "did more to Christianize American society than anything before or since." These produced "powerful undercurrents of democratic Christianity" that "distinguish the United States from other modern industrial democracies." Such undercurrents helped reduce the established distinction of the clergy as a separate class, gave greater credence to the spiritual experiences and impulses of lay people, and led to a broad spectrum of new organizational forms, some of which, ironically, were decidedly undemocratic.[16]

The nation's dynamic religious impulses found expression in the Second Great Awakening, the far-reaching evangelical Protestant revival that swept the United States roughly from 1780 to 1830. Donald G. Matthews argues that the awakening's social aspects played an important role in the new United States. Matthews explains that the awakening's organizing processes "helped to give meaning and direction to people suffering in various degrees from the social strains of a nation on the move into new political, economic and geographical areas." Martin Marty adds that the awakening's leading preachers sought to reform America as part of Christ's second coming, which would usher in a thousand years of peace and justice.[17] This dynamic atmosphere not only created waves of new religious innovators but also swelled the ranks of mainstream religious groups who might seek to limit them.

As the United States expanded its borders and, to greater or lesser degrees, welcomed new citizens, it needed to create cultural unity for a cohesive society. Especially with the opening of the West, American Protestantism went to meet and tame the perceived threat of barbarism. Churches acted as socializing institutions and have been called "the most effective organizations of acculturation in the West." Churches also helped impose order on a society torn by various developments: in the East, by problems such as Shays's Rebellion and the Whiskey Rebellion; in the West, by uncertainty as the government sought to settle new territories and to bring them into the Union. By spreading churches throughout the country, the Second Great Awakening encouraged democratic participation in church affairs; helped create a "common world of experience" across the nation, thereby fostering a national identity and a "distinct moral community"; and helped to unify American society. Later in the nineteenth century evangelical Protestantism helped shape reform movements that tried to make recent immigrants and Native Americans fit the mold of the national identity created earlier in the century.[18] In the following century, during the 1980s, evangelical Christians gained political power and made a vogue of their values, particularly as a vocal conservative influence in the Republican Party. As an important factor in creating a national identity for the United States, then, religion—particularly evangelical Protestantism—cannot be ignored.

The religious fervor surrounding the Second Great Awakening spawned religious mutations arousing the ire of eastern society, which effectively ejected religious splinter groups it found offensive. One such group founded in New York City, the Kingdom of Matthias, aimed to restore and strengthen what it felt were family values that had fallen by the wayside during the market revolution of the early 1800s. Specifically, the group followed a prophet calling himself Matthias whose visions directed him to establish and lead a strongly patriarchal group and allowed him to spread his influence and holiness through sexual unions with female followers. "Complaining neighbors, meddling Christians, his followers' kinsmen, and other persecutors of New York City" forced the Kingdom of Matthias to a more rural setting.[19] Even in rural New York, however, more interfering neighbors (led, oddly enough, by tavern patrons) eventually brought the kingdom to its knees and forced Matthias to seek greener pastures in western New York.

Matthias bounced around the countryside in a westering that took him, reportedly, to Kirtland, Ohio, where he sought to join forces with Joseph Smith and the Mormons. Finding little sympathy there, he continued his sojourn, which may have taken him to Arkansas before placing him back with the Mormons at Nauvoo, Illinois. Subsequent reports had him preaching to Indians in Iowa Territory. Placing the Kingdom of Matthias in historical perspective, Paul E. Johnson and Sean Wilentz categorize Matthias and a long line of other traditionalist American seers as constituting a group they call "wild American holy men."[20]

As the nation expanded westward, so did its spiritual concerns, although in the West non-Protestants met mixed receptions. The experiences of Jews in the West point up some difficulties faced by non-Protestant denominations, although the episodes fall short of violent intolerance. On the one hand, Jewish communities in Arizona and Nevada, for instance, clung tenaciously to their faith despite huge obstacles to traditional observances. Members did their best to observe Jewish customs, but a shortage of religious leaders often left them looking forward to periodic visits from San Francisco rabbis. Although they enjoyed what one historian calls a "significant absence of overt anti-Semitism," they may have experienced covert discrimination. On the other hand, because they constituted a small portion of the population, they may not have posed a significant threat to the dominant culture. Furthermore, the reasons offered for the lack of anti-Semitism indicate a group dedicated to goals held in common with the dominant culture. Arizona and Nevada Jews often worked as individual capitalist entrepreneurs; actively participated in secular fraternal and social organizations, such as volunteer fire companies; and received recognition for their high moral standards and civic involvement.[21]

Jews had similar experiences in California, home to some of the West's largest and most active Jewish communities. Members of these communities, which were large enough to support synagogues and rabbis, typically earned their livelihoods within the dominant economy and society, both of which they supported. Successful business careers like that of Levi Strauss helped San Francisco's Jewish community build the West's premier Jewish edifice, the Sutter Street Temple. Observers noted that the twin-spired cathedral-style temple drew the eye before all the Christian churches, and the historian Moses Rischin writes that the temple "came to symbolize the freedom, equality, openness, and fraternity of America and of the West for Jews and others." In fact, the economic successes of California Jews may have led San Francisco to become a hotbed of the anti-Zionist American Council for Judaism (ACJ). The ACJ promoted and encouraged Jewish loyalty to the United States, possibly to deny anti-Semites ground for attacking Jews. Most Jews in the West shared dominant-culture values and provided needed and valued services within the economy, which made them welcome additions to western society.[22]

Other Jews, however, differed from most of their coreligionists by trying to live off the land, the more traditional approach in the wider western society. These Jews helped found more than forty agricultural communities in America between 1881 and 1915 as part of an international Jewish back-to-the-soil movement. American Jews saw settlement on the land as a solution to a variety of problems, ranging from urban overcrowding to sluggish Americanization retarded by insular urban communities. They also hoped to inhibit anti-Semitism by changing stereotypes of Jews, to demonstrate Jewish commitment to the United States, and to effect a Jewish spiritual and physical revival. Examining one of these colonies—Clarion, Utah, founded 135 miles southwest of Salt Lake City in 1911—shows that although the colonies had indisputable religious ties, they subscribed wholeheartedly to dominant American values.

Clarion's founder, Benjamin Brown, sought between 150 and 200 married young men with sufficient savings to establish the colony. At first they would work the land communally and receive wages. Later land and equipment would be converted to private ownership, although the community would practice cooperative buying and selling. Unlike some other religious communes in the West, politics and religion would be private matters in Clarion. Although they received cooperation and advice from neighboring Mormon farmers who greeted the Jews as kindred spirits, dismal weather, poor soil, capital shortages, flagging enthusiasm, and other problems contributed to the colony's demise by about 1916. Other Jewish groups had similar experiences in the Dakotas and Kansas. The West defeated these Jews as it had thousands of others who had attempted to settle it, but religion did not seem to play a central role.[23]

Around the same time followers of mystic named Thomas Lake Harris established a religious communitarian colony in California that operated nearly a quarter-century without significant interference. Members of the Brotherhood of the New Life followed their leader to a valley north of San Francisco where they established Fountain Grove. Years earlier Harris had begun preparing his followers for Christ's return, which Harris would announce. The sect first established a commune in New York City, then moved to upstate New York near the Massachusetts border, and later settled in western New York on Lake Erie's shore. In 1875, allegedly following divine inspiration, Harris took his group to the Pacific Coast. Harris and company flourished at Fountain Grove until the 1890s, when a relative of a disgruntled former member published a biography of the former Harrisite containing allegations of sexual license and immorality. Those allegations, coupled with other misunderstandings of Harris's theories about the mystical and spiritual nature of sexual relations not only between humans but also between humans and God, contributed to Fountain Grove's demise. When Harris left to pursue his calling in Europe and New York City, his departure created a leadership vacuum his followers could not fill. In 1900 Harris sold his remaining interest in the commune to its members, who had meanwhile turned steadily away from spiritual pursuits to the commercial interests of running a winery.[24]

Further south on the California coast, Theosophists established a settlement in 1897 at Point Loma, near San Diego. Under the leadership of Katherine Tingley the group sought to form a society without distinctions of race, creed, sex, caste, or color; to promote the study of Aryan and Asian literature, religions, and sciences; and to investigate the mysteries of nature and psychical powers latent in humans. Although the Theosophists resembled a religious study group more than a religion, they directed their work at understanding what they felt to be divine knowledge. Generally, they got on well with their neighbors from San Diego, who frequented dramatic and musical productions by Point Loma's students. Horticulturists in the community produced remarkable fruit harvests and made pioneering breakthroughs in experiments with avocados and other tropical fruits, from which the rest of California benefited. Point Loma preserved private property, especially in the cases of wealthy members, but the prosperous community met most of the needs of its members. Unfortunately for the Theosophists, Tingley spent beyond the community's means, and when the Depression caused a dramatic decline in contributions from outside supporters, the community found itself in financial trouble. By 1940 most of the settlement's lands had been sold to satisfy creditors, and Point Loma's life as a Theosophist community ended.[25]

The West helped usher in the age of media evangelism thanks to the radio superstar Aimee Semple McPherson, who migrated to California seeking opportunity. "Sister Aimee" founded her Foursquare Gospel Church in Los Angeles in 1918 and went on to create a radio station, KFSG—"Kall Four Square Gospel"—to broadcast her Pentecostal message. Thanks to her attractive appearance, her proximity to Hollywood, and an alleged kidnapping that may have been a cover for a romantic escapade, McPherson commanded and held the media spotlight and paved the way for subsequent radio and television evangelists.[26]

In 1918 "Father" William E. Riker founded Holy City, a religious community of a considerably less admirable stripe, also in California. According to Riker, God sent him messages directing him to establish a community based on white supremacy. He bought land between San Jose and Santa Cruz where he and his followers operated a gas station, restaurant, print shop, and other small businesses. On four occasions Riker ran for California governor on a platform proposing that blacks and Asians be banned from owning or running businesses in the state and that they be relegated to what he felt was their proper role, serving the white race. Riker and Holy City attracted attention from outside newspapers, especially those in San Francisco, and Riker was charged with an array of crimes ranging from reckless driving to murder, but he won acquittal in every case. By 1952 only twelve members of his group remained, many aged survivors of the original thirty members.[27]

Hutterite migrants also experienced mixed results in the West. In the 1870s Hutterites from the Ukraine came to the Northern Plains to establish pacifist communes in which the individual submitted to group will. The Hutterites practiced progressive agriculture and welcomed technological breakthroughs. Their communal practices, centralized organization, and wealth irritated their non-Hutterite neighbors in South Dakota, however, and the state passed legislation restricting Hutterite land purchases. In the 1950s anti-Communist agitation contributed to several Hutterite colonies abandoning the United States for Canada.[28] Although some Hutterite colonies remain, the American West did not prove to be the land of freedom and opportunity for them.

Japanese immigrants on the West Coast, particularly those in California during the decade following World War I, found a Christian organization created by one of their compatriots waiting to save their souls and to help them cope with American society and culture: the Japanese Salvation Army. Masasuke Kobayashi, son of a samurai, came to the United States in 1902. Within three years of his arrival he became a Presbyterian and was baptized. First active in the YMCA, in 1910 he became general secretary of a Japanese-American interdenominational evangelistic board. In the course of a mass evangelism campaign in Japan in 1915, Kobayashi encountered the Japanese Salvation Army, whose militaristic tactics appealed to his samurai background. In 1918, after receiving instruction in the organization's ideas and structure, Kobayashi returned to the United States to establish the Japanese Salvation Army of America in San Francisco. He spread the organization to Hawaii and Washington State, providing such services as English classes, "Americanization" courses, and antigambling campaigns and establishing health services including a dispensary, a maternity hospital, a home for the elderly, and a shelter for "helpless Japanese girls."

Although Kobayashi and his organization appeared to be serving the interests of the dominant culture, they provided Japanese immigrants with a culturally Japanese adaptation of Christianity to help the new residents deal with life in America. Japanese immigrants to the United States faced systematic discrimination ranging from immigration restrictions to bans on owning land. Kobayashi himself was pelted with eggs on his arrival in America. He urged his followers to practice "Choteiko Shugi" (the principle of super-resistance). Kobayashi claimed Choteiko Shugi to be derived from the New Testament. For example, Jesus restrained himself from lashing out at his persecutors. Instead, he submitted to their attacks without compromising his character, and in the long run his tormentors received their "just desserts." To shame those abusing Japanese, Kobayashi urged his followers to cultivate traditional Japanese characteristics of *jinkaku* (personality), *hinsei* (moral character), and *jitsuryoku* (capability). Displaying such behavior in the face of abuse would show Japanese refinement and make the tormenters realize the shame of their actions. By combining Christianization with revered Japanese traits, Kobayashi allowed his followers to succeed in America by practicing dearly held Japanese values. The Japanese Salvation Army of California enjoyed popularity throughout most of the 1920s but fell out of favor in the late 1920s and 1930s. Kobayashi died in 1940 on the brink of the massive discrimination awaiting Japanese Americans during World War II.[29]

In 1959 Young Oon Kim brought word of a new religion to Oregon. Based on the visions of the Korean mystic Sun Myung Moon, which wedded Eastern religion and philosophy with elements of Christianity, the Unification Church sought to transform the world in preparation for the coming of a second messiah. The church struggled to gain members during the 1960s and 1970s, and mainstream America labeled the group a "cult" for supposedly brainwashing or hypnotizing youthful converts. By the mid-1980s it claimed about 5,000 members in the United States.

In its attempt to gain members and influence in the United States, the church ran afoul of the federal government. In the "Koreagate" scandal of 1974–75, the Korean businessman Tongsun Park, accused of trying to buy influence in the U.S. government, implicated Moon. A congressional investigation determined that the church had acted as a front for the South Korean government operating in the United States. In the aftermath of the investigation, federal and state government agencies attacked the church. The U.S. Immigration and Naturalization Service tried to stop Unification Church missionaries from entering the country. A decision from the District Court for the District of Columbia thwarted the attack by recognizing the church as a bona fide religion. The New York State Tax Commission tried to label the church a political organization to collect taxes on its New York real estate. This time the U.S. Court of Appeals in New York protected the church by ruling that it is primarily religious. In a third attack, Senator Robert Dole urged the Internal Revenue Service to investigate Sun Myung Moon's finances for tax improprieties. This time the government succeeded. The IRS successfully prosecuted Moon for tax evasion on $165,000 of church funds he had placed in personal bank accounts. Moon served eighteen months in a federal prison.[30]

Oregon attracted another unusual religious group in the 1980s, Bhagwan Shree Rajneesh and his followers (referred to collectively as "the Rajneesh"), who established the religiously based community of Rajneeshpuram near the village of Antelope. Fleeing India in 1981, the bhagwan (his title means "the enlightened/awakened one") stepped off a plane in the United States and announced, "I am the Messiah America has been waiting for."[31] The bhagwan attacked existing religious institutions, and his charismatic leadership provided the basis for the movement that would bear his name. He had been born in India in 1931, graduated from high school in 1951, and attended at least two colleges and a university while earning a B.A. and an M.A. in philosophy. In 1953, while pursuing his education, he experienced "enlightenment," which he later described as "a great storm of light, joy, ecstasy." The bhagwan taught philosophy at the University of Jabalpur, eventually becoming a professor in 1960. While teaching he studied meditation techniques associated with the Chinese philosopher Lao-tzu and in 1964 established his first meditation camp.

While continuing in the business of helping others seek enlightenment, the bhagwan developed his trademark technique, "dynamic meditation," and found himself the leader of a movement headquartered in Pune, India, which he began marketing worldwide. By the late 1970s the movement had developed an intricate international organization that one sociologist suggested resembled a multinational corporation. Simultaneously, the movement found itself embroiled in controversy in Pune. Local police investigated drug trafficking by members, and conflicts between the movement and its Hindu neighbors increased (the bhagwan claimed religious persecution, and others claimed that neighbors had been goaded into attacking the movement). The bhagwan and his followers fled these surroundings in 1981, determined to establish a new international headquarters for the movement in the Pacific Northwest of the United States.[32]

The organization bought a 64,000-acre ranch in north-central Oregon and set about building their community, known both as Rajneeshpuram and as the Big Muddy Ranch, between 1981 and 1985. During the settlement's brief life its population fluctuated from twenty-six to more than thirteen thousand (during summer festivals in 1983 and 1984) and then to thirteen in 1987. Residents of the nearest village, Antelope (population thirty-nine in 1980), felt overwhelmed and threatened by their new neighbors, particularly when the religious communalists gained political control of Antelope and changed its name to Rajneesh. The seekers also quickly ran afoul of state and local authorities as they charged headlong into conflict with land-use regulations geared for agriculture and small populations. The differences between the Rajneesh and their American neighbors produced bitter battles and enmities. The Rajneesh accused local and state officials of participating in an international conspiracy against them, while Oregonians labeled the Rajneesh evil and erected plaques on The Dalles courthouse and at the Antelope post office commemorating the efforts of those who repelled the Rajneesh-led attempt to take political control of Wasco County.[33]

Ultimately Oregonians and the United States destroyed the Rajneesh through the federal and state legal systems. They attacked the Rajneesh for violating boundaries between church and state in administering Rajneeshpuram and Antelope/Rajneesh and in 1985 charged the bhagwan and his followers with crimes ranging from electronic eavesdropping conspiracy to arson and attempted murder. The bhagwan was "allowed" to depart the country voluntarily, and several of his lieutenants served time in federal prisons. The commune fell into disarray in the following years, despite promises from the bhagwan's disciples to carry on. In December 1988 Wasco County put the Big Muddy Ranch on the auction block, and the Connecticut General Life Insurance Company, holder of the ranch's mortgage, bought the property.[34]

In addition to providing a home to native prophets and a variety of innovators and refugees, the expanding nation's vast spaces caused concern about another group: Roman Catholics. Ray Allen Billington tells a chapter of this story in his book *The Protestant Crusade: A Study of the Origins of American Nativism*. According to Billington, the dominant Protestant culture of the nineteenth century aimed at limiting the power and development of the Catholic church in the United States. He traces the origins of anti-Catholic sentiment in America to the first English colonies in New England. In addition to opposing Catholicism on theological grounds, early Americans distrusted Catholics socially and politically because of their loyalty to the pope. During the early national years Protestant zealots expressed their anti-Catholicism through newspapers, books, and mob violence, such as burning a Boston convent. Anti-Catholic mobs acted so frequently in New England that many parishes there established around-the-clock patrols to protect their churches. As the nation moved westward, the dominant culture transported its anti-Catholic tendencies. It struggled to ensure Protestant domination in the Mississippi Valley. Some worried that all America west of the Alleghenies would become a French or Spanish Catholic country, thanks to Catholic advances there and divisions among Protestant denominations.

Protestant opponents of creeping Catholicism linked preservation of their religion to the state, the Constitution, and national security. They pushed for Bible reading in schools to avoid a nation of godless voters and to make the scriptures known to Catholics, whom they feared had been duped by Latin-speaking priests serving Rome. Protestants also feared group voting by Catholics, whom they suspected of voting as instructed by their priests. A Catholic archbishop gave credibility to these fears in 1850 when he publicly declared that the Church of Rome fully intended to convert both pagan and Protestant nations, including the United States and its officials from legislators to the president. Anti-Catholics countered that Catholicism is an idolatrous religion incompatible with democratic institutions in the United States.[35]

The struggle over American values simmered even within the Catholic church. When he was appointed bishop of Monterey and Los Angeles in 1853, Thaddeus Amat undertook a campaign to purify the Mexican American form of Catholicism by ridding it of its folk customs, such as selling burial shrouds, which he feared would discredit the church in the view of the majority American society.[36] Filipino immigrants faced similar problems. Most Filipinos who came to the United States practiced Catholicism, but when they got to California's Central Valley, they found that local Catholics did not readily accept them. The Filipinos responded by forming their own Protestant church. As far as fitting into United States society was concerned, however, denomination apparently made little difference, according to one early Filipino immigrant who, recalling the early decades of the twentieth century, wrote, "We were treated like dirt by the Americans, regardless of whether we profess to be Catholics or Protestants."[37] By the 1850s, then, a well-established tradition of fearing foreign religions antithetical to American values had developed among Americans, and suspicions of Roman Catholicism would continue to surface in twentieth- and twenty-first-century electoral politics, especially when a Catholic ran for president.

The vignettes related thus far reflect relatively mild conflict and could even be construed as supporting the claim that diverse religious groups coexisted peacefully in the West. The exceptions to the rule—where the mythic West, various fringe religious movements, and the federal government collided with destructive results—prove more complicated. One way to approach them is to begin in the middle, introducing the episodes from the perspective of people who attempted to stave off disaster by acting as intermediaries, as religious culture brokers, between the religious groups and the government.

Thomas Leiper Kane placed himself between the forces of Mormonism and those of the United States. Much as they suspected and feared Catholic loyalty to Rome, many mainstream Americans suspected and feared Mormons for their seemingly slavish, unrepublican devotion to Brigham Young. Born of a wealthy and highly respected eastern family, Kane had been a friend to the Mormons for years. Millard Fillmore relied on Kane's assessment of Brigham Young's moral character and standing when deciding to name Young Utah's first territorial governor. When Mormon-U.S. relations appeared doomed in 1857, Young called for Kane's help. Young asked Kane to recommend statehood for Utah or, in case that did not work, to request that the recently inaugurated James Buchanan appoint Mormons to vacant federal posts in Utah. Buchanan refused both requests.

The president did, however, grant quasi-official status to Kane as a negotiator, and Kane rushed to Utah for talks between Mormon leaders and General Albert Sydney Johnston, commander of the Utah Expedition, as well as Alfred Cumming, whom Johnston had been directed to install as the new governor of Utah Territory. Johnston's command received Kane coolly, suspecting him of spying for the Mormons. Relations with the military never warmed, but Kane eventually convinced Cumming to precede the army into Utah in a peaceful attempt to assert federal authority. Once in Utah, Cumming persuaded Brigham Young that he would neither meddle in Mormon church affairs nor consider Young's followers rebels against the U.S. government.[38] Establishing that level of trust closed much of the gap between the U.S. government and the Mormons and, in this case, avoided bloodshed. Danger had drawn nigh yet been averted, but in the following decades the Mormons would not escape federal presence untouched.

In dealings with the latest version of a Native American revitalization movement, the U.S. government's cultural policies for the West touched Lakotas more forcefully than they had the Mormons. Dakotas and white settlers fought each other in the Minnesota conflict of 1862, leading the federal government to imprison hundreds of Dakota men for their part in the hostilities. Many of these men learned to read during their incarceration as they studied with Christian missionaries versed in the Dakota language. In addition to teaching the Dakotas English, the missionaries converted some of the men to Christianity. Once freed, some pursued missionary careers among the Dakotas and Lakotas.

Rev. Louis Mazawakinyanna ("Iron Wing" in English) became one of the most prominent of the Christian Dakotas. Born in 1836 in Minnesota, Mazawakinyanna served four years in prison beginning in 1862 in the aftermath of the hostilities near Mankato. While jailed, he learned to read—using the Bible as his text—and became a devout Christian. In 1868 he was licensed as a missionary, and in 1870 the Dakota Presbytery ordained him. As a Presbyterian minister Mazawakinyanna joined a corps of converted Sioux who made regular contributions to the Dakota-language newspaper *Iapi Oaye*, many of which strongly advocated Christianity, especially to the unconverted Sioux. When the Ghost Dance religion became popular among his target audience in 1890, he found himself wielding his pen in the midst of a holy struggle that turned deadly at Wounded Knee Creek. Mazawakinyanna reported that a number of Sioux thought God had not been strong enough to guide them through their tribulations and had not served them well. Looking for a better, more responsive religious experience, they began practicing the Ghost Dance religion, which promised an Indian messiah who would improve their lives and remove the evil influence and presence of whites. Mazawakinyanna explained that Wovoka, the Ghost Dance prophet, was a false messiah, and tried to rally his people to the real (Christian) God. If only people would forsake this false religion and go to church regularly, he wrote, they would go to heaven.[39]

Mazawakinyanna and his counterparts, Indian or not, did their best to encourage the Lakota Ghost Dancers to adopt the dominant society's values. But events would not follow that path. The Indian agent at Pine Ridge feared the new religion, as did whites living near the Lakota reservations in western South Dakota. Their accounts of the Ghost Dance found a ready audience in the media, and tensions and emotions built toward hysteria. Whites called for the U.S. Army to quash the religion. Before the year's end, the Seventh Cavalry did just that when it left more than two hundred Ghost Dancer corpses on the frozen plains.

More than a century later the attorney Dick DeGuerin traversed the southern Great Plains near Waco, Texas, on his way to an early spring visit with his client Vernon Howell. Howell needed DeGuerin's help because the federal government was holding him and more than one hundred of his disciples at gunpoint in their home. Howell, known better as David Koresh, had assumed the mantle of leadership of the Branch Davidians, an offshoot of the Seventh-day Adventist Church that had been operating in the Waco area for decades since its founder fled his parent church in Los Angeles searching for a more welcoming place to establish a righteous community. Since taking charge of the group, Koresh had taught his followers that he had been chosen to lead them to the Promised Land, a journey that would begin with his violent death at the hands of the evil secular government based in Washington, D.C. On February 28, 1993, when agents of the Bureau of Alcohol, Tobacco, and Firearms (BATF) stormed the Branch Davidian compound in an armed assault, Koresh's followers saw proof of his prophesy. After the Davidians repelled the BATF assault, other government agencies entered the conflict and surrounded the Mt. Carmel compound prepared for a long siege.

During the siege DeGuerin met with Koresh frequently, sometimes daily, and acted as an intermediary between the two stalemated groups. The attorney told federal authorities that Koresh primarily wanted to discuss the Bible, to explain the Branch Davidians' beliefs and actions to the authorities, who were treating the standoff as a hostage situation. The authorities dismissed Koresh's messages as "Bible babble." DeGuerin maintained that his client spoke and behaved rationally and normally throughout the event and that however outlandish his beliefs appeared by conventional standards, he was no charlatan. Government negotiators would have none of that.

As the siege dragged on, days turned into weeks and weeks turned into a month. In early April DeGuerin and another attorney representing the Davidians apparently had legal details of a surrender worked out with government agents. Only the timing had to be arranged, but that would be up to Koresh, who awaited a sign from God. DeGuerin and other Davidian supporters argue that he had received that sign and was preparing to exit the compound peacefully. But the government's patience had reached its limits. On April 19 federal forces stormed the Mount Carmel compound a second time, this time with tear gas and military equipment, including tanks. Suddenly a fire blazed within the compound. Like the first shot at Wounded Knee, its source remains controversial. Whatever its origin, it left seventy-four charred corpses of men, women, and children (twenty-one of them, aged one to thirteen years) in the compound. Another six had died in the initial raid, along with four dead and twenty wounded BATF agents.[40] Despite DeGuerin's attempts to negotiate a settlement, eighty of approximately 130 Branch Davidians lay dead.

Each of these three middlemen—Thomas Kane, the Reverend Louis Mazawakinyanna, and Dick DeGuerin—attempted in various ways to inject reason into volatile situations. Their roles in these incidents suggest the multiple perspectives at work in these conflicts between religious groups and the federal government. This issue remains both perplexing and submerged because of the interrelationships of culture, time, and space and the reliance on explanations and stereotypes rooted in myth. The United States, particularly the American West, has a reputation for welcoming diversity. It also guarantees remarkable freedom of religion, which has spawned a number of unusual—by mainstream standards—religious groups. Many of these groups have found a comfortable home in the West, at least for a time. Three groups, however, pushed American society past its tolerance and produced extreme shows of force that radically changed one group and nearly destroyed two others.

These three collisions reveal limits in an otherwise free and open society. Brigham Young took his Mormon followers west to avoid persecution and to practice their religion freely. They wished to be left alone to practice Mormonism and to pursue their version of the American dream. But their dream included establishing a theocracy and led to bellicose and antisocial behavior the United States could not ignore. The Ghost Dancers likewise wished to practice their religion, but in addition to constituting religious activity, the Ghost Dance spawned behaviors deemed threatening, uncivilized, and even criminal. The Branch Davidians went so far as to buy their own land as a refuge. But a government unsympathetic to their beliefs and practices they were alleged to espouse—namely, weapons violations and child sexual abuse—held them hostage with an overwhelming show of force that contributed to many of the Davidians' deaths.

Each of the groups discussed here practiced at least one behavior that rightly concerned the government. Religion motivated those behaviors. During the nineteenth century the U.S. government worked to alter Mormonism and to extinguish traditional American Indian religious beliefs. Religious values motivated those U.S. policies and show that a religious mainstream had developed in the East and was being applied to the West. By the late twentieth century no government policy or policies sought to alter or extinguish the Branch Davidians, but the record left by the Branch Davidians, their neighbors, news coverage, and the agents who besieged them shows that remarkably little had changed since the 1890s when it came to attitudes about religion. All three episodes support Limerick's four Cs of western history. Mainstream values still ruled the West and indicate that the region may not welcome diversity and individuality as much as its mythology would have us believe.

2 Uncle Sam and the Saints

A recent writer . . . proposed (to use his own words) not a crusade, but a *civilizade,* against this polygamous community, to put an end to what seems to him a retrograde step in civilization.

—John Stuart Mill, *On Liberty*

Our enemies are determined to blot us out of existence if they can.

—Brigham Young, "A Series of Instructions and Remarks"

We will clean up our rifles, our pistols and swords,
And we will ever be ready to march at the word,
We will trust in the Lord and take good aim,
And the kingdom of Heaven we will it maintain,
And the kingdom of Heaven we will it maintain.

—Asa Smith Hawley, "Autobiography"

ON JULY 24, 1857, more than 2,500 members of the Church of Jesus Christ of Latter-day Saints gathered in Big Cottonwood Canyon for their annual "Pioneer Day" celebration. This occasion took on special importance because it commemorated the tenth anniversary of their arrival in the Salt Lake Valley. That decade had been a tumultuous one for the Saints as they struggled to create homes for themselves in what had become Utah Territory. In the summer of 1857, however, the pioneers took time to mark their accomplishments. In addition, they looked to their place in the greater polity. For example, they had contributed soldiers to the U.S. Army's campaigns in the Mexican-American War. Just weeks before the Cottonwood Canyon gathering, moreover, communities across Utah had paused to celebrate the Fourth of July. Celebrants toasted national symbols, including President James Buchanan ("May he ever continue the friend of the 'hardy Pioneer'") and the Constitution ("Be all pain to her enemies, but *champagne* to her friends"; "May its broad wings shelter Utah"). To note their own accomplishments, the Saints erected three spacious, wooden-floored shelters. Those who negotiated the traffic and parking situation created by 464 carriages and more than 1,300 draft animals danced to music provided by the six bands in attendance. Revelers who took a moment to glance up might have noticed U.S. flags flying from the two highest peaks visible from camp or from the two highest trees.

Given the excitement and the crowd, the arrival of a wagon carrying four harried travelers might have gone unnoticed. The four men had come west from a station of the Mormon Y. X. Express Line bearing important news for Brigham Young, who as church president and territorial governor was the most important man in Utah. Not finding him in Salt Lake City, the men drove hard to Big Cottonwood Canyon. Tension between Utah and the United States had been simmering for years, and the news born by the four travelers indicated it had reached crisis: the U.S. Army was on its way to Utah.[1]

The Utah War receives little attention from most American historians. President James Buchanan initiated the episode in 1857 when he dispatched a sizable portion of the U.S. Army to Utah Territory to install federally appointed territorial officials. Federal territorial officials typically did not require a large, heavily armed escort to assume their posts, but in the East the Utah Territory appeared to be in chaos, if not on the brink of rebellion. Mormons in Utah practiced polygamy, had driven off previous federal officials, and had created a theocracy on the U.S. frontier led by a man whom Buchanan and others perceived to be ignoring laws as it suited him. That man, Brigham Young, had led his followers out of the United States after they had suffered more than a decade of persecution in Ohio, Missouri, and Illinois, where the Mormons' prophet Joseph Smith had been murdered. Young and his followers saw the West as a haven where they could practice Mormonism safely and create God's kingdom on earth. Their brief sojourn outside the United States ended when Utah became a territory, but once back within the nation's bounds, they put their faith in the Constitution, which they viewed as a divinely inspired document. It would, they hoped, preserve their spiritual and worldly pursuits. Their opponents, however, perceived them as so religiously deviant that the Constitution could not protect them. The Utah War, whose military engagements and negotiations were limited to 1857–58, marked the blustery beginning of a decades-long, highly contentious relationship between the U.S. government and Utah Territory that fundamentally altered Mormonism and society in Utah. The rhetoric employed by all parties involved shows that religion played an important role in their interactions.

As the nation spread, the U.S. government created political units in its own image. The West reflected this phenomenon more so than much of the East, where states created a political system out of thirteen separate colonies. It took a revolution, a failed government under the Articles of Confederation, and a civil war before the United States reached a consensus on what these political units would be. The U.S. government used that image as a model as it molded western territories into American states.

When it came to religion, what was acceptably "American" had certain limits: those of Christianity or of a Judeo-Christian ethic. When a group pushed beyond those limits, even in the West, which was widely viewed as an haven for individuality, the government acted to ensure that American institutions would take root and flourish. Otherwise, as David Brion Davis asks, "What was to prevent liberty and popular sovereignty from sweeping away 'the old landmarks of Christendom, and the glorious old common law of our fathers'?"[2] Members of the Church of Jesus Christ of Latter-day Saints, commonly called "Mormons" or "Saints,"[3] experienced the government's regulating influence in several forms.

The demand that Mormons be "Americanized" was "a demand for undivided loyalty to the United States government, for the acceptance of the country's democratic processes under the Constitution, including the separation of church and state," according to Gustive Larson. The Mormon–U.S. conflict certainly involved these elements, but Larson and others hedge on the principle that achieving these goals meant changing Mormonism.[4] The government objected to certain tenets of Mormonism and thus destroyed them in an effort to create an American West. When Mormon Utah joined the Union in 1896, it was a vastly different place than the one the Mormons had built; it was American.

Mormonism traces its roots to New York's "Burned-Over District" in the 1820s. Joseph Smith claimed that the angel Moroni visited him on September 21, 1823, and revealed golden plates containing inscriptions that would become the Book of Mormon. At first Moroni would not let Smith take the plates, but in 1827 he gave them to Smith along with the "Urim and Thummim," so-called seer stones that allowed Smith to translate the inscriptions into English.[5]

Smith finished translating the plates in 1829, and the following year he published the first editions of the Book of Mormon, which was named after Moroni's father, Mormon, said to have been an ancient American soldier-historian.[6] The book's introduction claims it is a "volume of holy scripture comparable to the Bible" that gives "a record of God's dealings with the ancient inhabitants of the Americas."[7] The book tells about the family of Lehi, a Hebraic patriarch who escaped slavery by leaving Jerusalem before the Babylonian desolation of 587 B.C.E. Lehi's family crossed the Atlantic Ocean, arrived in the Americas, and broke into two factions hostile to each other: the Nephites, who generally held the righteous ground, and the Lamanites, who generally were wicked. Christ appeared to these people in America, creating more than two centuries of harmony. The two factions turned against each other again, however, with the Lamanites—ancestors of the American Indians—killing all the Nephites but one, Moroni, who buried the writings of his historian-warrior father, Mormon. Mormonism judges America "a land choice above all other lands," whose discovery by Columbus and subsequent history are shown, in prophecy, "as fulfillment of God's will."[8]

The Book of Mormon elicited a variety of responses from readers. Some viewed it as a harmless piece of fiction. Others reviled it as heresy. Still others read it and believed it to be the truth. To believers, the book established Smith as the prophet of a new religious path that offered hope and order in a chaotic world. After all, this was a time of social and religious change. The American Revolution had sundered links with established social orders, and Jacksonian America was bringing more democracy to more people. Changes in American Christianity resulting from the Second Great Awakening made religious authority subject to democratic processes and increasing skepticism. Events in America seemed increasingly further removed from the world depicted by Christianity. Joseph Smith's story, which included a new era of direct communication with God, placed America and its people at the center of a new story that made sense according to recent events.[9]

To Mormons, recognizing this special, central role for America included honoring the Constitution. Mormons would use the atmosphere of religious freedom created by the Constitution—which they believed to be a divinely inspired document—to create God's kingdom on earth. Once in place, Zion's perfected "theodemocratic" government would supersede the imperfect American constitutional government, preparing the way for Christ's return.[10]

Mormonism holds as an important tenet the belief that, beginning with Joseph Smith and continuing through successive church presidents, God has resumed communicating divine will to humans, a phenomenon that had ceased at the deaths of Christ's original apostles. This belief contributed to the Mormons' inability to separate the world into secular and religious spheres; the two are intertwined, and Mormons tended to follow their ecclesiastical leaders in all matters of life. This attitude originated in a revelation purportedly received by Joseph Smith: "All things unto me [God] are spiritual, and not at any time have I given unto you a law which was temporal."[11] Mormons could expect advice from the pulpit and tended to heed that advice on all matters.[12]

Almost from the beginning of their group's existence, Mormons conflicted with neighbors who did not share their religious views. Many non-
Mormons, whom Mormons sometimes call "Gentiles," felt Mormon beliefs
were "superstitious, disgusting, repellent . . . even 'un-American.'"[13] Early
anti-Mormons described the Saints as "the very dregs of society . . . , lazy, idle,
and vicious," suggesting that class differences dogged early Mormons.[14] Persecutions by neighbors drove the Saints to a succession of frontier regions in
search of a haven where they could practice their religion.

Experiences with the American legal system in the East taught Mormons
to suspect the fairness of frontier justice and fear the cost of getting tangled
in lawsuits, which could quickly drain church coffers. As they moved from
New York to Ohio to Missouri and then to Illinois, the Saints began to fear
the prospect of endless, costly legal battles in a hostile judicial system. In Kirtland, Ohio, they found themselves in a legal quagmire involving, among
other things, violations of Ohio banking laws. As they left Ohio and its conflicts, members of the priesthood leadership felt they had been treated un-
fairly by the non-Mormon judicial system, adding to the Saints' dismay of
"Gentile" institutions.[15]

As the Mormons moved west, their relations with Indians also raised suspicions among their neighbors. The Book of Mormon says American Indians had once practiced an advanced Christianity taught to them by Jesus
Christ after his crucifixion. Over time, according to Mormonism, they
strayed from God. Mormon theology made the Saints responsible for bringing the Book of Mormon to Indians and teaching them the ways of their
once-Christian ancestors. Their neighbors in Missouri, Illinois, and Iowa,
however, believed the Mormons were "agitating among the Indians" and
feared an Indian-Mormon alliance, a concern that would resurface among
federal officials after the Mormon exodus to Utah.[16]

The nature of Mormon society also stirred fear among many who viewed
their Mormon neighbors as "economic, political, and religious threats."[17]
They despised Mormon economic isolation, bloc voting, and religious ex-
pansionism, which meant competition for goods, power, and souls. Indeed,
religion itself led to divisions, for Mormonism appeared to involve unacceptable beliefs regarding morality and theology, including notions of the
afterlife. It also incorporated an economic philosophy and a strategy of community building bound to create tension with non-Mormon neighbors.[18]

In addition to enduring differences with their immediate neighbors,
Mormons in the mid-nineteenth century faced hostility from mainline
American religions. In 1851 Mormon missionaries in Hawaii reported that

a Congregationalist missionary had criticized the deceased Joseph Smith during a Sunday sermon, denouncing him as a "notoriously bad character," a polygamist who pretended to see angels, and a "very wicked man."[19] On the mainland, evangelical Christian denominations followed the Mormons to Utah. They wanted to convert "deluded" Mormons from what they believed was a non-Christian religion.[20]

Mormons experienced their most vicious persecutions in Missouri and Illinois. They tried for seven years to build communities in Missouri, only to be forced successively from Jackson and Clay counties to Caldwell and Daviess counties in the northwest part of the state.[21] Mormons and their non-Mormon neighbors clashed for a number of reasons, all related to religion. In his history of Missouri's so-called Mormon War, James H. Hunt wrote that he aimed to give a true, unbiased account of the violence but also admitted that he wanted to present Mormonism in such a way that anyone could see its shortcomings and view it with contempt. He sought, among other things, to educate people so as to prevent their seduction by a belief system that he believed produced infidels.[22] Hunt clearly did not compose an unbiased account, but his work provides valuable insight into anti-Mormon thought and the type of literature to which non-Mormons might have turned for information about the Saints.

Tension between Mormons and their Missouri neighbors escalated as both sides engaged in vigilantism. Problems worsened during 1838 with Mormon refugees from Kirtland, Ohio, swelling the ranks of the Missouri Mormons. Non-Mormons, fearing increased Mormon power, reacted with hostility, leading the Mormon leader Sidney Rigdon to call for—in a July 4 sermon, no less—"a war of extermination" against Missourians. Tensions escalated throughout the summer, reaching all-out war in September and October. Missouri governor Lilburn W. Boggs responded on October 27, ordering that Mormons "be exterminated, or driven from the State if necessary for the public peace." Three days later, at the Mormon settlement of Haun's Mill, Missouri soldiers killed eighteen Mormons. Missouri forces surrounded Joseph Smith and a large body of Mormons two days later, forcing their surrender and ending the armed conflict. Missourians drove about 15,000 Mormons from the state that winter amid extraordinary suffering. The Missouri evacuation explains much about the Saints' construction of a defensive city-state at their next home, at Nauvoo, and about their nineteenth-century interactions with the United States.[23]

Mormons appealed to the federal government for justice in their various Missouri legal problems. The federal government refused to become involved, however, arguing that Missouri's legal system provided adequate mechanisms. The Mormons disagreed, feeling that state and even federal legal mechanisms would not protect them as long as the laws were administered by individuals hostile to their community. If the law were to protect them, many believed, it must be built to Mormon specifications and administered by Mormons.[24] The Saints simply had to find a place where they could make that happen.

Having fled Missouri, the Mormons established the city of Nauvoo on the banks of the Mississippi River in Hancock County, Illinois. A liberal charter granted by a state legislature eager to attract settlers allowed Mormon leaders significant latitude in building Nauvoo into a virtual city-state. For example, they were permitted to recruit a militia, the Nauvoo Legion, staffed with Mormon officers. By 1844 Nauvoo's population of about 10,000 made it the state's second-largest city.[25] This large, well-armed city and the "peculiar" ways of its inhabitants who voted in monolithic blocs made Nauvoo's Gentile neighbors uneasy.

Thomas Coke Sharp, editor of the *Warsaw (Ill.) Signal,* expressed non-Mormon fears in his newspaper. Sharp, a (some said *the*) leading anti-Mormon in the area during the 1840s, used the *Signal* as his bully pulpit to oppose Mormon rule in Nauvoo, even urging the group's removal from Illinois. Sharp's rhetoric repeats much of the sentiment expressed by non-Mormons in Missouri. Mormons heard yet another call for their extermination. They saw themselves separated from "citizens"—in Sharp's mind, the non-Mormon and presumably Christian people of Illinois. Not only did Mormons not qualify as citizens; Sharp cast them in an evil religious light by labeling them "infernal devils." Lastly, Sharp summoned the imagery of American individualism, asserting that "every man" would make "his own" comment regarding the un-American, herdlike Mormons.[26]

Tensions reached a flashpoint when Joseph Smith suppressed an opposition newspaper, the *Nauvoo Expositor,* by having the Nauvoo Legion destroy its offices. Governor Thomas Ford responded by requesting the disarmament and demobilization of the Nauvoo Legion, and Smith complied. In return, however, Smith requested state protection from his enraged enemies.[27] Illinois proved unequal to the task. On June 24, 1844, a mob killed Joseph Smith and his brother Hyrum in the supposed safety of the jail at Carthage, Illinois.

Joseph Smith's death fragmented the church. Brigham Young assumed leadership of its main body.[28] Young, like Smith a native of Vermont, had converted to Mormonism in 1832 and rose through the church ranks, becoming a president of the Quorum of the Twelve Apostles, the highest-ranking officers in the church after the president, for which he earned the

title "Lion of the Lord." In Nauvoo he was among the first to practice polygamy, taking his second wife in 1842. After Joseph Smith's assassination,
Young assumed the church presidency, which he held until his death in 1877.[29]

A brief calm followed the murders, but Mormon-Gentile relations soon
soured. In 1845 the Illinois legislature repealed Nauvoo's charter, and the federal government indicted Brigham Young and other high-ranking Mormons
on suspicion of counterfeiting. In 1846, two weeks after his indictment (no
reliable evidence implicated Nauvoo's Mormon leaders in the crime) and
amid rumors of federal military intervention, Young announced that the
Saints would abandon the United States to found Zion outside its borders.[30]

The outbreak of the Mexican-American War in 1846 smoothed the way
for Mormons heading west. The United States, needing troops, accepted
more than five hundred volunteers, known collectively as the Mormon Battalion, from the Saints camped in Iowa on their way out of Illinois. This not
only boosted the ranks of the U.S. military but also allied Mormons with the
United States and ended President James Polk's concern that they might fight
for Mexico. Government service brought food, clothing, and pay to the men
of the Mormon Battalion, many of whom shared this compensation with
their families, thus aiding the Mormon exodus.[31] Ironically, in waging war
against Catholic Mexico, the United States found Mormonism tolerable.

As the Mormons headed west, they saw themselves in the same light as
they did those settlers who had abandoned Europe to find religious asylum
in America. According to Brigham Young, the move west fit into a divine plan
for the Mormons. "Joseph [Smith] intended to go West; he designed to raise
a company to come to the very country we now occupy," Young told a gathering of Mormons some years later.[32] Young and those who followed him went
not only westward but into "a primordial sacred time," according to the historian Jan Shipps. By wandering through the western wilderness to reach their
own promised land, Shipps argues, the Saints "conjoined experience and
scripture to take possession of that special relationship to God which once
had been the sole property of the Jews." Thus began Mormonism's "Golden
Age," when the Saints made themselves a chosen race and created what
amounted to a nation-state powerful enough to be perceived as a threat by
the government of the United States. The Mormons wanted "to quit 'Babylon,'" to escape the evils and persecutions of American society, and to build
their Zion in the safety of the West.[33] But that West existed only in myth.

Brigham Young led the Mormons west to the Great Basin, which was then
part of Mexico. To govern their settlement, the Mormons established the
"state" of Deseret—as they saw it, the government of God on earth. The

Saints staffed Deseret's government from the ranks of their church. Because most Utah settlers at the time were Mormons, and because Mormons accepted the concept that religious leaders should influence civil affairs, church and local government worked together to achieve common objectives. Generally speaking, the local government hierarchy was staffed by church members and mirrored the church hierarchy. Young became governor, joined by a secretary of the territory and supreme court judges, all of whom came from the highest ranks of church leadership. In addition, every member of the legislature was a church leader. The Deseret legislature met when Young needed it and did little beyond formalizing church policy.[34]

Officially Deseret operated only briefly, for Mexico soon ceded the territory to the United States. The federal authorities then organized the Utah Territory and imposed a new form of government on the Saints. Despite the existence of the territorial government, however, Deseret's machinery continued to function behind the scenes until 1872.[35]

Fortune smiled on the Saints during Utah's early years as a territory, when President Millard Fillmore helped them install considerable church authority in the territorial government. Fillmore appointed Brigham Young governor of Utah Territory and named another Mormon and two residents of Utah to other important positions. By naming Mormons and Utah residents to four of seven federal positions he appointed, Fillmore gave greater local control to the Saints than they probably would have received from either of his two immediate predecessors in the White House.[36]

In creating Zion the Mormons built a unique judicial system. Echoing Paul's advice to Corinth's Christians, Mormon leaders taught that the Saints should resolve their disputes within their own community rather than turn to secular institutions. For the remainder of the nineteenth century, Mormons tended to do just that.[37]

County probate courts of early Utah hold special interest because of their extraordinary powers. The church-dominated territorial legislature appointed county probate judges. These men presided over county probate courts, which included two selectmen and whose powers extended to executive and legislative matters at the county level. Even considered on strictly judicial terms, the county probate courts had exceptional powers. For example, after non-Mormons who were critical of the church were placed on the territorial supreme court, the Mormon-dominated territorial legislature gave these probate courts civil and criminal jurisdiction concurrent with that of federal district courts. As one might guess, probate judges usually held influential positions in the church, too.[38] This state of affairs frightened proponents of republican government or at least gave them justification to act against the Mormons—to defend the American way of government.

Even though the Saints wanted to escape their persecutors and to establish the kingdom of God on earth, they also held strong loyalties to the United States, at least for the time being. Church doctrine in fact demanded loyalty to the law of the land in which the Mormons lived. Before the founding of Utah Territory, Joseph Smith received a revelation in 1833 commanding respect for the constitutional law of whatever land the Saints inhabited. A subsequent revelation indicated that the Lord had established the Constitution of the United States.[39] The Mormons had clear, divine orders to be good citizens of the land in which they lived.

Prophecies recorded by Joseph Smith explain the apparent paradox presented by Mormons seeking their own government within the United States. In remarkably prescient passages within the just-mentioned revelations, Smith recorded conditions under which the Mormons might have problems with secular government and methods they should use to handle them. One passage indicated that although the laws were good, the people who carried them out might not be. Another instructed the Saints to use established civil channels to protest against those officials who might harm or threaten their interests. If the civil government did not provide satisfaction, the revelation assured, the Lord would bring his fury on the nation to set things right.[40] The U.S. Constitution and laws of the land were sacred to the Mormons. The execution of those laws and those chosen to execute them, however, could and would cause problems. Before those revelations had aged twenty-five years, the Mormons found themselves at odds with federally appointed territorial officials, primarily in the judiciary.

Even as President Fillmore empowered Mormonism by naming Young and other influential Mormons to high offices, he also vexed them by appointing a number of political hacks to office in Utah, particularly in the territorial judiciary. The non-Mormon appointees Lemuel G. Brandebury (chief justice), Perry G. Brocchus (associate justice), Broughton D. Harris (territorial secretary) and Henry R. Day (Indian agent) hoped to accrue wealth and power through their federal jobs. On arriving in Utah in 1851, Day learned that as governor, Brigham Young served ex officio as superintendent of Indian affairs, which meant that he controlled all Indian business. The justices discovered that the all-Mormon legislature had named probate judges—all Saints—to handle cases within the jurisdiction of the territorial courts. As for Harris, he found that Young, who took office while the non-Mormon appointees were still en route to Utah, had conducted a census, a task normally undertaken by the secretary, and had held a delegate election.[41]

Even before the federally appointed territorial officials arrived, then, the stage had been set for conflict with Mormon officials. The report Brandebury, Brocchus, and Harris sent to President Fillmore in December 1851 shows that little had changed in the months after their arrival. It also provides insights into the coming U.S.-Mormon conflict. The officials described Utah as having a homogeneous population, almost entirely Mormon, with the church controlling virtually every aspect of people's lives, the legislature, the judiciary, and the military; minting money stamped with the phrase "Holiness to the Lord"; openly sanctioning plural marriage; and requiring strict obedience to the church.[42] According to this report, the Mormons had already made substantial progress toward creating their kingdom of God on earth before the U.S. federal presence could be brought to bear. Because, political hacks or not, the territorial officials were most likely good republicans, they found much to dislike in Utah.

Friction between the federal appointees and the Saints quickly created a crisis. Judge Brocchus, addressing the semiannual meeting of church officers, attacked Mormonism and insulted the Saints. More fuel found the fire when Secretary Harris invalidated the August delegate election. Within days, on September 28, 1851, Brandebury, Brocchus, Day, and Harris left Utah, taking with them the territorial seal, public papers, and $24,000 in cash intended for territorial business. Once back in Washington, the officials reported that the Mormons were resisting federal laws and that the army should be dispatched to enforce order. Secretary of State Daniel Webster told the "flying officers" to go back to their jobs or resign. They resigned.[43]

By 1851 the federal government had already come to perceive the Utah Mormons as posing serious problems, and these perceptions now became even more inflamed. The Saints' Indian policy, communalism, and polygamy all attacked fundamental aspects of American life, including Judeo-Christian doctrines. The U.S. government continued to disagree with the Mormons over Indian policy, just as non-Mormons in Missouri had earlier. Most in the United States wanted to convert Indians into mainstream Christian farmers, while the Saints wanted to make them Mormons. In 1855 Garland Hurt, the Indian agent for Utah, complained to the commissioner of Indian affairs that the Mormons had sent "a large number of missionaries" among the Indians, leading them to turn against the United States. Hurt also reported another item that would stir emotions in the government and in the East: the Mormons believed that they were the only true Christians on earth.[44]

The practice of plural marriage provided one of the most sensational sources of Mormon-U.S. conflict. More often referred to as polygamy, this tenet of Mormon theology, publicly announced in 1852, widened the rift between the Saints and the American mainstream and provided the basis for the federal government's nearly fifty-year crusade against them. Mormons believed they were answering God's call to multiply and replenish the earth via an institution rooted in the Bible. Mainstream America, however, believed the Mormons were building a Sodom in the Great Basin. From the time of the announcement through the church's denunciation of plural marriage in 1890, Mormon polygamy held America's attention from the White House to the halls of Congress to the national media.

Non-Mormons in the Victorian United States believed the entire social order rests on men's abilities to control their desires. Polygamy smacked of unbridled sensuality, which many feared would undermine morality, the foundation of civilization and of the nation's social order. In addition, given its connotations of slavery, it threatened to debase women and womanhood, who were supposed to be the glue that held American homes together. A wag might suggest that mainstream Americans, knowing the power women added to society through their family contributions, feared that Mormon super-families, fueled by contributions of several wives per family, might come to exercise undue influence on American society. To Mormons, plural marriage made perfect sense within their theology and would not bring chaos. On the contrary, it would speed salvation and the construction of God's kingdom on earth.[45]

For unknown reasons, the 1852 official announcement sanctioning polygamy did not cause an immediate stir but exploded on the political scene in the 1856 election. Perhaps the Democrats in power had little stomach for tackling a domestic issue such as polygamy when it would likely require tackling another volatile domestic issue, slavery. Perhaps it remained quiet because the men appointed to replace the "runaway officials" did not care to make an issue of polygamy's legality. Maybe the replacement of the former territorial secretary with a Mormon played a role. Overall, a cast of territorial officers consisting of Saints and cooperative Gentiles and an all-Mormon legislature allowed Brigham Young to rule Utah absolutely from 1851 until 1858.[46] During this period the Saints enjoyed independence vis-à-vis the federal government much like the American colonies' pseudo-independence from Great Britain known as "salutary neglect." As their colonial forebears had done, the Saints made the most of the opportunity.[47] When the United States decided to reassert its authority in Utah, conflict, even war, appeared imminent.

The beginning of the end of home rule in Utah can be traced to the 1855 appointment of W. W. Drummond to replace Leonidus Shaver—one of the cooperative Gentiles—as associate justice of Utah's territorial supreme court.

Drummond left his wife back East and instead brought his mistress, whom he allowed to share his bench as he conducted court business. This offended the Mormons, who considered adultery to be among the worst sins. In addition to perpetrating this personal affront, Drummond assaulted the legal fortress the Saints had created. He declared the Utah Judiciary Act unconstitutional and ordered probate courts to give up their criminal and civil jurisdiction.[48]

Justice Drummond created even more trouble for the Mormons when he resigned. In his resignation letter Drummond complained that Utah's Mormons obeyed no law other than that handed down by Brigham Young; laws passed by Congress, he alleged, carried no weight. He also made vague charges about secret Mormon organizations dedicated to resisting U.S. laws, court records that had been destroyed with the knowledge and approval of the church, and federal officers in the territory who suffered constant insults, harassment, and annoyances from Mormons.[49] Drummond's resignation drew more unfavorable attention to the Mormons and may have contributed to President James Buchanan's decision to send the army to Utah. Drummond's public enmity came at a bad time, just as Mormonism was entering a fervent revival in the basin.

By the mid-1850s Mormon leaders believed their move to Utah had isolated them enough to let them begin establishing the kingdom of God on earth. A series of disasters (drought, grasshopper infestation, hard winter, poor crops) in 1855 and 1856 convinced church leaders that God was not pleased with the state of spiritual affairs in Utah and was punishing the Saints. A smallpox epidemic reinforced that notion. The situation, they believed, called for spiritual renewal and reform.[50] From the spring of 1856 through the spring of 1857, the Saints experienced a revival that strengthened the spirit of many Mormons, but it also drove some marginal believers from the faith and, along with a number of non-Mormons, from Utah Territory.

Elements of the Mormon Reformation alienated outsiders, many of whom already considered the Saints strange and threatening. The doctrine of blood atonement, for one, made many question the Mormon belief system. This doctrine requires perpetrators of certain sins to be willing to be executed as an offering to heaven. Many outsiders saw in this yet another example of fanatical religious dementia.[51]

The Mormon Reformation also focused attention on polygamy. Although it had been known for years that some Mormons practiced plural marriage, the Reformation urged all Mormons to embrace the practice. The church now taught that monogamists, even worthy ones, would not dwell in the highest chambers of heaven; a popular Reformation song reminded Saints that those coveted places were reserved for the plurally married. By the end of 1856 requests for polygamous marriages had increased dramatically, as had the church's approval rate for those unions.[52] Although they did not surface until 1858, newspaper reports of polygamy and the Reformation reminded Americans of this Mormon idiosyncrasy. The *New York Daily Tribune*'s correspondent wrote that the essence of the Reformation was "the forcing of polygamy upon the entire population—no longer as a matter of choice, but as a rite pleasing to God and essential to salvation—and also the inculcation of hatred toward the Government of the United States, and toward all Gentiles as a religious duty."[53]

The intensification of Mormon practices during the Reformation may have contributed to dislike, anti-Mormon hysteria, or even hatred among non-Mormons, particularly considering that Brigham Young and others threatened destruction on enemies of the church. In April 1857, as the Reformation came to a close, Young told church officials that Gentiles and apostates had to leave that spring or he would remove them. On July 4, 1857, Young wrote, "The way Lawyers, loafers, special pleaders, apostates, officials and filth has been cast out is a caution to all sinners, that here they would be in the wrong place."[54]

The Reformation also bore consequences for federal officials, who may have contributed to the spirit that spawned the movement. One of the first to feel its effects was Judge George P. Stiles, himself a Mormon and a former associate of Joseph Smith. The church tried Stiles for adultery and, finding him guilty, ostracized him. He responded with anger toward Mormons who came before him on the bench. Perhaps in retaliation for Stiles's hostility, burglars broke into his office and that of a Gentile lawyer and stole court records, dumping some into a privy and burning them. Reformation zeal also led to conflicts with David H. Burr, the surveyor general, and Dr. Garland Hurt, an Indian agent. Having difficulty performing their jobs, they complained to Washington that the Mormons were in rebellion.[55]

From the Mormon perspective, the Reformation appeared successful. Crops improved in the fall of 1856, and "weak" Mormons and others fled Utah. The exodus included the second contingent of federal officials to flee the state—Stiles, Drummond, Burr, and Hurt. By the spring of 1857 Brigham Young declared their exit to have been the result of the Almighty's fire burning out the ungodly. Among many Mormons these events and actions aroused heightened religious consciousness and fanaticism. This in turn made Mormons feel that they must stand united against a sinful world.[56] Unbeknownst to Young or any of the Saints in Utah, even as they celebrated what they considered the success of the Reformation, the largest peacetime army yet assembled in the history of the United States—a sixth of the entire army—was already on its way to Utah to put the Saints in their place.

By 1856, thanks partly to the Republican platform dedicated to eradicating slavery and polygamy, the "Mormon Question" had become a centerpiece of national political discourse. The first antipolygamy bills appeared in Congress. In debates about slavery and admitting Kansas to the Union, congressmen asked whether allowing Kansas—and southern states—to have slavery would not mean allowing Utah to have polygamy—and allowing territories subsequently entering the Union to have both. In this highly charged atmosphere, Utah's residents decided to make another bid for statehood, which brought even more scrutiny to their lifestyle and how it would, or would not, coexist with the rest of America.[57]

The debate over Utah's statehood helped tie slavery to polygamy as political issues. Some Democratic newspapers favored admitting Utah, polygamy intact, to the Union. Some pundits argued that compared to "Bleeding Kansas," also nearing statehood, polygamous Utah looked like a paragon of order. If chaotic Kansas could be considered for admission, why not orderly Utah? This debate also put some southern politicians on the spot. Those who argued that territories should be admitted regardless of their domestic institutions (code for slavery) found themselves in the uncomfortable position of allowing polygamy under the same rationale. Unfortunately for Utah, this argument presented the Union with a double whammy: favoring polygamy also required favoring slavery, or at least its legality.

Shortly after the Democrats nominated James Buchanan for president and adopted a platform dedicated to popular sovereignty, Republicans tried to capitalize on the day's issues by nominating John C. Fremont and adopted a platform dedicated to purifying the territories of "those twin relics of barbarism—Polygamy and Slavery." Fremont rallies often featured banners trumpeting slogans to that effect. At a Fremont parade in Indianapolis, one float carried a figure dressed as Brigham Young accompanied by six wives— white ones, black ones, and bald ones—each with an infant. The Young character held a banner that read, "Hurrah for the Kansas-Nebraska bill—it introduces Polygamy and Slavery."[58] Thus Mormons saw their religion dragged mockingly into national politics.

While the Republican position may have made good political sense, it also reflected the moral values of the Republican Party and of the mainstream East. Mainstream America saw polygamy as "a growing evil," like slavery. That meant the Church of Jesus Christ of Latter-day Saints, espouser of one of the evils and tolerant of the other, was evil. Fighting social evils meant fighting the church and the Mormons in Utah's territorial government and waging war against an evil, un-American religion. Though the Democrats had carried the election in 1856, they could not afford to be seen as friends of the Saints.

When he took office in 1857, President James Buchanan had just finished campaigning against the fledgling Republican Party, dedicated to eradicating slavery and polygamy. According to the historian Elbert Smith, Buchanan's foremost concern on assuming the presidency was ensuring that the Republicans did not win the office in 1860. Buchanan must have known that he would inherit major political headaches from slavery and "Bleeding" Kansas. Politically, Buchanan could not afford to risk a strong policy in Kansas or on slavery, even if he were so inclined. Utah held more promise. Robert Tyler, son of a former president, advised Buchanan to use an anti-Mormon crusade to divert attention from abolitionism. Buchanan may also have been influenced by federal appointees who had abandoned posts or lost money in Utah and sought vengeance against the Mormons.[59]

Buchanan could have found support for his Utah policy in the eastern press, which expressed considerable anti-Mormon sentiment. In May 1857 the *New York Times* stated that affairs in Utah had reached the point where the federal government had to act. The paper recommended immediately sending a new governor, "backed by an imposing military force—to tender the Constitution with one hand, while a drawn sword is held in the other."[60] Even in Utah Mormons knew national public opinion ran against them. Hosea Stout, an influential Mormon, wrote in his diary on June 14, 1857, "It appears that there is now throughout the U.S. the most bitter, revengeful, and mobocratic feeling against us that has ever been manifested." An 1857 letter-writing campaign by W. W. Drummond, arguing that only federal troops could restore order in Utah, likely fueled both sides of the debate.[61] The polygamy issue gave Buchanan an opportunity to act decisively on a high-profile issue, seemingly with little political risk to him and, perhaps, with considerable reward.

The Mormons themselves helped hold the nation's attention. For instance, church leaders made statements that appeared strident and rebellious to people in the East. Brigham Young uttered the best known of these comments when he declared in 1853, "I am and will be Governor, and no power can hinder it until the Lord Almighty says, 'Brigham, you need not be Governor any longer.'" During the following years, Young figured that if he understood Joseph Smith properly, he could precipitate conditions that would bring the Savior's return and initiate the millennium. This contributed to his decision to pursue a bellicose position with respect to the United States, including manufacturing weapons and stockpiling supplies and ammunition as early as 1856. Young believed God would inspire the Saints to prevail over any force the United States could muster.[62] Anti-Mormons could hardly have asked for better evidence that Utah harbored religion-crazed renegades worthy of federal force.

Considering all these factors, the newly elected Buchanan decided to reassert federal authority in Utah by replacing Brigham Young as governor, appointing officials to replace those who had fled, and sending a powerful army to escort these appointees to Utah to ensure their installation. Sadly, Buchanan made poor use of this opportunity by appointing political hacks to many of the Utah positions, a trait that he displayed throughout his administration and that caused more trouble in Utah. With Utah officials having received no notice of these new appointments or of the large armed force that would be escorting them, Buchanan's policy went into effect on May 28, 1857, when General Winfield Scott, heeding his commander-in-chief, ordered troops from Fort Leavenworth to march on Salt Lake City.[63]

The decision to send an armed force to Utah occurred in a complex atmosphere involving a number of considerations. Buchanan explained his decision in legal terms, alleging that religious persecution played no role. He argued that Utah's residents had for years shown insubordination to the Constitution and the laws of the United States. He sent the army to Utah to enforce the laws, to protect the new federal officers arriving there, and to help them perform their duties. Furthermore, Buchanan argued that by opposing U.S. authority, the "misguided people" of Utah stood in "rebellion against the government to which [they] owe[d] allegiance" and that by "levying war against the United States," they were guilty of treason.[64] These curiously strong words came from the same president who took no action against southern states that seceded from the Union before his term ended. At first blush Buchanan's rhetoric seems to focus on law and order, but a closer reading suggests religious underpinnings for his motives, even if he did not admit them. If the people of Utah were indeed "misguided," it was because of Mormonism.

By claiming that the federal action against Utah had no religious basis, Buchanan showed that he failed to understand Mormon theology and society. His proclamation specifically denied any religious element to the expedition's purpose. He also wrote that if Mormons obeyed the laws, they could

pursue whatever faith they chose. Buchanan also asserted the federal government neither directly nor indirectly sought to disturb Mormon worship
or to influence religious opinions among the Saints.[65] Whether he meant it or
not, Buchanan's attention to religion showed it was on his mind. Regardless
of the veracity of his claims, this federal action marked the beginning of a
thirty-three-year federal crusade against Mormon religion and culture.

When it came time for Buchanan to justify his Utah policy to Congress,
he followed much the same tack. He mentioned religion only when beginning his speech, saying, "We have much reason for gratitude to that Almighty
Providence, which has never failed to interpose for our relief, at the most
critical periods of our history."[66] After Buchanan expressed thanks to God
for smiling on America, he made a case for sending troops to Utah to suppress the rebellion and force Mormon obedience to the Constitution and
U.S. laws. The president neglected to mention that he had not tried to negotiate with the Mormons, who held the Constitution and its laws sacred,
and that the territory had been peaceful prior to the Utah Expedition.

In Salt Lake City the *Deseret News* reported the Mormon version of the
conflict with the U.S. government. Owned by the Church of Jesus Christ of
Latter-day Saints (LDS), the newspaper served as its mouthpiece but also gave
a fairly accurate account of the United States' position and policy.[67] Early in
the conflict, shortly after news of the Utah Expedition became public, the
paper's editor asked, "Why Utah?" California and Nebraska, among other
places under federal jurisdiction, had much more serious problems with law
enforcement and insurrection than did Utah, the paper argued. Why not dis-
patch troops to those places, editor Albert Carrington queried, instead of to
Utah, where "all is peace, industry, law, order, virtue, sobriety"? Carrington's
answer was Mormonism. Self-servingly he argued that the evil government
had determined to corrupt virtuous Mormons to become as lawless and blood-
thirsty as the federal government and mainstream America or exterminate
them in the process.[68] Speaking for the church, the *Deseret News* showed that
the Saints believed the U.S. government was attacking them only for their religious beliefs. However overwrought or unjustified Carrington's rhetoric, it
points to the basic fact of a contest of values being waged in the West.

Given the Mormons' experiences with armed forces ranging from mili-
tias to armed mobs, they expected the worst from the approaching army.
Revelation provided many guidelines for Mormon policies, and reaction to
the prospective invasion of their Great Basin kingdom proved no exception.
Revelation's influence appears clearly in the records of the Nauvoo Legion.
Mormon doctrine provided guidance for resolving conflicts with the United

States, should they arise. Because the governmental systems erected under the Constitution had God's blessing, doctrine urged Saints to address their problems within those systems. When a problem arose, Joseph Smith's revelation from God urged the Saints to use the legal system to resolve it. Should the legal system fail, they should take their case to the governor and, if necessary, to the president of the United States. Should the entire system fail, God would "vex the nation" in his fury at its wrongdoing. As the Nauvoo Legion prepared to face the advancing U.S. Army, the influence of that revelation appeared in its orders. The commander briefly summarized the Saints' persecutions to date, citing attacks on Mormon homes and women and religious intolerance. He argued that the Mormons had sought justice within the legal apparatus established by the state and found neither justice nor sympathy from judges, governors, or the U.S. president. Those avenues having been exhausted, he wrote, the time had come for the Saints to invoke a higher power and defend themselves from additional transgressions. The orders can be compared to the Declaration of Independence, which outlines a series of offenses committed by a distant, tyrannical government as a justification for harsh action. Another Nauvoo Legion commander signed a report with the words "May God direct our efforts and Israel prevail." Mormons believed they had faced their persecutions to that time as dictated by scripture. Having received no redress from following the prescribed channels, they believed it was time to fight their persecutors and expected God's sanction in doing so. As Andrew Love wrote in his diary on April 1, 1858, "There is no rest for the people of God untill [*sic*] they are strong enough to assert their rights and maintain them at the point of the sword."[69]

Brigham Young responded to the expected invasion with bluster and threats. On the day Young is alleged to have learned of the military threat (evidence indicates he knew of the army's advance well before the date he officially announced it), he wrote in his diary: "The feeling of Mobocracy is rife in the 'States,' the constant cry is kill the Mormons. *Let them try it.*" Young later confided to his diary that unless the U.S. government adopted a more conciliatory attitude toward Utah and the Mormons, he would consider stopping overland migration through Utah and "make every preparation to give the U.S. a Sound drubbing."[70]

The drastic actions Young apparently considered included independence for Utah. He interpreted the army's approach as an act of God that would cut ties between the Saints and the rest of the United States. Young's writing on this topic provides another example of the way Mormons interpreted a bedrock principle of American politics—in this case, contractarianism—

in such a way as to incur the wrath and retribution of the government. Briefly stated, the position is this: good and virtuous men conduct good government; God inspired the U.S. Constitution, which will foster good government worthy of Mormon support and loyalty when administered by virtuous men; when nonvirtuous men administer the Constitution, however, poor government will result, in which case Mormons should strike out on their own.[71] As Buchanan had invoked "Almighty Providence" in his message to Congress, Young looked heavenward for guidance, but from the vastly different perspective provided by Mormonism.

Young declared martial law in September 1857 and prepared the Mormons to defend themselves against their invaders. Young's declaration appeared on a broadside announcing a hostile force about to invade Utah to destroy the Saints. As a statement of Mormon resolve and justification for their actions, the declaration deserves special attention. After a strong opening, Young recounted the trials, tribulations, and persecutions the Saints had experienced while living in the United States. As he put it, the Saints had suffered while residing in "the boasted abodes of Christianity and civilization."[72]

After that tirade Young told the Saints that they faced more persecution for their religious beliefs. "Our opponents have availed themselves of prejudice existing against us because of our religious faith," Young wrote, "to send out a formidable host to accomplish our destruction." In exhorting the Saints to action, Young again emphasized freedom of religion.[73] Through these passionate pleas, Young prepared the Saints to defend their religion against the invading force.

Young's message came through clearly, judging by subsequent Mormon records. A selection of Wilford Woodruff's writings shows Young's influence on church members and the extent to which Saints interpreted the events surrounding the Utah Expedition as a religious conflict. Woodruff, a high-ranking Mormon who worked as church historian at the time of the Utah Expedition, later became president of the church and in 1890 issued the "manifesto" that ended its sanction of plural marriage. On August 28, 1857, Woodruff wrote in his diary that the U.S. government had sent an army to destroy Mormonism. Furthermore, he charged non-Mormon Americans with being wicked enemies of God who were determined to prevent the establishment of God's kingdom on earth. Woodruff still held this view months later, as revealed by a November 19, 1857, diary entry titled "Reflections," in which he repeated stories of Mormon persecutions at the hands of Americans. According to Woodruff, when it became apparent that the Mormons would prosper in the West, the United States dispatched an armed force to accomplish its "Hellish purpose" of destroying the Saints.[74]

Although anti-Mormons might argue that this proves Mormonism antithetical to republican values, Woodruff, a loyal Mormon, appears to be repeating church policy as articulated by Brigham Young. Other high-ranking Mormons echoed these sentiments. S. W. Richards, regent of the University of Deseret, wrote that news of the army and "the universal cry and voice of the nation that the Mormons must quit the practice of their religious institutions . . . indicate to us that the present intentions of Gov. towards us are extremely hostile."[75] While some caution must be exercised in interpreting these words, they suggest that at least the Mormon leadership shared, or parroted, the notion that the U.S. government was attacking them because of their religion.

Writings by Mormons lower in the church hierarchy show similar patterns, indicating broad acceptance of the invasion as a religious matter. The impending invasion inspired Asa Smith Hawley to write a song whose lyrics offer one of the most creative and comprehensive responses to the event. Hawley's ballad puts the invasion in the context of Mormon persecutions in Missouri and Illinois and warns the current persecutors that the Saints will resist forcefully and that the invaders' bones will "molder and bleach on the Plains."[76] On September 17, 1857, David Candland made an entry in his journal explaining why Young had declared martial law: "The United States had sent her troops here for the purpose of annoying us & Making us succumb to the Civil law whose object was & is to force us to relinquish our cherished holy religion." Two months later Esaias Edwards recorded his belief that the U.S. government sought to kill off the Saints.[77]

Still others, perhaps continuing to feel the Reformation's excitement, interpreted the invasion as God's test of their faith. On August 30, 1857, after mentioning the troops marching on Utah in his diary, Andrew Love wrote, "Trials & purification we must abide or no celestial glory, now is a time to watch & pray & live our religion."[78] The Saints believed their respite from religious persecution had ended and that the U.S. government would now extend its long arm to accomplish in the Great Basin what the mobs of Missouri and Illinois could no longer do.

Newspaper reports carried Mormon responses to the Utah Expedition to eastern readers and clearly expressed the conflict's religious overtones. In September 1857 a newspaper correspondent wrote that travelers along the transcontinental trail reported the Saints reacting defiantly to the news of the Utah Expedition. The travelers reported hearing a Mormon song with the following chorus:

> We'll serve the Lord to-day;
> The Prophet we'll obey;
> You may mind just whom you'll please,
> We will mind what Brigham says.

What Brigham said, according to the newspaper's report, was that the U.S. Army intended to make whores of Mormon women and that Young threatened personally to kill the army's commander and send him to hell.[79]

Despite President Buchanan's assurances to the contrary, the Utah assembly saw the federal action as a clear threat to their religious liberty when it memorialized Congress. In addition to citing the Missouri and Illinois persecutions, the memorial listed the murders of the founder and prophet Joseph Smith and his brother Hyrum and the assassination of Parley P. Pratt, a high-ranking church official killed in Arkansas earlier in 1857. In addition, the territorial legislature asked Congress to protect the Mormons' religious and political rights, which they believed had been trampled. The memorial emphasized the U.S. Constitution's protection of religious liberties, which those in Utah took to be under attack. The nation may have wished them to deny their God and their religion, but the Saints assured the nation they would not do it. Brigham Young reemphasized the Mormon persecutions two months later when addressing a special council at the Tabernacle, telling the assemblage that their relations with the United States had amounted to "being driven from the Christian world by Christians."[80] Seen from Utah, the advancing army and its purpose offered a drastically different appearance than they did when viewed from Washington.

Knowing they were outgunned and therefore must not start a shooting war, the Mormons prepared for a defensive stand and a battle of attrition. The Nauvoo Legion received orders to annoy and harass, but not kill, their enemy. Mormon guerrillas destroyed three U.S. government supply trains, ran off stock, and burned thousands of acres of grazing land along the army's route. Another element of their defense involved limiting the army's capabilities by driving off its draft animals. Army officers worried about lost animals and cut communication lines.[81]

This strategy resulted in few or no human casualties and accomplished two important objectives. First, it convinced the U.S. government that invading and occupying Utah would not be easy; in fact, it would be downright expensive. Second, by preventing the army from reaching striking distance of Salt Lake City, the Mormons bought time to devise another strategy.[82]

According to one eyewitness to a Mormon raid, the Saints had mixed results as they tried to drive off the army's animals. He reported that when the army was camped within a day of South Pass, in central Wyoming, six mounted Mormon raiders awakened the camp at night with a terrific yelling and firing of guns that stampeded every horse and mule. The mules ran about three miles, but then the army buglers sounded "stable call"; the mules recognized the signal as a call to eat, so they ran back to camp, as did the six still-saddled horses of the Mormon raiders.[83] Another veteran of the expedition told a different story in which Mormon guerrillas succeeded in making life miserable for the advancing army. According to that account, Mormons fired the grass and scrub daily as the army approached camp. Every night before pitching their tents, the soldiers had to fight fires. The tactic forced the army to drive its animals farther to find feed, expending considerably more time and energy than would have been the case otherwise. Moreover, it created strong resentment among the soldiers.[84]

The Mountain Meadows Massacre gave the Mormons another reason to keep the army out of Utah. In early September a wagon train consisting of travelers from Missouri and Arkansas crossed southern Utah, allegedly antagonizing Indians and Mormon settlers. Of all Mormon Utah, the southern settlements may have been the most disturbed by the news that the U.S. Army was headed for the territory. Most of the settlers there had been with the church through the troubles in Missouri and Illinois. Some had survived the massacre at Haun's Mill in Missouri in 1838; others had lost family members and friends there. Partly because of their remote location, the southern settlements arranged to defend themselves by organizing a company of minutemen in January 1856.

When news of the U.S. army's advance reached them, the southern settlements mobilized. In addition to urging general readiness, Mormon leaders admonished settlers there to prepare for a possible winter campaign by conserving supplies. In particular, church authorities forbade selling or trading foodstuffs to "any Gentile merchant or temporary sojourner." Mormons had sent missionaries to the Indians since their arrival in the Great Basin, but with a major military clash impending, Indian relations took on a new significance. The Mormons did their best to ensure cooperation on the part of Utah's natives. One Mormon referred to them as "the battle-ax of the Lord," which the Mormons might be able to use against an enemy, such as the advancing U.S. force or unwelcome immigrants. The southern Utah

Mormons also knew that Parley P. Pratt, a member of the Quorum of the Twelve Apostles, had recently been murdered in Arkansas—by the jealous and angry husband of one of Pratt's plural wives, whom she had not legally divorced—creating much anguish and likely sentiment for revenge.[85]

Into this "zealous south," as Juanita Brooks called southern Utah, rolled the Fancher party, a wagon train of people emigrating from Arkansas and Missouri. Few would survive. More than one hundred men, women, and children from this group were murdered on September 11, 1857, in a spasm of violence known best as the Mountain Meadows Massacre. On that horrible day, Mormon militia and Paiute Indians killed about 120 men, women, and children of the Fancher party. Eighteen children survived. After the disaster, the murderers explained their actions by citing various motivations, including suspicion that the Fancher party might be allied with the army advancing on Utah, a desire to avenge Parley Pratt's murder in Arkansas and the Mormon expulsion from Missouri in 1838, and a desire to loot the wagon train. The conflict between the U.S. government and the Mormons cannot be discussed without considering the massacre, and the massacre cannot be understood separately from the conflict between the United States and the Mormons. Controversy swirls around the event's interpretations, including charges that Brigham Young ordered the massacre and its subsequent cover-up. Young eventually excommunicated three men for their participation at Mountain Meadows. One, John Doyle Lee, was tried, convicted, and executed.[86]

The atmosphere in Utah had grown yet more charged the week before the Fancher train arrived in Salt Lake City. In August 1857 Young whipped his followers into an anti-American lather with his sermons. Even though the Saints loved the U.S. Constitution, he said, the corrupt U.S. government had persecuted them, and now Young declared, "I am at the defiance of all hell [and] Governments, but especially ours." The week prior to the Fancher train's arrival, Young's rhetoric became even more pointed when he declared, "God has commenced to set up his kingdom on the earth, and all hell and its devils are moving against it." As Indian agent for the territory, Young had a duty to protect overland travelers. As he prepared the Saints for conflict with the U.S. Army, however, he sent representatives to area tribes to encourage them to attack wagon trains. He could thus threaten to halt overland travel.[87]

Some sources suggest the Fancher train brought disaster on itself. They reported that its members went out of their way to antagonize Mormons in the settlements through which they passed. They named their oxen after Brigham Young and other high-ranking Mormons and loudly cursed the beasts by name when passing through towns. Furthermore, they boasted of what they would do to the Mormons once the army arrived. When Mormons refused to sell them food, the emigrants reportedly stole what they wanted. To be fair to the latter, however, it must be admitted that the Mormons did not treat them well, either. Harboring immense bitterness from their persecutions, they refused to supply the settlers as they prepared for the final push through rough country on their way to California.[88]

More recent studies suggest that such accusations were fabricated as part of the grisly event's cover-up and in the pressurized atmosphere created by the U.S. Army bearing down on Utah. Records do not corroborate the charges leveled against the Fancher train, and some incidents attributed to it were committed by earlier emigrants and attributed to the Fancher group to help explain the massacre. The truth about what happened may never be known, but the facts seem not to justify a single death, let alone more than one hundred.[89]

The murder of as many as 120 emigrants by Mormons and their Indian allies occurred in mid-September 1857. Thirteen years passed before any form of justice was meted out to the perpetrators of the massacre, and even then it was a sham at best. The church excommunicated two men, John D. Lee and Isaac C. Haight, for their actions in the affair. Within four years the church reinstated Haight, but John Lee remained an outcast. After the Poland Act of 1874 took criminal jurisdiction from the probate courts and installed it in the federal courts, Lee became the target for both the church and the government. Federal officials arrested Lee and tried him in 1875 for his part in the massacre. The trial ended in a hung jury, but Lee was tried again in September 1876. During the intervening months, leaders of the church allegedly agreed to help convict Lee if the court would drop charges against all others. Lee died at the hands of a firing squad on March 23, 1877.

Brigham Young supposedly had no direct responsibility for the massacre, although he apparently had made it clear that he wished Indians and others to attack emigrants, which would signal his ability to cripple overland travel. As for the other participants, their motives may never be known. Juanita Brooks suggests that they acted out of hysteria, believing themselves to be at war. That explanation probably carries some truth. One must also acknowledge that the recently ended Mormon Reformation, the years of persecution, and simple revenge and hooliganism all played a part. Finally, one must consider the possibility of a grand end-time scheme. Various signs may have convinced Young that the Second Coming had drawn near. Given Joseph Smith's prophecy that in the last days Indians would unite with the Saints to defeat unbelievers, Young may have believed that if the Saints re-

mained righteous and brought on certain conditions, God would usher in
the millennium. At the very least, he believed God would lead the Saints to
victory over any opponent the United States could throw at them. This would
help explain why Young pursued what seems to have been an irrationally bellicose policy toward the United States and perhaps sought to provoke conflict not only with the Fancher train but also with the United States.[90]

Fortunately, the army's late start and Mormon harassment prevented the
U.S. force from reaching Utah in 1857. The army made winter quarters in
Wyoming at Fort Bridger (or that portion of Fort Bridger that the Mormons
had left standing) and waited for spring to renew its advance. The troops
stored what supplies they had in a stone enclosure remaining from the fort
and erected a tent city, which they dubbed Camp Scott. The troops had
enough supplies to survive the winter, but only on reduced rations of flour,
salt, and meat.[91] Mormons interpreted the soldiers' hardships as God's fa-
vorable response to their actions. "The Lord has accepted our offering has
confused & stopped our enemies & we have not had to kill them or even
fire a gun at them," recorded one Mormon in his journal.[92]

The record left by soldiers and other non-Mormons leaves no doubt that
they identified Mormons primarily as a religious group. The Gentiles who
left a record of their opinions about the Saints included average citizens and
army officers, the secretary of war, and even the president.

Some Gentiles who came with the U.S. Army changed their minds about
Mormons and Mormonism after arriving in Utah. One such person was William Wallace Hammond, who served as a civilian laborer hauling supplies to
Utah for the army. After the freighting company for which Hammond
worked reneged on its promise to pay employees on arrival in Salt Lake City,
he enlisted in the army and participated in the expedition. Hammond found
Utah and the Mormons so much to his liking that he married a Mormon
woman and converted to Mormonism in November 1859.[93]

Another soldier who found his view of Mormons and Mormonism
changed by his experiences reported anonymously for the *Philadelphia Daily
Evening Bulletin* using the nom de plume "Utah." The amateur journalist provided glimpses into the life of an enlisted man in the Second United States
Dragoons on the Utah Expedition. Although "Utah" had enlisted to help enforce federal supremacy over the Mormons and favored the Whigs and Republicans in politics, he gave even-handed accounts of the Mormons, reporting good and bad about them and about the U.S. Army. The fairness of
his reports is astonishing given economic conditions in Pennsylvania, the
man's home state. High unemployment in the East created by the Panic of

1857 made the military an attractive employment option. In addition, anti-Mormon sentiment made army service attractive to those wishing to teach members of the curious religion a lesson. "Utah" wrote that at the time of the expedition, there was "little congeniality of feeling between the Mormon people and *the people of the United States.*" Indeed, despite their general need for cash, members of the First Pennsylvania Regiment gave up a month's pay to help offset the cost of shipping them to Utah.[94]

Exposure to the Mormons convinced the soldier-journalist that they were not the monsters of popular conception in the East. His first letters show him agreeing with the prevailing opinion, that Brigham Young and his followers needed to be taught a lesson—a harsh one, if necessary. On May 28, 1858, he described Brigham Young as a criminal and his followers as fanatics. He wrote, "The cause of morality demands the extermination of this nest of adulterers, and no further time should be wasted in attempts at compromise or windy discussion." Nor should time be spent on attempts to convert the Saints or change their minds. The only message to which the Mormons would respond, he believed, would be one delivered at gun- or swordpoint.[95]

Popular opinion in the East, and the soldiers sent to enforce it, called for firm action against the Mormons. Ironically, "Utah" affirmed the common Mormon opinion of both federal officials and the tool—the army—sent to enforce federal wishes and U.S. morality: they were both corrupt. He referred to the soldiers of the Utah Expedition as "missionaries that are to reform the Mormons" but pointed out that in his unit, at least, the high number of thieves, drunks, gamblers, and other moral degenerates rendered them unfit to enforce any morality worthy of the name.[96]

Meeting Mormons in person changed this soldier's opinion of them for the better, and as early as September 1858 "Utah" reported his transformation. Encountering a caravan of Danish Mormons headed for Salt Lake City, which he referred to as "the Mormon Jerusalem," he took the opportunity to interview its leader. The caravan's leader persuaded him that the United States misunderstood the Mormons. The Dane said that the Mormons "wanted nothing but freedom of conscience, and the privilege of worshipping God in their own manner," and "carried in their bosoms an inherent respect for the land of Washington . . . that could never be extinguished though Brigham himself should head the anarchists." The conversation "much pleased" the soldier-journalist and gave him "a much higher estimate of the Mormon character."[97]

By the end of September 1858, "Utah" agreed even with the Mormon assessment of Judge W. W. Drummond's low character. It may have helped that he heard corroborating evidence from non-Mormons he considered reliable." By October his opinion of the Mormons had changed to the point that he wrote, "Those who rant about the ignorance, bigotry and fanaticism of the Mormons are merely slanderers of the lowest grade."[98] But perhaps neither "Utah" nor Hammond was representative of non-Mormons in Utah during the nineteenth century.

John Ginn, a Gentile member of an army supply train, provides a more typical experience. On encountering the Mormon commander at Fort Bridger, Ginn wrote that the Saint was "an unusually kind and intelligent man for a religious fanatic."[99] After leaving the supply train, Ginn went to Salt Lake City, where he was treated as a prisoner of war. He described one of his guards as a "young Englishman of the lower class, wholly wrapped up in and saturated with Mormonism." Another guard he described as "an ignorant brute" who could not "talk anything but nonsense."[100]

As Ginn's captors began to trust him, they allowed him to stay with the mother of John Taylor, who later succeeded Brigham Young as president of the Church. "Old Mother Taylor was a kindly and rather intelligent old lady for a woman steeped to the eyes in Mormonism," Ginn wrote of his hostess. Ginn listened as Mother Taylor plied him with Mormon doctrine, which he considered but dismissed as "absurd."[101] Ginn coexisted with his captors/hosts but always identified them as religious fanatics lacking common sense or the ability to discern that they were under the spell of a false religion, if he went as far as calling it a religion. Ginn's record also shows an acute awareness of lower-class Mormon immigrants from abroad.

Ginn had plenty of skeptical company among the U.S. soldiers in the expedition. One Mormon militiaman, probably a member of the Nauvoo Legion, wrote that when he was captured by the U.S. force, his captors asked him what he thought of Mormonism. "I would rather die than deny my religion," he replied. The U.S. soldier responded: "Damn your religion; we don't care about it if you will not fight the government. We shall go to Salt Lake City. Jesus Christ can't keep us back."[102] U.S. soldiers had an intense, often crass, awareness of Mormonism.

Comments by the army's officer corps show that anti-Mormon sentiment was not restricted to the enlisted ranks. The first commanding officer of the expedition, Gen. William Selby Harney, reportedly said that to solve the Utah problem, "he would capture Brigham Young and the twelve apostles and execute them in a summary manner and winter in the temple of the Latter-day Saints."[103] Before Harney could act on this policy, command of the Utah Expedition went to Col. Albert Sidney Johnston.

J. H. Carleton, an officer in the First Dragoons, which were sent to Utah following the Mountain Meadows Massacre, wrote that as the Mormon-American conflict blossomed in 1857, "the most bitter hostility against the Gentiles became rife throughout Utah among all the Latter-Day Saints."[104] The hostility this assessment (perhaps falsely) reports may have been somewhat justified if Carleton and his comrades projected their feelings in a way noticeable to the Saints. He wrote, for example, "Crime is found in the footsteps of the Mormons wherever they go, and so the evil must always exist as long as the Mormons themselves may exist."[105] Carleton (no doubt along with many mainstream Americans) also interpreted the Mormon persecutions and travels in a remarkably different fashion than did the Saints. Writing of the Mormons in Missouri, while in "their infancy as a religious community," Carleton stated, "From the crimes and depredations they committed, they became intolerable to the inhabitants, whose self-preservation compelled them to rise and drive the Mormons out by force of arms." He described the reaction of Illinois citizens in similar terms and applauded the murders of Joseph and Hyrum Smith, whom Carleton called "shallow imposters" and "arrant miscreants."[106] Carleton concluded his report by predicting that the United States would see considerably greater trouble and expense in Utah for having allowed the Mormons to remain within U.S. borders. "They are an ulcer on the body politic," he wrote. Then he offered the cure: "It must have excision, complete and thorough extirpation, before we can ever hope for safety or tranquility."[107]

One of the most extensive records left by a member of the armed forces may also be one of the most valuable for gauging the sentiment of mainstream America at the time of the Utah Expedition. John Wolcott Phelps, born in Vermont on November 13, 1813, began his army career at West Point. After graduation in 1836, he fought against the Creeks and Seminoles, participated in the Cherokee "Trail of Tears" in 1838, and served under General Winfield Scott in the Mexican-American War. Phelps resigned his commission in 1859, but in 1861 he returned to the army as a brigadier general to lead Vermont volunteers in the Civil War. Immediately following the Civil War, he became president of the Vermont Teachers' Association. Phelps traveled widely within North America and Europe, earned a reputation as a scholar and linguist, and wrote several books. In 1880 he ran for president of the United States as the American Party candidate.[108] Phelps's credentials as a part of the mainstream elite—officer, education leader, politician—make his record of the Utah Expedition worthy of thorough investigation and consideration.

If Captain John Wolcott Phelps accurately reflects the army leadership's view of Mormonism, the invading force held the Saints and their theology in contempt. Reflecting on Mormonism's origins—Joseph Smith's translating script on golden plates that only he could read, and even then only with the help of stone spectacles through which he alone could see—Phelps mused: "Where else than in America could such a flat and puerile invention become enshrined as an established belief[?] From what trunk except one of the most vigorous of free institutions could such a fungus of absolutism arise?"[109]

In defending Utah against the approaching U.S. Army, Mormon forces burned the plains, but an article in the *Deseret News* quoted Brigham Young as saying that prairie-dwelling people typically burn grass in the fall. This, to Phelps, demonstrated Young's disingenuous side, which he blistered in a December 1857 letter wherein he compared Mormonism to a snake coiled in the desert and concluded that it, like the snake, should be smitten immediately.[110]

Phelps clearly identified Young as a religious leader and saw his actions as an affront to American values and legitimate religion, whatever that might be. Furthermore, he saw it as so dangerous a threat as to be worthy of destruction, and by the U.S. Army no less.

Shortly after writing this scorching indictment of Mormonism, Phelps attacked the religion again in a letter to his brother Charles. Again using the snake metaphor, Phelps labeled secret societies the vitals, Mormonism the body, and Brigham Young the head. Part of Phelps's disgust derived from allegations that Mormon agents seeking territorial status had attempted to barter support for slavery in exchange for the South's support of Utah's application. "Such is Mormon arrogance," Phelps wrote; "it calculates, as the price of our slave dissensions, to force us, twenty and odd millions of Christians, to respect polygamy if not to worship at the Mormon shrine." A Christian land such as the United States, Phelps argued, was no place for polygamy.[111]

Dealing with the problem at hand presented Phelps an uncomfortable choice: allow Mormonism to wither and thereby preserve the greatest amount of self-government in the United States or use force to repress it and thus sacrifice ideals on which the country had been founded. Phelps had mixed feelings about using force. The Whig side of him opposed it, hoping to preserve self-government, but the military man in Phelps answered, "act with decision and effect or act not at all."[112]

Assessing the prospects for peaceful coexistence of Mormons and Americans—Phelps differentiated between the two—he made a gloomy forecast. Fundamental value conflicts, with the Mormons rooted in their religion and

Americans rooted in their republican heritage steeped in evangelical Protestantism, would keep the twain apart. As Phelps saw it, Mormonism appealed to base instincts and passions. He viewed Mormon leaders as ignorant and brutal and thought poorly of rank-and-file Mormons, whom he described as the dregs of old Europe. He saw America (and presumably Americans) as being too young, vital, and filled with aspirations to succumb to Mormonism's base appeal.[113] According to Phelps, the people he had been dispatched to police barely qualified as human. His writing reflects his suspicion and distaste not only for Mormonism but also for Mormons.

Although Phelps believed the government should use force with extreme caution, he also thought that the Mormon situation presented a clear case of its appropriate use. He wrote, "There never was, perhaps, a more striking instance than this Mormon question presents, where the prompt interposition of the arm of power was necessary for suppressing the vicious and depraved and giving protection and countenance to the good." Phelps found it outrageous that the army had been brought so close to ridding America of the serious Mormon threat to republicanism and to the virtue of American women without accomplishing its mission.[114] To this officer in the U.S. Army, the failure to stamp out religious freedom in the Great Basin insulted American values.

After spending about two years with the Utah Expedition, Capt. Phelps compared Mormonism to Catholicism. Phelps, one must remember, had also fought in the Mexican-American War, which could be interpreted in part as an anti-Catholic crusade. He found both Catholicism and Mormonism opposed to American republican values. "The depraved politics and exceeding sophistication of the Utah affair," Phelps wrote, "naturally lead the mind to the Catholic Church." When a council of officers in Utah selected a Catholic priest as chaplain, largely because the majority of the command had recently emigrated from Catholic countries, Phelps objected. He saw foreigners and Catholics as threats to American institutions and Catholicism especially as incompatible with republican government. On the same day when he complained about Catholics, Phelps wrote a letter in which he claimed that the Mormons had "entirely abandoned the light of Heaven and the traditions of our race, and [were] following out their own ingenious devices." Phelps blatantly compared Mormonism to Catholicism in a letter to his brother Frederic in which he complained of an experience he had in Mexico; having asked a member of "the lower classes" a simple question, he received as an answer only a blank stare. To get an answer, Phelps wrote, he had to have a third party repeat the question while giving some assurance that

it was in fact a plain question and not some device that might lead to persecution from the church or some political faction. The assurance given,
the citizen would at last give a direct answer to the simple question. Yet
Phelps felt that the Mormon Church outdid the Catholic Church in this respect, of controlling its adherents' minds and behavior.[115]

Phelps saw Mormons as threatening American values both politically and
religiously. Their religion strayed from what was acceptable to mainstream
America. Realizing that the Mormon hierarchy paralleled the Catholic hierarchy in many ways and that many Saints had recently arrived in Utah from
Europe, Phelps disapproved of both Mormon society and Catholicism for
many of the same reasons. The army, he felt, had a duty to protect republican society and its cherished ideals of freedom of thought and action from
the threat posed by the decidedly antirepublican values of bloc voting and
the Saints' adherence to group rather than individual ideals.

By the time the army entered Salt Lake City, the Mormons had fled, leaving an empty city. The army's march through a dramatically deserted Salt
Lake City gave Phelps and no doubt others more grist for their anti-Mormon
mills. As the army marched through the city's wide, deserted streets, it passed
the shuttered and sometimes boarded windows of the Saints' homes. Reflecting on this eerie atmosphere, Phelps wondered with awe and perhaps disgust at what type of man or power could create such a situation and what
type of people would allow it.[116] Phelps regarded the Mormon leaders as
despots and believed their followers were foolish dregs of society who had
been duped into believing the Mormon message.

Further reflection led Phelps to conclude that Brigham Young and the
Mormon leadership at large had manufactured a perverted version of the
American dream that they sold to Europe's downtrodden. Europe's lower
classes, he speculated, suffered the ills of a tired, old society still ruled by royalty. The masses looked heavenward for an explanation and promises of a better life. In this state of mind, they supposedly presented easy marks for Mormon missionaries working in Europe. Fresh from the United States, renowned
land of opportunity, the missionaries promised equality and prosperity in
their western Zion. There, according to Phelps's analysis of Mormonism's appeal as preached by the missionaries, "all are brethren," and "the deformed,
morally as well as physically, are restored to health by the prophets of the
Lord." Furthermore—and here the bogeyman of polygamy reappears—"the
hump-back dwarf can have as many pretty wives as if he were a perfect Ado-
nis, and the most unpardonable criminal can become the brightest of the
Latter-day Saints."[117]

Phelps's indictment of Mormonism did not end there. On arriving in Zion, converts found themselves in the midst of a desert, and according to Phelps, they were stripped of property to repay their debts to the church's emigration fund. Furthermore, the church leadership then deluded converts, offering them charming foreign mission posts and boggling their minds with secret signs and elaborate ceremonies. He detested what he saw as Brigham Young's complete control over the hearts and minds of those who arrived in Utah. The Bible played a crucial role in Phelps's analysis. European royalty used the Bible as justification for their superiority in this world and for keeping the masses down. Common folk had to die to achieve equality. Under those circumstances, he argued, was it any wonder that Mormon promises of equality and prosperity found a welcome audience?[118]

Phelps's analysis and criticism leads to an interesting speculation. Could Mormonism have been offering a conservative alternative to Karl Marx's then-recent prescription for the ills of an industrializing society? Mormonism offered not a Marxist reordering of society but rather a return to a strong paternalistic family system and opportunities on the land instead of in factories. Nathan Hatch, a historian of religion, characterized the Book of Mormon as "a document of profound social protest, an impassioned manifesto by a hostile outsider against the smug complacency of those in power and the reality of social distinctions based on wealth, class, and education." Mormonism gave to common people "the right to shape their own faith and to take charge of their own religious destiny."[119] Oddly enough, these poor founders who offered an egalitarian religion built a rigid church hierarchy topped by a theocrat. On a societal level, then, Mormonism threatened American republicanism and individualism. Religiously, Mormonism, which conferred the priesthood on the masses (of men), offered opportunities for salvation and equality in this life not available in Europe, where the Bible and religion supported monarchs and monarchy. But religious and social opportunities could not be separated within Mormonism, causing concern in mainstream America.

Even ardent supporters of mainstream America who held reservations about using force to preserve Protestant and republican values saw its merits in the case of Utah. Phelps fell into that category, and he hoped the army could help set things right. As he saw it, the army's presence in Utah would loosen Young's hold on his followers, allowing them to think clearly and to interpret the scriptures accurately, and would generally create an atmosphere in which "Christian society" would flourish.[120] Phelps hoped the army could shake Young's authority enough that his "deluded" followers could see the light and return to mainstream Christianity and American values. Ironically, Phelps, who opposed the tight church-society link inherent in Mormonism, supported the symbiotic relationship between evangelical Protestants and the U.S. Army.

By late 1858 Phelps had become frustrated with the government's Mormon policy. He wanted to destroy Brigham Young's influence and, presumably, the Mormon Church. Were he to have enacted policy, he would have established the army's headquarters at Provo rather than in the middle of the desert at Camp Floyd. Thus placed, the army would have encouraged business in Provo and simultaneously displayed United States strength. Making Provo the center of commerce and power would, he hoped, sap Brigham Young's strength, and "the power of Brigham would have been ruined immediately." But the army did not follow that policy. Instead, Phelps wrote, "[the] policy would seem to be to keep [Young] and his religion conspicuous and influential," a policy he labeled "quackery."[121]

By mid-1859 Phelps and others were growing increasingly frustrated. He worried that all in Utah must gradually come under Mormon law or have no law. He believed that the rebels had co-opted the army. In fact, Phelps wrote later that month that Brigham Young's power seemed "to be as great as ever," by which he meant far too great. He found it particularly disturbing that Mormons had to get Young's permission to "rent their own houses to the Americans." Elsewhere, Phelps reports that he told a man he appeared to be an American and then asked him if it were possible that he could be a Mormon, as if the two were incompatible. Phelps reflected, "Born in New York and a resident of Illinois—what can it be, ignorance or crime, or both, that has brought him into such a community as this?" He concluded, "Their religion is a worship of the senses, and it produces upon them something of the same softening effect that is produced by whiskey drinking and opium eating."[122]

These words emphasize two problems. First, they reveal the breadth and depth of control that the church's president-prophet exercised over rank-and-file Mormons. The idea that someone would have to request a higher authority's permission when dealing with, say, private property ran counter to basic American values of free enterprise and the right to property proclaimed in the Declaration of Independence. In the view of outsiders such as Phelps, Brigham Young held a religious, social, and economic dictatorship in Utah. Second, Phelps again separates Mormons from Americans, as if in leaving the United States, the Saints had forsaken their American citizenship. By casting them in the light of "other," as foreign, he made it easier to demonize the Mormons and presumably to act forcefully against them.

Later that year, when a territorial judicial appointee refused to hold court in western Utah because it lacked jails and courtrooms, Phelps took the government to task for not providing the basics needed for a republican society. The United States, Phelps believed, should have used its army to preserve mainstream values and institutions. As he saw it, the mission of the army and the territorial officials in Utah was "to vindicate the laws of christian [*sic*] society and civilized government."[123]

Spending time among the Mormons did not soften Phelps's opinions of them or his dedication to the idea that the United States should exercise firm action against them. If anything, his feelings about the Saints had hardened. Phelps came to see Mormonism as a money-making scheme and criticized James Buchanan for backing down from the challenge of religion, which he viewed as a parasite on Puritanism.[124] Phelps recognized Mormonism as a uniquely American institution, albeit a twisted mutant in his mind. He still resented the army's not having been given the command or opportunity to destroy it, and he resented what American politics had become to allow Mormonism to survive and even thrive.

President Buchanan's secretary of war, John B. Floyd, echoed these sentiments in his annual report for 1857, showing that anti-Mormon sentiment reached from the enlisted ranks through the officer corps and as high as the cabinet. Floyd was the cabinet officer most intimately involved with executing Buchanan's Mormon policy, and his opinions reveal the motives behind Washington's policy. For one thing, Floyd disapproved of the government established in Utah. "They have substituted for the laws of the land a theocracy, having for its head an individual whom they profess to believe a prophet of God," Floyd wrote. He also accused the Mormons of behaving in an unChristian fashion. "They have practiced an exclusiveness unlike anything ever before known in a Christian country, and have inculcated a jealous distrust of all whose religious faith differed from their own," he reported to Congress. Floyd disapproved of Mormon "harems," which he charged were filled "chiefly from the lowest classes of foreigners." He also charged they used "religious fanaticism, supported by imposture and fraud," to "enslave the dull and ignorant," while more intelligent members held fast to the group because polygamy allowed them to sate their lusts. Floyd's assessment of the Mormons touched a number of issues significant for mid-nineteenth century Americans.[125] Like other contemporary anti-Mormons, Floyd identified the Saints primarily as a religious group and worried about the threats they posed to republican virtue and Christian morality, including polygamy, to which he referred indirectly. In Floyd's mind, conflict between Mormons and Americans was inevitable because of their opposing ideologies.

Floyd voiced other concerns common among non-Mormons. He acknowledged rumors that the Mormons were "instigating the Indians to hostilities against our citizens." Following this charge, he added a roundabout mention of the Mountain Meadows Massacre, though he stopped short of directly accusing the Mormons of participating in that event. Lastly, Floyd broached an issue that may not have occurred to rank-and-file Americans of the day but that concerned the U.S. government mightily: the Mormon community sat astride the principal route connecting the United States with its Pacific Coast settlements.[126] Mormonism stood in the path of the American republic as two interpretations of manifest destiny clashed in the Great Basin. The U.S. government thus had a variety of reasons to act against the Saints, but religion lay at the heart of the conflict.

The Mormon strategy of buying time proved effective partly because it brought Congress into the picture. Buchanan had dispatched the army while Congress was in recess. When it convened in December 1857, it demanded that Buchanan justify his expensive crusade. Buchanan produced an impressive array of evidence against the Mormons, although much of it had not been written or known at the time he deployed the army. Under Buchanan's leadership the national debt ballooned from $25,000,000 to $65,000,000, thanks considerably to the Utah War, which cost about $15,000,000. With Congress refusing to appropriate more money for the venture, despite its continued hostility to the Saints, Buchanan had to bring the episode to a close.[127]

Sampling responses of congressmen shows a variety of opinions of the Utah Expedition. C. J. Faulkner of Virginia opposed Buchanan's request to recruit volunteers to reinforce the expedition. Faulkner said he did "not condemn the sentiment of opposition to the religious abominations of Mormonism," but he opposed sending volunteers to Utah, fearing that their anti-Mormon emotions would lead them to commit atrocities against the Saints. Instead, Faulkner favored increasing the size of the regular army so that professionally trained soldiers could be sent to do the job.[128]

Other congressmen favored the use of force for different reasons. Samuel R. Curtis of Iowa supported using force mainly for the reasons Buchanan stated, to suppress rebellion.[129] Although he mentioned the rebellion, New York's John Thompson emphasized the un-Christian nature of Mormonism and thus supported increasing the army primarily to send a powerful message about the religion's acceptability. He called the Book of Mormon the "Koran of Mormonism," not wishing to lend it any dignity or credibility by calling it the Bible of Mormonism or even to point out that Mormons follow the Bible as well as the Book of Mormon and believe in Jesus. Thompson associated the Mormons with the Kingdom of Matthias—the polygamous group discussed earlier—as he tried to discredit the Saints. He also pointed out Mormonism's theocratic "despotism," which he said "combines all the traditional force of Mohammedan absolutism with the shifting policy of Jesuit craft." Thompson further warned that "every convert is a zealot; every zealot a hero!" As if these elements of Mormonism were not enough to frighten mainstream America into action, he raised the specter of "downtrodden, famishing masses from Wales, Scotland, Sweden, Germany, France, and all parts of the other world," "begrimed with the soot of the dark mine, or pale from the faintness of the heated factory," flocking to the Garden of Eden in the American West that Mormon missionaries had promised them.[130]

Fortunately, Buchanan had prepared a safety valve for the conflict. When Thomas Leiper Kane volunteered to mediate, Buchanan accepted, allowing the longtime friend of the Mormons and member of a well-connected Pennsylvania family to travel to Utah and see what he could arrange. Kane joined the Utah Expedition in February and focused his energies on the new governor, Alfred Cumming. Kane convinced Cumming to seek a peaceful solution.[131]

Cumming left the army and visited Salt Lake City alone as a show of trust and friendship. Cumming's bravery and trust in the Mormons made a strong impression. Wilford Woodruff wrote, "Had Gov. Cumming . . . remained behind the bristling bayonets of the army, he would have been . . . dispised [*sic*], by every American citizen in the Territory." During this visit Cumming and Brigham Young laid the groundwork for a settlement. In fact, Cumming felt so well received that he wrote to Col. Johnston, "I have everywhere been recognized as the governor of Utah . . . with such respectful attentions as are due to the representative of the executive authority of the United States in the Territory." Cumming also reported that Brigham Young extended every courtesy when he addressed a gathering of nearly four thousand Mormons who listened attentively to his speech. Cumming saw a gathering dedicated to its religion and prepared to follow the U.S. Constitution.[132] This hardly describes a rebellion worthy of one-sixth of the U.S. Army. No doubt the army's presence shaped the Saints' mood, but Cumming also acknowledged their devotion to their religion and to the Constitution, which he did not have to do.

Students of Kane's diplomatic efforts have debated his significance in the affair. The Mormon assessment gives him much credit and shows again how the Saints viewed the crisis in religious terms. Wilford Woodruff heaped praise on Kane for his efforts. In March 1859 Woodruff described Kane as an instrument of God sent to save the Saints from the invading army's wrath.[133] The Mormons viewed the Utah Expedition as a crusade against

them that, they believed, had been halted by an act of God in the form of
Col. Thomas Kane.

Meanwhile, Buchanan sent peace commissioners to offer the Saints
amnesty, although they would have to consent to an army occupation of Utah.
The commissioners arrived in Salt Lake City on June 7, 1858. Young stalled as
long as he could, but after two days of meetings, on June 11 and 12, he accepted
the terms. By July 7, with President Buchanan's amnesty proclamation in effect, the Utah War ended. The occupying army, or Department of Utah, grew
to a force of about 3,000 and performed duties such as guarding prisoners
and assisting federal marshals, roughly the same type of duties the army had
been performing in Kansas for some years. Unlike the situation in Kansas,
where only the governor could requisition troops, in Utah federal judges and
marshals had the power to requisition troops until 1859.[134]

This peaceful resolution marked the end of one phase of the dialogue between Mormon Utah and the United States. The United States had quelled
a perceived rebellion and taken measures to improve safety for travelers
crossing through Utah Territory. As Joseph Smith's prophesy, the Reformation, and Brigham Young's bellicose policy attest, the Mormons cannot be
seen as helpless victims in their relations with the United States. The relationship's next phase brought fewer threats of violence but remained tense
thanks to religion and the role it played in shaping the West.

Although the threat of violent conflict had passed, considerable potential for cultural conflict persisted as long as the army remained in Utah. As
early as September 1858 an official in the Church Historian's Office complained that the army brought with it "all the paraphernalia of modern
Christianity, civilization and order, its stream of corruption, its accumulated
icebergs of degradation and filth." One non-Mormon who served in the expedition confirmed this assessment, noting that a large percentage of the soldiers in the expedition were carousers recently arrived from England, Scotland, Ireland, and Germany who could find no work other than in the army.
In addition, soldiers sometimes made provocative remarks to Mormons, typically focusing on polygamy. For their part, Mormons goaded the soldiers by
suggesting Utah might soon join the union, Mormonism intact.[135] Beyond
reflecting social relations in occupied Utah, this episode reinforces the argument that religion lay at the base of the conflict and that among religious
issues, polygamy dominated the minds of those in the U.S. force.

Further evidence for this argument comes from letters written by Elizabeth Wells Randall Cumming, the governor's wife. Elizabeth Cumming had
strong ties to mainstream American society—her grandfather was the pa-

triot Samuel Adams. In a May 1858 letter to the governor's sister, Elizabeth Cumming wrote, "Alfred likes some of the Mormons there—some of the leaders—not their Mormonism—but their courage, intellect." Soon thereafter, in June, she wrote, "Alfred sends love, & says he is going to convert Mormons to some good *ism.*" In another letter, penned in September 1858, she recorded her own impression of the Mormons, describing them as "generally ignorant, fanatical, superstitious, & possessing a profound disdain for the religious belief of the rest of the world." Although Elizabeth Cumming clearly did not approve of Mormonism, she noted that its adherents, especially women, cared deeply about their religion.[136] The Cummings, then—the governor and first lady of Utah appointed by the U.S. government—noted that Mormons lived by deeply held religious convictions, but they also disapproved of those convictions and recognized their mission to change them, to convert them to another, more acceptable "-ism."

The occupation also changed religious and economic life in Utah, at least in the short run. According to Esaias Edwards's journal, some of the non-Mormons who entered Utah with the army wanted to assassinate Brigham Young. Regardless of that report's veracity, Young felt enough of a threat that he secluded himself in his house much of the time during the early occupation and preached very little. In August 1858 Edwards wrote, "There is at present a famine for the word of the Lord."[137]

Economically, non-Mormon merchants took advantage of the disruption to Mormon agriculture and commerce brought by the invasion and of the disruption to local production caused by the evacuation of Salt Lake City. According to Esaias Edwards, these merchants charged high prices and demanded cash payments or payment in wheat at low prices. Edwards wrote, "[Zion] languishes at present."[138]

The Utah Expedition also brought a precipitous decline in Mormons emigrating from Europe. After showing steady growth through the early 1850s and peaking in 1855 at about four thousand, Mormon emigration from Europe dropped an astonishing 90 percent in 1858, totaling only several hundred. Emigration rates began recovering in 1859 and climbed to near their record levels in 1862 and 1863 before dropping off again.[139] Assuming that anti-immigration feelings played a role in anti-Mormon sentiment in mainstream U.S. society, the U.S. government's Utah Expedition clearly satisfied public opinion, at least for the short term.

At the close of the Utah War, even part of the non-Mormon press reflected the belief that the action had been religiously motivated. In July 1858 *Harper's Weekly* concluded, "Had [the Mormons] been Christians there would

have been no trouble; had we recognized Mormonism and polygamy as law-
ful institutions, we should have sent no army across the plains. . . . the United
States made war upon the Mormons because their domestic institutions were
deemed inconsistent with the organization of the confederacy, and the whole-
some growth of self-governing communities on United States Territories."[140]
Even outside Utah, some people recognized and were willing to say that the
U.S.-Mormon conflict hinged on the religious underpinnings of social organization.

Despite the hardships brought on by the conflict and the presence of the
army of "civilization" and others deemed undesirable by the Saints, most
Mormons seemed to remain loyal to their religion. By Brigham Young's estimate, "a great majority" remained "faithful and true," while comparatively
few left the faith—"less than might be expected under the circumstances." Yet
Young bemoaned the fact that many Mormons did not live as piously as the
faith asked. John Taylor, who would succeed Young as president of the church,
assessed the episode and concluded God had protected the Saints and delivered them safely from the challenge. He predicted the Saints' Kingdom of God
would resume its growth.[141] From a spiritual perspective, the Saints weath-
ered the invasion well. Brigham Young believed most people's faith had endured, while John Taylor suggested the episode may have even strengthened
it for many. Indeed, Captain Jesse Gove of the Tenth Infantry wrote to his wife
to say that he believed the Mormons had not truly changed but only paid lip
service to making changes. He still favored hanging about a hundred of them
as an example to the rest. That, he believed, would bring real change to Utah.
Given the sentiments common to many in the army, the Utah Expedition
must have been a frustrating experience, and it is to their credit that, as Robert
Coakley put it, the army conformed "strictly to the directives of civil authority."[142] Although the Utah Expedition might not have delivered the results desired by many of the soldiers and people in the East, the government's
assault on Mormonism had fallen short only for the time being.

Even with the army occupying Utah, the Saints continued their efforts
to attain statehood and, they hoped, the self-rule statehood would bring. The
importance of the Saints' religious beliefs in motivating their worldly actions
has already been made clear, but that did not preclude savvy political opera-
tions. Shortly after the army established its base in Utah, Brigham Young resumed the statehood campaign. In an October 1858 letter to a Mormon in
St. Louis, Young outlined a strategy for increasing Mormon influence and for
gaining public sympathy. Tactics included encouraging immigration to Utah,
advocating the principles of popular sovereignty, promoting railroad and tele-

graph development, and writing brief articles for newspapers over a wide geographic area. The newspaper pieces, according to Young, should try to win sympathy for the Saints. For example, he suggested writing about the way the U.S. government had taken the mail contract for service from Missouri to Salt Lake City from a Mormon contractor—resulting in no eastern mail for a year—and awarding it to non-Mormons who had submitted a higher bid for the route.[143]

The threat of armed conflict between the Saints and the United States had passed, but the battle for Utah had not been decided. The United States faced a true republic-threatening rebellion, the Civil War, which temporarily diverted attention from Utah to the South. For twenty years following the Utah War, Mormon-American conflict in the Great Basin simmered in the local courts. Beginning in the 1880s, however, the United States opened a new offensive against the Mormon Church and polygamy that would not end until the Saints submitted to mainstream will, abandoning a tenet of their religion and basically promising to behave culturally and politically like mainstream Americans.[144]

For the purposes of this study, the legal details of those court battles are less important than the nature of the army's occupation of Utah and what it revealed about U.S. motives. The *Valley Tan,* a newspaper published in Great Salt Lake City by Kirk Anderson, one of the many non-Mormons to flood into Utah on the heels of the army, voiced the opinion of mainstream America, or at least of those representing mainstream America in the Great Basin. It gave the *Deseret News,* the church's newspaper, its first opposition. It also showed how the ghosts of Missouri continued to haunt the Saints, because Anderson was a former Missouri newspaperman.[145] The contents of the *Valley Tan* leave little doubt that all in the basin, Mormons and non-Mormons alike, knew that religion lay at the heart of the conflict between the United States and the Saints.

Early in its run the *Tan* showed its partisan stripes in a comment on the large police force the Mormon leadership had created to maintain peace in Salt Lake City. The paper complained that the squad was an "ecclesiastical patrol," not a police force. Whatever one called it (the city legislation creating the force called it the "city watch"), the force had great success making life orderly in Salt Lake City.[146]

Change in the White House also brought change to Utah policy that endured until the 1880s. Presidents Abraham Lincoln and Andrew Johnson both had too much to worry about in the East to devote much effort to reconstructing Utah. The status quo suited them, as long as Utah left the route

to California open. The same could not be said for Congress. Once the Radical Republicans took control of Congress in 1864, news of antipolygamy and
anti-Mormon bills found its way to Utah.[147]

Radical Republicans wanted to reconstruct Utah with regard to polygamy and its courts, just as they were reconstructing the South with regard
to slavery and politics. To this end they introduced a series of antipolygamy
bills from 1856 through 1869, but the bills failed to change Mormonism. Federal antipolygamy legislation dates to 1856 when, at the height of both the
Mormon Reformation and plural marriage activity to that date, Vermont
congressman Justin R. Morrill introduced the first bill to suppress polygamy.

Studying Morrill's character and opinions on Utah illuminates Republican motives behind the legislation. In a speech given on February 23, 1857,
Morrill marshaled evidence that the Mormons were aggressively and possibly dangerously un-American. According to Morrill, Brigham Young threatened (in the name of Jesus Christ, no less) that any U.S. president to lift a
finger against the Mormons would die an untimely death and go to hell.[148]
This not only underscores the perceived Mormon threat but also points up
the central role religion played in the conflict.

To Morrill and mainstream Americans, a significant portion of the Mormon threat came from the Saints' enmity toward republican government
and Christianity. Much as Brigham Young did, Morrill linked the religious
with the political in promoting his mission to Congress. In rallying support
for his bill, Morrill accused the Mormons of wishing to live in a monarchi-
cal system to entrench their patriarchal society. To stir outrage Morrill
charged Young with having sixty to ninety wives, so many that Young himself had lost track—and that while serving as territorial governor and defying the United States.[149] These unique Mormon characteristics, he implied,
threatened American ways.

These arguments would stir many Americans to dislike or even fear what
the Mormons were doing in Utah, but Morrill saved even more shocking evidence, his depiction of Mormon polygamy, for last. First, he told how Mormons stealthily, under cover of the Constitution, established polygamy and
allowed it to take root. Using religion as a guise, Morrill charged, they maintained this "Mohammedan barbarism revolting to the civilized world." To
further fuel his argument, Morrill added that the Mormon system included
easy divorce. This might seem counterintuitive at first, but rather than view
divorce as an escape for women, he painted it as a way for lusty Mormon men
to abandon wives and as another affront to the institution of marriage. He
concluded that the Mormons might as well use religion to protect canni-

balism or infanticide. In Morrill's opinion, no one could twist the Constitution to defend such an atrocity, thus ruling out any argument that controlling or suppressing Mormonism would restrict religious freedom. As he put it, if the Constitution forbade Congress from passing laws affecting the establishment of religion, the same interpretation applied to states, which were creations of Congress. Armed with that logic, Morrill urged Congress to bring American-style order to Utah.[150]

Morrill's first antipolygamy bill failed, but his second became law on July 7, 1862. The Morrill Act said that no one having a living husband or wife could marry anyone else in a U.S. territory. It also revoked an act of the Utah Territorial legislature incorporating the church, as well as all other acts by the territorial legislature that supported polygamy, and prohibited any religious or charitable organization in a territory from acquiring or holding real estate valued higher than $50,000—holdings in excess of that amount went to the federal government. With that legislation, Morrill and the Republicans integrated law and faith in their attempts to reform or reconstruct what they saw as a corrupt society developing in Utah. As the legal historian Sarah Barringer Gordon sees it, the federal government "directed a fundamental reordering of a society based explicitly and unabashedly on religious law to one based on the humanitarian impulses of a competing legal system and its silent yet potent Protestant subtext." Polygamists faced almost no threat from Morrill's bill because the probate courts refused to use it. Other bills designed to suppress polygamy, often coupled with judicial reform measures, surfaced in Congress in 1863, 1866, 1867, and 1869, but none became law.[151]

During the early 1870s the government crusade against polygamy dragged Brigham Young into court on a charge of adultery. Leading the charge was Utah Territory's chief justice, James B. McKean, the son of a Vermont Methodist minister and himself a leading Republican. Judge McKean considered polygamy a cancer on the nation's Christian conscience. In the fall of 1871 officials brought Young to court on charges of violating a territorial law against adultery and lewd and lascivious cohabitation. When Young appeared in court, McKean noted from the bench that while the case might be known formally as *People v. Brigham Young*, its real title, as far as McKean was concerned, was "Federal Authority versus Polygamic Theocracy," and he added, "a system is on trial in the person of Brigham Young."[152] Although the court could not obtain a conviction against Young, government anti-Mormon activities had found their way to the most exalted Mormon.[153]

The final assault on polygamy began taking shape in 1877. Brigham Young died that year, and John Taylor succeeded him as leader of the church, first

as president of the Quorum of the Twelve Apostles and then as church pres-
ident. Taylor led the church through nearly a decade of intensifying pressure
from the federal government but refused to compromise church practices.
His motto, "The Kingdom of God or nothing," indicates his stubbornness.[154]
It also showed he would follow in Young's footsteps, resisting the United
States in defense of his religion.

Meanwhile, developments in the East spelled impending doom for the
Mormon society as constituted in the Great Basin. In 1879 the U.S. Supreme
Court laid the groundwork for a concentrated federal legal assault on polygamy with its decision in *Reynolds v. United States* (1879). The Court ruled that
certain conduct, even if religiously inspired, can be controlled by civil authorities and that polygamy constitutes a threat to public order. Gordon called
the intersection of order, democracy, and religion developed in the U.S. legal
system "a democratically constructed yet indelibly Protestant public morality." Polygamy, defined as a social evil by the United States, stood beyond First
Amendment protection. The *Reynolds* decision opened the way for Congress
to enact a series of increasingly severe antipolygamy laws aimed at the Saints.[155]

The press, mainstream evangelical Christian denominations, and reformers also renewed their antipolygamy campaigns. In the U.S. Senate the
Methodist chaplain used that chamber as a bully pulpit for his anti-Mormon
ideas. The *Deseret News* reported in 1881 that Episcopalians, Methodists, Baptists, Presbyterians, and Congregationalists had begun a "Sectarian Crusade"
against the Saints carried out by schools and missions founded and supported
by those denominations.[156] The reformer Kate Fields carried the antipolygamy
message to the people, drawing sellout audiences to hear her "Mormon Mon-
ster" lectures through the mid-1880s. Polygamy, Fields told her audiences, was
a monstrosity, a "rock that need[ed] blowing up with the dynamite of the
law."[157] Public opinion against Mormonism had gained a new power.

More significantly, however, Vermont's Senator George F. Edmunds became the new standard bearer in Congress's anti-Mormon crusade. Edmunds,
elected in 1865 as a Radical Republican, introduced legislation to reform Utah
politics and attack polygamy.[158] The Edmunds Act became law in 1882 and
took the government's antipolygamy crusade to new heights. Widening the
antibigamy act of 1862, the Edmunds Act of 1882 prohibited polygamy, a
change from the earlier act's prohibition of "bigamy." The Edmunds Act
tightened a loophole in the previous legislation, which barred a man with one
wife from marrying another. The new law added a prohibition against a man
marrying simultaneously two or more women. It also provided penalties for
cohabitation, allowed the mere approval of polygamy to be grounds for dis-

missing a person from jury duty, marked children of polygamous marriages as illegitimate for legal purposes, and barred polygamists and illegal cohabitors from voting or holding public office. To enforce the act, Congress established the "Utah Commission," which registered voters and supervised territorial elections. Only citizens registered by the commission could vote.[159]

Capitalizing on the momentum his first bill produced by disfranchising polygamists and removing them from the territorial legislature, Edmunds introduced even harsher legislation when Congress convened in the winter of 1885–86.[160] The resulting Edmunds-Tucker Act, which brought the harshest anti-Mormon measures yet, aimed at restricting Mormon civil rights and dismantling the church. The act limited Utah probate courts to matters concerning estates and guardianship and empowered the president of the United States to appoint probate judges. It extended the life of the Utah Commission and gave it the power to administer a qualifying oath to potential voters. In addition to enacting these indirect limits on church power, the law took vicious, direct action against the church itself. Edmunds-Tucker ended the Perpetual Emigrating Company (an organization designed to promote and facilitate emigration of poor Mormons to Utah), abolished the Nauvoo Legion, and dissolved the Church of Jesus Christ of Latter-day Saints as an incorporated body. Church assets went to a receiver. To administer these provisions, the government hired hundreds of officials, effectively creating a bureaucracy to dismantle the church.[161]

That same year, one day after the anniversary of the Saints' arrival in the Great Basin, LDS president John Taylor died, creating an atmosphere conducive to change in church leadership. To Mormons, even nonpolygamous ones, the need for change was apparent. Antipolygamy laws affected only a relative few of the total Mormon population, but they constituted an important segment. The church approved polygamous marriages only for those deemed worthy—those who prospered. In other words, polygamy existed disproportionately among the elite in Mormon society, which meant that many church leaders were among the polygamous. Thus, when vigorous government prosecution of polygamists began to put its leadership behind bars, the policy crippled the church. Some church leaders not yet incarcerated opted to go underground or to leave the country to avoid prosecution. John Taylor, for example, went underground during his presidency, shuttling among hideouts in Utah for nearly two and a half years. Making matters worse, the government taxed the church to such an extent that by November it went into receivership. U.S. government officials took over church buildings, including the president's office.[162]

Statistics on polygamy convictions show the effect of increasingly strin-
gent antipolygamy legislation. In the twenty years following the passage of
the antibigamy law of 1862, two Mormon polygamists were indicted. After
the Edmunds Act passed in 1882, polygamy convictions rose steadily. In 1884,
4 polygamists were convicted. The number jumped to 55 in 1885, 132 on 1886,
and 220 in 1887. By the end of 1888 nearly 600 Mormons had been fined or
imprisoned.[163]

Mormons' responses to these actions showed their readiness to compromise if that would help get the U.S. government to cease its persecution,
but Benjamin Harrison's election to the presidency in 1888 halted whatever
progress had been made. Scholars regard Harrison as one of the United
States' most religiously oriented presidents. The historian William C. Ringenberg argues that Harrison's "religious perceptions and convictions provided an intellectual and moral framework that vitally influenced how he
viewed issues and the manner with which he approached them." Before becoming a lawyer, Harrison nearly embarked on a religious career, citing the
potential pleasure of evangelizing the world." With respect to religion and
the state, Harrison believed that God had created America as a model to show
the world what could be achieved through a constitutional government guar-
anteeing individual freedom. As president, Harrison saw himself as assisting
the development of God's special plan for America.[164] The U.S. presidency
had fallen to a man who would not tolerate a Mormon America within a
mainstream Christian America.

Although he granted amnesty to individual polygamists, Harrison took
a stand against Mormonism by not encouraging Congress to approve Utah's
bid for statehood. Even though Utah's population base was more than sufficient for statehood and nearly all the surrounding territories had already
become states, polygamy disqualified Utah in Harrison's eyes. In his speech
accepting the Republican nomination in 1888, Harrison opposed statehood
for any territory fostering institutions antithetical to civilization or republican government. Despite the Saints' abandonment of polygamy in 1890,
Harrison did not endorse Utah's bid for statehood during his term. Given
his amnesty program for individual polygamists, which indicated his warm-
ing toward Utah, he probably would have supported statehood during a second term had he been reelected.[165]

Harrison appointed a new governor for Utah, one who believed stricter
action necessary to bring the Mormons into line. This appointment coincided
with a fresh run of anti-Mormon bills in Congress. In response, the church
sent a delegation to Washington to suggest that if the bills were delayed, the

church would ban the practice of polygamy. On September 28, 1890, the public learned that the church forbade plural marriage. In addition to ending support for plural marriage, the church abandoned blood atonement, murder of apostates, and the power of bishop's courts over probate courts. It also promised not to dictate members' voting behavior and not to support linkages of church and state. Furthermore, in 1896 the Mormon religious authorities decreed that men holding "high positions in the Church" not "accept political office or enter into any vocation that would distract or remove them from the religious duties resting upon them" without approval of their peers and superiors in the church. The church was abandoning formal politics. When Utah gained statehood in 1896, its constitution prohibited polygamous or plural marriages. By attacking Mormonism until it changed, the government forced the Saints into the modern age, from sacred time into historical time. Forced to abandon sacred practices such as polygamy, the Saints had to find acceptable ways to practice their faith and to set themselves apart from the world. Ritual practices such as tithing, wearing distinctive undergarments symbolic of their covenants, and following the Word of Wisdom (a revelation concerning health that called for Mormons to abstain from alcohol and tobacco) took on important new significance.[166] The U.S. government had completed the mission it began in 1857. Through military intervention and coercive legislation, the government had reformed the face of Mormonism and made the religion's adherents American enough to join the Union.

The church ceased sanctioning plural marriages with the announcement of a "manifesto." To the outside world, it seemed Mormons had finally come to their senses. Within the Mormon community, however, the manifesto created uncertainty and a division between polygamists and the official church. Furthermore, church authorities secretly continued to authorize and perform polygamous marriages through 1904, although in dramatically smaller quantities. The manifesto apparently pleased the U.S. government; in 1893 and 1894 presidents Harrison and Cleveland issued pardons to convicted or indicted polygamists who promised to obey U.S. law in the future.[167]

Fundamentalist Mormons, citing Joseph Smith's revelation regarding plural marriage, continued the practice while the mainstream church moved increasingly further from it. In 1935 the Mormon church excommunicated a group of fundamentalist polygamists in Short Creek, Arizona. Despite continued persecution of polygamists in northern Arizona and southern Utah in the twentieth century, however, the practice continues, and law-enforcement officers in both states routinely ignore it. Utah attorney general Paul Van Dam addressed the issue in a 1991 television documentary, saying the state knew of tens of thousands of polygamists, who were clearly violating the law. Yet the state did little if anything about it, because experience showed that arrests would not stop them from practicing what they considered a crucial element of their faith. The government, both state and federal, as well as the church had come a long way. The state convinced the LDS Church not only to abandon a fundamental tenet but to help punish transgressors and enforce the state's laws, which the church adopted. But those living the fundamentalist version of Mormonism persist and are finally tolerated by the state.[168]

According to Howard Lamar, the conflict between Utah's Mormons and the United States teaches us about the values of both sides in equal measure. As Lamar puts it, the contest pitted "a so-called WASP-American view of American values and a Mormon adherence to and espousal of values which they, too, could argue were 'as American as apple pie.'" Mormons took certain spiritual and temporal traditions of early nineteenth-century America further than any other group. Their dedication to millennialism and communitarianism exceeded that of any other religious or utopian group from the Burned-Over District, and they rigorously pursued it in their efforts to build a Mormon Zion through the end of the century. Their travails in the Midwest helped them forge a coherent society that they transplanted to Utah and elsewhere in the West, where they turned their ecclesiastical organization into a government. After decades of government coercion, however, the church abandoned those tenets that incited federal persecution. Mormons, and anyone else who doubted it, learned that morally speaking, the Constitution is a Protestant document and the United States a Protestant nation.[169] Others would learn a similar lesson. At the same time that the Mormon prophet received his revelation to Americanize his religion, a religious group in South Dakota was enjoying a spirit of revival and beginning to flourish. It, too, would soon suffer for exceeding the toleration of mainstream America.

★

3   Uncle Sam and the Lying Messiah

> When Good Thunder and Kicking Bear came back in the spring
> from seeing the Wanekia [the son of the Great Spirit, or "One Who
> Makes Live"], the Wasichus [whites] at Pine Ridge put them in prison
> awhile, and then let them go. This showed the Wasichus were afraid of
> something.
>
> —Black Elk, *Black Elk Speaks*

JUST BEFORE DAWN on December 15, 1890, a group of Lakota police officers gathered on the Standing Rock Reservation to pray for divine guidance in the dangerous mission they were about to undertake. Lt. Bullhead led the Christian prayers of the ceska maza, or metal breasts (the term refers to their badges). After finishing their prayer, the ceska maza saddled their horses and rode toward the camp of the "religious fanatics" whose leader they had been ordered to capture and under no circumstances allow to escape.

One of the ceska maza, Lone Man, had once followed this leader, the most feared and respected among all the American Indians whom the U.S. government considered to be especially dangerous. Lone Man's loyalty to this man had led him into battle against Colonel George Armstrong Custer and then into Canada, fleeing from the U.S. Army. Since then the two had parted ways. Lone Man had abandoned aspects of his old Lakota life, including what he now saw as a superstitious religion and other old-time customs, and had cast his lot with the United States by becoming an Indian policeman. The leader, Tatanka Iyotanke, clung to familiar ways, resisting efforts by the federal government and mainstream white culture to efface Indian lifeways. He embraced a new religion that promised to revitalize the old ways and to improve his people's world. Because Tatanka Iyotanke embraced the Wanagi Wacipi—because, that is, Sitting Bull embraced the Ghost Dance—the United States wanted him removed from Indian country or dead. The ceska maza prayed for success in carrying out that mission, and their prayers were answered. Within hours Sitting Bull lay dead, and exactly two weeks later the

Seventh Cavalry killed hundreds more Ghost Dancers, including some who had fled Sitting Bull's camp during the raid by the Indian police.[1]

In South Dakota, cultures had collided with horrifying results. A new religion entered the world and spread among Indians living in the West. When the Ghost Dance reached the Lakotas in 1889–90, they made it their own, as did many other Indian nations, but they added a militant twist that frightened whites and their government. In an atmosphere swirling with fear, ignorance, and a history of violent conflict (including perhaps the greatest Indian victory or one of the most embarrassing defeats in U.S. history, depending on one's point of view), tensions escalated during November 1890. White neighbors, government officials, and the media fed the panic, and in response hundreds died, including one of the most feared Lakota resistance leaders. Although the heavy-handed government response failed to destroy the new religion entirely, it drove the Ghost Dance underground temporarily and sapped it of its vitality.

A number of factors contributed to the disaster, but underlying them all was a missionary zeal to eliminate one culture and its religion and replace it with another culture and its religion. Of the hundreds of thousands of Indians who experienced the United States spreading European civilization through the West, few experienced it more violently than the Lakotas who adopted the Ghost Dance movement. As had been the case with Mormons, many factors contributed to the tension between American Indians and the United States, and the record left by the participants shows that religion again played an important role in fostering conflict, this one producing horrific violence in December 1890.

Prophets appear in many faiths, including those of Native Americans. One of the best known and most misunderstood is Wovoka, the prophet behind the Ghost Dance religion, which swept the American West in the late nineteenth century, reaching the Lakotas and other Plains tribes in 1889 and 1890. During his childhood Wovoka, a Paiute known as Jack Wilson in the English-speaking world, picked up spiritual influences that would shape his prophecies. His father was thought to hold spiritual powers and followed the teachings of Wodziwob, prophet of the first Ghost Dance movement, which dated to the 1870s.[2] The U.S. government would undertake an active campaign to discourage this religion in the West and to impose its own values of Christian civilization.

During an eclipse of the sun, probably on or about January 1, 1889, Wovoka fell asleep and had a vision that formed the basis for the Ghost Dance. According to the most reliable sources, he never said he was an Indian messiah, but he did claim to be a prophet who had received divine revelation. The core belief of that revelation predicted that soon all Indians, living and dead, would be reunited on a regenerated earth to live a life of happiness and plenty free from death, disease, and poverty. The white race, and the evils it brought to the Indian world, would disappear forever, probably during an earthquake that would not harm Ghost Dancers. As this message spread to tribes from California to the Great Plains, it assumed a variety of new interpretations owing to imperfect translations and individual opinion. Despite the various interpretations, however, Ghost Dancers consistently sought to make themselves worthy of the upcoming deliverance, and they were urged to discard warlike accoutrements and to practice honesty, peace, and goodwill to all people, even whites as long as they were around. Wovoka urged his followers to perform a five-day dance to be repeated at six-week intervals. He also explicitly warned his followers not to make trouble with whites, presumably because supernatural forces would deal with them in due time.[3]

The Ghost Dance inspired fear in the white community. Whites, who generally failed to distinguish religious dances from war dances, interpreted the Ghost Dance as the Lakotas' preparation for a fatalistic clash with whites to expel them from this world.[4] The federal government responded by sending troops to quell the religious ceremony, an act that ultimately led to the death of Sitting Bull, the great Hunkpapa holy man who personified Lakota resistance to the threat of American expansion, and to the massacre of a great many Lakotas (at least 146 and possibly more than 250) at Wounded Knee Creek on December 29, 1890.[5] Historians often use these events to symbolize the last gasp of traditional Indian ways in the face of an expanding imperial nation.

Ideally, Ghost Dancers could have practiced their religion peacefully in the United States. But the Great Plains of the 1890s remained far from ideal, particularly for the people who had lived there longest. They faced a nation bent on remaking them into what it considered ideal citizens. To accomplish this, the federal and state governments would see to Native Americans' secular and industrial education while churches established and maintained religious missions. "By this harmonious and yet separate activity of the government and the churches," wrote T. J. Morgan, commissioner of Indian affairs in 1890, "all of the Indians will eventually be brought into right relations with their white neighbors, and be prepared for the privileges and responsibilities of American Christian citizenship."[6]

Within civilian circles an unfortunate admixture of religion and politics may have contributed heavily to the state of affairs in Indian country that perhaps made Lakotas and others ripe for interest in the Ghost Dance. In 1890, shortly before the Ghost Dance sparked hysteria in the white community, Agent Hugh D. Gallagher, who apparently enjoyed good relations with the Indians at Pine Ridge, was replaced with Daniel Royer, who has been widely viewed as incompetent during his tenure as agent there. Because he was a Democrat and a Catholic, Gallagher suffered when T. J. Morgan, a Protestant Republican, became commissioner of Indian affairs in Washington, D.C. Indeed, Morgan may have cut rations to Pine Ridge to harm Gallagher's reputation.[7]

Robert Pugh, an issue clerk at Pine Ridge before and during the Ghost Dance phenomenon, condemned Morgan's work. Morgan, whom Pugh described as a Baptist preacher, turned a deaf ear to requests for supplies at Pine Ridge. "Told that the Indians are hungry, [Morgan] inquired what kind of religious reading would be best for them," Pugh told Judge Eli Ricker, a student of the frontier who interviewed participants in notable events such as Wounded Knee. Continuing, Pugh said, "[Morgan] acted as though a diminished ration would create a spirited appetite."[8] As it happened, the diminished ration may indeed have contributed to a heightened spiritual appetite among the Lakotas, but the Ghost Dancers certainly did not try to satisfy it in a fashion Morgan would have approved.

Beginning in 1870, when a number of Indian agents were to be replaced, President U.S. Grant and subsequent presidents made the new assignments based on recommendations from religious groups. The federal government "apportioned [the agent positions] among the prominent religious organizations of the country." The Bureau of Indian Affairs enhanced its harmonious relations with its mainstream Christian religious partners and endorsed their work by requiring many of its charges to observe the Sabbath. Pupils at government-sponsored Indian schools were required to attend Sabbath observances, although conscientious objectors among employees could be excused from religious exercises.[9]

The superintendent of Indian schools recognized the unusual nature of this arrangement and commented on it in his annual report. He asserted that there exist "broad grounds of essential ethics and positive religious truth on which all who accept, in any form, Jesus Christ as the great teacher, can stand and work in harmony." He also appealed to the "Christian sense of the American people," asking their assent to the idea that "every teacher, without hindrance, may breathe forth a Christly spirit and exhale the perfume of true piety . . . which rises far above cant and dogmatism."[10] Working hand in hand, the U.S. government and Christian missionaries sought to force Christian values on America's indigenous population.

The values and tactics of the Christian missionaries were recorded in the newspapers *Iapi Oaye* and *The Word Carrier,* printed in Dakota and English, respectively, at the Santee Agency in northeast Nebraska, which doubled as a Protestant mission.[11] The missionaries John P. Williamson and Stephen R. Riggs founded and edited the papers. One of Riggs's sons, Alfred L. Riggs, edited the paper almost continuously from 1883 through 1916, including the Ghost Dance era among the Lakotas. The missionaries' editorial stance championed the advance of Christianity by any means necessary, including virtual crusades by the U.S. Army. These views appeared in 1876 as the paper reported the battle at the Little Bighorn River and Sitting Bull's involvement there. The paper excoriated the government's Indian policy for coddling "lawless" Indians, such as Sitting Bull and his followers. Had the government forced law and order on the Indians years earlier, the paper argued, it would have faced a minor confrontation but would have established discipline and obedience among the "lawless."[12]

It should be noted that the battle at the Little Bighorn involved more than a military conflict. It should be considered a cultural and possibly even a religious conflict as well. Although the missionaries commenting on the events may not have known it at the time, Sitting Bull had prophesied the battle and its outcome, adding to his prestige among Lakotas. At a Sun Dance he organized in early June 1876, Sitting Bull had a vision in which he saw a large number of soldiers attacking an Indian camp; some Indians died, but all the soldiers perished. Before the month ended, Sitting Bull's prophecy came to pass when a massive force of Lakotas and their allies wiped out Colonel Custer's forces.[13]

The missionaries at Santee clearly viewed the Lakotas as uncivilized troublemakers. "There were a great number of Dakotas," the paper asserted in an unattributed editorial, "who, in order to be worth anything, must have a good thrashing."[14] Accordingly, the editors urged continued warfare against the "hostile Sioux," generally the Lakotas. "Sitting Bull and his people must be *humbled* and *beaten* and *captured,*" the editor demanded.[15] The missionaries went further in May 1883 when they predicted that Sitting Bull would ultimately "plow the ground with his stubby horns."[16] To the credit of its Christian foundation, the editors cautioned against the indiscriminate slaughter of women and children. Limiting attacks to strikes against warriors would place "the Lord and right on [the troops'] side."[17]

In 1882 and 1883 the missionaries called for allotment, leasing of Indian lands, and outright cession of reservations. The editors felt this would speed Indians toward "civilization" as they observed the example of their hard-working, agricultural white neighbors.[18] A headline in the English portion of the paper succinctly offered recommendations for preventing further conflicts: "Raise no more Indians." Again criticizing the government, the paper urged cessation of ration issues to Indians who raised children "as wild, as ignorant, as much indisposed to labor, and as ready and eager to go on the warpath as themselves." Instead, the paper hailed education as the Indians' path to civilization. Through compulsory education in religion, trades, and the arts, including instruction in their native language, the paper sought to "train up Indian children so they [would] not be Indians," thus making "Life and Salvation" available to all Native Americans.[19]

The government also used the recently established Indian police and courts of Indian offenses as tools of acculturation. As the U.S. government administered increasingly more Indian reservations in the second half of the nineteenth century, it entered a new phase of imposing its morals and laws on indigenous populations. Early incarnations of Indian police forces took the form of ad hoc paramilitary groups of men from a given reservation chosen for their loyalty to the agent. In 1878 Congress felt the need for a more permanent solution to disorder on reservations and allocated funds to hire Indian police. Agents now used a candidate's loyalty to the "civilization" programs of the United States to test his suitability. Before the year ended, one-third of all agencies had their own police forces. By 1880 that proportion had grown to two-thirds; by 1890 virtually every agency had an Indian police force.[20]

In addition to being able to work and command respect among their people, Indian police almost always belonged to the "progressive" faction of a given tribe—that group most sympathetic or resigned to U.S. policy (as opposed to "traditionalists" or "conservatives," who are often described as opposing U.S. policy).[21] This made sense, considering the act authorizing their creation called for them to be used "for the purposes of civilization of the Indians." This meant Indian police officers could have only one wife and that they should look like agents of civilization—cutting their long braids, forsaking face paint, and wearing boots rather than moccasins, among other things. The nature of their duties also led them to oppose dancing, to enforce school attendance, to oppose the work of medicine men, and to support the agent and progressive Indians against conservatives. When one Indian police officer summoned a medicine man to treat his sick children, the agent removed him from the force.[22]

Shortly after authorizing Indian police forces, the U.S. government created the courts of Indian offenses. Secretary of the Interior H. M. Teller created the courts in 1883 to punish offenders apprehended by the Indian police. Troubled by the continuation of traditional practices on reservations, particularly "heathenish dances" that "stimulate warlike passions," Teller instructed Hiram Price, commissioner of Indian affairs and an active Methodist, to draft a set of rules and regulations to end such practices. Teller also believed something should be done to end plural marriages and to reduce the influence of medicine men. Price complied, and Teller approved his recommendations and circulated them to agents. In choosing judges for the courts, the agents were to select Indians who were "intelligent, honest, and upright," "of undoubted integrity," and not polygamists. The cases most often heard by the courts involved adultery, rape, polygamy, cohabitation, licentiousness, bastardy, and fornication. The Indian police and courts of Indian offenses, then, carried out the government's acculturation policy at the grassroots level and sought to establish morality based on the nation's mainstream religious values. Agents supplemented their influence through additional regulations. In 1888, for instance, the Pine Ridge agent banned funeral rites, leading some on the reservation to complain that white men harassed them even in death.[23]

Although these might seem innocuous, secular matters to twenty-first-century Americans of European descent, they amounted to significant efforts to control Indian society and culture. In these Indian communities all social and political ties carried strong religious overtones. With respect to maintaining peace and order, the supernatural played a larger role in Indian communities than it does in contemporary American culture. Indians did not, as it were, separate church and state.[24] Examples of this program of control can be found at the Cheyenne River Agency in South Dakota. The agency's three court of Indian offense judges represented "the civilized or Christian element," reported Agent Perain P. Palmer. Palmer wrote in his annual report that one judge was a Roman Catholic and two were members of the Protestant Episcopal Church. These judges heard about 125 cases during the year comprising the Wounded Knee massacre and made 73 convictions for offenses that included infidelity to marriage vows, illegal marriage, and encouraging the Ghost Dance. Punishments included confinement in the agency prison for periods ranging from two to ninety days, depending on the offense. Palmer also reported that Cheyenne River's police and agency farmer played important roles in "subduing" the Ghost Dance there.[25]

At Pine Ridge acculturation policy included work by Phillip Wells, a part-Indian government farmer in the Medicine Root district. Wells fought the Ghost Dance at Pine Ridge, showing that government cultural programs incorporated religious aspects even if they were not among the stated goals of particular secular programs. When the Ghost Dance appeared at Pine Ridge, Agent Gallagher consulted with agency employees about stopping the dance. Most advocated "stern measures and even force." According to Wells, Gallagher used agency farmers to discourage the Ghost Dance and agency police to arrest leaders. Wells claimed that he argued against force and that, although he had help from an Episcopal clergyman, he alone among agency farmers kept his district free of the "disturbing ghost dance."[26]

As for the U.S. Army, certainly some of its members felt that Indians in general and Ghost Dancers in particular must be rid of their superstitions. Captain John G. Bourke of the Third Cavalry wrote a letter to the press stating as much. Bourke's letter appeared in the *Omaha Morning World-Herald* in the midst of the Ghost Dance controversy. He wrote, "The life of the Indian rested upon his religion and . . . the medicine man was the one individual in the tribe whose actions and motives must be understood and frustrated." The solution, he believed, rested in breaking the medicine men's power, and as he put it, "no effort [would be] too great or too small to effect this."[27] Although he went on to advocate means such as education and trickery, citing a case of a magician surprising some Sioux by pulling a ten-dollar gold piece from a medicine man's mouth and another from Little Big Man's nose, Bourke believed strongly that Indian religion and Indian holy men must be undermined. Bourke hoped that Indians would respect property and travel "the road to wealth, which means conservatism, peace and prosperity."[28] Although Bourke did not speak officially for the army, he was representative of its officer corps and voiced a popular sentiment of the day. Government agencies and agents, then, enforced Christian morality on the Lakotas and made political prisoners of those practicing native culture and religion.

In carrying out this policy, the government contended not only with traditional Native American religion but also with a religious revival that swept up western indigenous groups during the late 1880s and early 1890s, with the Ghost Dance as its central feature. In Oklahoma Arapahos and Cheyennes adopted the Ghost Dance during the summer of 1890. Their neighbors, including the Pawnees, Poncas, Otos, Missouris, Kansas, Iowas, Caddos, Wichitas, Kichais, Delawares, and Kiowas, also practiced the religion.[29]

Ghost Dance advocates spread the religion with evangelical zeal that would have done their Christian counterparts proud. West of the Rockies, the religion spread among the Paiutes—Wovoka's people—and their neighbors. The religion moved quickly into California and the home regions of the Bannocks, Shoshones, Gosiutes, and Utes. The Ghost Dance did not catch on with most of the tribes of the Columbia Basin or those in the region that became

Arizona and New Mexico. Tribes to the east learned of the religion from members who visited Wovoka to learn about the Ghost Dance. Black Coyote (Watangaa) of the southern Arapahos brought the religion to his people in the spring of 1890. He also sought a permanent travel pass from the U.S. government to allow him to visit other Indian agencies at will to spread the religion.[30] Native American Ghost Dancers on the plains faced suppression from the U.S. government, but nothing like that faced by the Lakotas.

Lakotas constitute a division of the "Sioux," which is a French rendering of an Ojibway word roughly meaning "the Lesser Adders," the latter's derogatory term for their western neighbors. When used to refer to a political unit, *Sioux* refers to peoples in three geographic groups who speak three dialects of the same language—Dakota, Nakota, and Lakota.[31]

The Santees, or eastern Sioux, who speak the Dakota dialect and are sometimes called Dakotas, include four tribes: Wahpeton, Mdewakanton, Wahpekute, and Sisseton. Of the various Sioux groups, the Dakotas were probably the first to meet Europeans. The French traded with the Dakotas as early as 1660, and the United States opened official relations with them in 1805 when one of Zebulon Pike's expeditions entered their homelands in what is now Wisconsin and Minnesota. In 1863, in the wake of a conflict near Mankato, Minnesota, the United States unilaterally abrogated its treaties with the Dakotas and forced them to move west to what are now the states of North and South Dakota. During these hard times some Dakotas accepted Christianity as they became dependent on the U.S. government for food and as their social and political organization began to disintegrate. In 1866, after the Dakotas had spent a miserable term at the Crow Creek Reservation in Dakota Territory, the government moved them, again by force, to the Santee Reservation in northeast Nebraska Territory, where their reservation remains.[32] The Dakotas' new Nebraska home also became the headquarters for an assimilation campaign waged by Indian and white holy men on Dakotas and Lakotas.

The smallest division, the Yanktons, who traditionally lived northernmost among the groups and speak the Nakota dialect, includes the Ihanktunwan (also known simply as Yankton) and Ihanktunawanna (or Yanktonai, meaning "little Yankton"). When Europeans arrived in the upper Midwest, the Yanktons practiced a woodland culture similar to the Santees'. By about 1700 they had moved onto the prairies of what is now southwestern Minnesota and northwestern Iowa. They began moving into the area that became southeastern South Dakota around 1800 and traded with Americans coming up the Missouri River. They also traded with their Lakota relatives, allowing the Lakotas to obtain American trade goods while continuing to avoid direct trade with whites. In fact, Lakotas reportedly used this situation to raid American merchant traffic on the Missouri without facing the consequence of losing access to American goods. Pressure from the U.S. government to cede their lands and move onto reservations, combined with other factors, led the Yanktons to move to reservations by 1860, with their main reservation standing along the Missouri River in southeastern South Dakota.[33]

The Tetons, or western Sioux—also known as Lakotas because they speak the Lakota dialect—constitute the largest of the three groups and includes seven bands: Oglala, Sicangu (Brulé), Hunkpapa, Sihasapa, Itazipco (Sans Arcs), Oohenunpa (Two Kettles), and Miniconjou. Lakotas moved from the prairies of what is now central Minnesota onto the plains during the mid-eighteenth century and had reached as far west at the Black Hills by 1765. Having adopted horses and guns into their culture with astonishing success, the Lakotas achieved unprecedented wealth, power, and mobility by the first half of the nineteenth century.[34]

The Lakotas, the last of the Sioux to submit to reservation life, probably felt cultural changes and threats later and more acutely than their eastern relatives. After their rise to power during the early part of the nineteenth century, Lakotas encountered a new, aggressive, and expansionist power on the plains—the United States—and entered into a violent and contentious relationship with the new republic. Settlers came, and the buffalo, a staple of the Plains Indian economy, fell victim to U.S. government scorched-earth policy, greed, overhunting, and other hazards of U.S. settlement.[35] By the end of the nineteenth century, the United States had taken most Sioux lands, and the Sioux had become wards of a powerful alien state. The Lakotas most involved in the Ghost Dance included Oglalas at Pine Ridge, Sicangus at Rosebud, Hunkpapas at Standing Rock, and Miniconjous at Cheyenne River.

Missionaries, general education, and industrial training had made the Dakotas and Yanktons "hostages to civilization," an improvement over their previous condition in the eyes of the government. Most Lakotas, however, struck government officials as "wild" compared to their other Sioux relatives, even after the Lakotas had spent more than a decade on the reservation.[36] To make matters worse, sometime in late 1889 or early 1890 Lakotas at Pine Ridge Agency heard a message of salvation—a new religion promised a return to the good times enjoyed so recently. The U.S. government saw things differently, fearing that the new religion would reinforce the un-Christian "wildness" it so desperately wanted to eliminate from America's indigenous peoples.

Word of the Ghost Dance reached the Lakota reservations during the summer of 1889. That autumn councils at Pine Ridge, Cheyenne River, and Rosebud selected emissaries to visit Wovoka, collect information about the Ghost Dance, and report back to their various reservations. The Pine Ridge council chose Good Thunder, Yellow Breast, Flat Iron, Broken Arm, Cloud Horse, Yellow Knife, Elk Horn, and Kicks Back. Rosebud sent Short Bull and Mash-the-Kettle; Cheyenne River sent Kicking Bear. The Lakota pilgrims traveled to Wovoka's Nevada home, going part of the way by train. Once on the Paiute Reservation, they spent roughly a week learning about the Ghost Dance. They returned to their reservations in March 1890 to relate their findings.[37]

As did nearly all Indians who visited Wovoka, the Lakota delegates reported the Ghost Dance through the prism of their experiences and beliefs. By performing a certain ceremony, they believed, they could conjure an Indian savior who would resurrect fallen Lakotas, bring back the buffalo, and leave the land in Indian hands forever. Nearly all tribes that adopted the Ghost Dance held at least those tenets in common. Lakotas distinguished themselves, however, by adding militant overtones. Rather than retain Wovoka's pacifist teachings, Lakotas believed that white people were evil and that the "messiah" would vengefully exterminate them.[38]

The Lakota incarnation of the Ghost Dance contained another element that would disturb whites—supposedly bulletproof vestments known as ghost shirts. The earliest record of ghost shirts worn in concert with the Ghost Dance occurred in June 1890 at Pine Ridge. Although several other tribes that practiced the Ghost Dance adopted the ghost shirt, only the Sioux imbued it with bulletproof qualities. On the day of Sitting Bull's murder, a Ghost Dancer named Crow Woman made a dramatic display of the garment's effectiveness. Clad in a ghost shirt, Crow Woman rode past an encampment of soldiers who fired on him but missed. Twice Crow Woman repeated the feat, and each time the soldiers failed to hit him. For the Lakotas observing the event, it proved the ghost shirt's power. (This test apparently contradicted an experiment conducted on Pine Ridge in November in which a volunteer named Porcupine received a nearly fatal wound while testing a ghost shirt against bullets.)[39] The advent of ghost shirts and the bravery they instilled in those who wore them inspired fear in the white community, which responded by sending troops to quell the religious ceremony, an act that ultimately led to the death of Sitting Bull.

Ghost Dancers and whites viewed the world in fundamentally different ways. Statements by Lakotas about their own spirituality reveal some of those differences. For example, a Lakota named Iron Hawk encapsulated Lakota spirituality in a 1907 interview at age seventy-three: "God gave us a spirit to work, to sleep, to do all good things in our generations. He [an Indian] knows that his life is from God; that he lives in Him; that it has been so from his birth. He says this is his own idea—his own mind. He has known from his birth that he was to be a friend to every body and everything—to all animals of their kind as well as to all human beings. . . . I am raised to know every-thing—to have knowledge of everything."[40] This represents a seamless worldview in which all things are related, in contrast to the worldview, com-mon among non-Indians, that divides existence into separate sacred and sec-ular realms.

Some agents reported that the Ghost Dance had not found favor among the Indians at their agencies, but their reports reflect important assumptions that Christian whites made about native spirituality. The agent at Sisseton reported that the Ghost Dance had not been introduced there, but even if it were introduced, it would likely not be welcomed. "As a large majority of the Indians here are Christians," the agent explained, "it is not at all likely that an effort to introduce the ghost dance would meet with any success." The agent assumed lineal "progress" on the part of his charges—once they had adopted Christianity, they would not revert to a native religion. He also assumed that the Sisseton Sioux had accepted a pure Christianity that they would not augment with any elements of their own, centuries-old spiritu-ality or with elements of a new religion steeped in native culture.[41]

Phillip Wells's description of the dance (as recorded by Eli Ricker) indi-cates how easily Christians perceived it as dangerous and threatening. Ghost Dancers were "wrought up to high pitch of excitement and went through various indescribable contortions, . . . and when going into trance uttered unearthly moans and groans and all manner of utterance and noise, the most inconceivable discord and tumult smiting the air, while they clawed the air and flung froth from their mouths, the numerous performers in the Sty-gian conceit keeping their regular cadence."[42]

Drawing on his interview with Wells, Ricker called the Ghost Dance "strange, weird, and grotesque, not to say pathetic, worship" and pointed out that the rapidly spreading movement produced results deemed undesirable by those interested in "civilizing" the Lakotas.[43] Statistics provided by the American Missionary Association for its Indian missions in the Dakotas show that after five years of steady growth in most categories, the number of schools, pupils, and Sunday-school students dropped during the year in which the Ghost Dance enjoyed its greatest popularity among the Lakotas. Numbers declined precipitously in categories concerning young Indians—that is, those with impressionable minds, whom the missionaries sought most to influence. From 1889 to 1890 the number of pupils declined 19.9 percent, while the number of Sunday-school students dropped a staggering 51.9 percent to the lowest level on record. Meanwhile, Lakotas threw themselves into other dances, too. Ricker spoke for many other whites when he concluded that the Ghost Dance had a "demoralizing" effect on the Lakotas.[44]

Government agents gave mixed responses to the Ghost Dance among the Lakotas but generally tried to end it as quickly as possible. Cheyenne River agent Charles E. McChesney dismissed the religion and did not interfere with Kicking Bear's efforts to spread it. From almost the moment the new religion arrived at Rosebud and Pine Ridge, however, officials tried to stop it. At Pine Ridge, when Agent Gallagher first learned of the Ghost Dance in April, he met with Good Thunder and two other leaders. When they refused to discuss the religion, Gallagher jailed them. After two days they agreed to stop promoting the dance, although they still refused to answer his questions about it. For the time being, it seemed, Gallagher had snuffed out the Ghost Dance.[45]

By August 1890, however, the religion had resurfaced. Worried about the effect of the Ghost Dance, not to mention the gathering of an estimated 2,000 dancers on White Clay Creek, Gallagher ordered his Indian police to break up the dance and disperse the dancers. When this raid on the Ghost Dancers failed, Gallagher himself went to the dance grounds accompanied by twenty Indian police. Ghost Dancers met the agent's party "stripped for fight," armed with Winchester rifles, and "prepared to die in defense of the new faith." Whatever transpired, Gallagher reported that the dancers "were finally quieted," although, given the circumstances, that seems likely to be Gallagher's positive interpretation of a confrontation he may well have lost.[46]

If Gallagher indeed quieted the Ghost Dance at Pine Ridge, he did so only temporarily. In October the new agent, Daniel Royer, reported that more than half the agency's Indians had joined the dancing. Continued requests from the agent to cease dancing brought the same response: the dancers stripped and prepared to fight. Royer felt that he and the Indian police had lost control of the situation and hoped that he could get the military to help restore order.[47]

Meanwhile, at Standing Rock, Sitting Bull invited Kicking Bear to teach the Ghost Dance at his camp on Grand River in October. Kicking Bear, of the Cheyenne River Agency, was a leading Lakota Ghost Dance apostle and among those Lakotas who had visited Wovoka in Nevada. Sitting Bull's invitation to him brought the new religion into the jurisdiction of James McLaughlin, U.S. Indian agent at Standing Rock and longtime adversary of Sitting Bull. In his memoir McLaughlin called Sitting Bull an "unreconstructed Indian—which he remained to the day of his death." In his criticism of Sitting Bull, McLaughlin focused on the Hunkpapa's moral conduct, particularly his multiple wives. According to McLaughlin, the older Lakota men clung to polygamy and their polygamous households, which undermined morals and the civilization process more generally. Sitting Bull, he wrote, had two wives until the end of his life, and maybe more.[48] Sitting Bull, prophet, polygamist, and defender of the old ways, stood squarely in the path of McLaughlin and his duty to advance U.S. policy.

On learning of Kicking Bear's arrival at Standing Rock, Agent McLaughlin ordered thirteen Indian police to arrest him and escort him from the reservation. This force failed to complete its mission, but when McLaughlin sent another contingent of Indian police to order Kicking Bear back to Cheyenne River, the apostle apparently complied. Sitting Bull, however, refused to abandon the religion. He reportedly told the police that the Great Spirit had spoken through Kicking Bear, instructing Sitting Bull and his followers to perform the dance if they wished to continue living.[49]

Agent McLaughlin saw his old nemesis, whom he characterized as "a polygamist, libertine, habitual liar, active obstructionist, and a great obstacle in the civilization" of the Indians at Standing Rock, as the primary instigator behind the Ghost Dance. McLaughlin claimed, "A great many of the Indians of this agency actually believe [the Ghost Dance]," and he called the new religion an "infection . . . so pernicious that it now includes some of the Indians who were formerly numbered with the progressive and more intelligent." According to McLaughlin, Sitting Bull, "high priest and leading apostle of this latest Indian absurdity," caused the Ghost Dance to be welcomed at Standing Rock. If it were not for Sitting Bull, McLaughlin believed, Standing Rock Indians would have rejected the religion.[50]

Echoing his counterparts on other reservations, McLaughlin called the dance "demoralizing, indecent, and disgusting." Having failed to stop the religion through intimidation, McLaughlin decided to try a new tack: removing Sitting Bull from the agency. McLaughlin recommended arresting the Hunkpapa leader and confining him in a military prison far away from Standing Rock, preferably before spring, when, according to the Ghost Dance eschatology, the white race's demise would occur—presumably, most whites no doubt thought, via an "Indian outbreak" directed against them. With Sitting Bull and other Ghost Dance leaders gone, according to McLaughlin, "the advancement of the Sioux [would] be more rapid and the interests of the Government greatly subserved thereby."[51] His plan to neutralize Sitting Bull would soon come to fruition.

The agent at Rosebud tried to starve the Ghost Dancers into submission.

When the dancers refused his request to stop dancing, he informed them that he would withhold their rations until they acquiesced and went home. This apparently worked in the short run, but when the agent left on a trip and appointed a temporary substitute agent, the dancing began again, with the dancers "defying all control."[52]

As summer gave way to fall in 1890, the new Ghost Dance religion found a receptive audience among some sectors of the Lakota population. The Lakotas performing the Ghost Dance no doubt looked forward to the coming spring, when whites and the evils of their world would be swept from the earth, ushering in a new and better era for Indians. As news of the religion spread, however, so did whites' fears that the Ghost Dance was no harmless religion but rather a movement that would spark a new era of warfare with the people who had soundly defeated Custer fourteen years earlier. That possibility aroused intense interest. In November newspaper reporters began descending on Lakota country hoping to get a hot story. They were not disappointed.

Newspapers and U.S. Indian agents played an important role in creating an image of the Ghost Dance and its adherents that aroused hysteria among both citizens and government officials. Although the Utah Expedition may have faded from the popular memory by 1890, morality in the West remained an issue, as is demonstrated by the ongoing controversy over polygamy discussed in the previous chapter. The national press still issued reports on the Mormon saga in the fall of 1890. In Ogden on November 21, five Mormons, identified in the press as "mormon [*sic*] polygamists," pled guilty to charges of unlawful cohabitation. A newspaper covering the incident smugly reported, "The best informed people here consider Mormonism dead beyond resurrection."[53] The United States appeared to have gained the upper hand in vanquishing the "evils" of Mormonism, but another "menace" to U.S. values, the Ghost Dance religion, had come out of the West not far from Mormon country. Against the backdrop of continued questions about morality in the West, the Ghost Dance's spread that autumn terrified white neighbors, but not for long—the U.S. government saw to that.

Although concern about the Ghost Dance had been growing, it escalated in November 1890, particularly in the media. Early that month news stories, although calm, indicated that the media and mainstream America held the Ghost Dance in contempt. The *Omaha Morning World-Herald* reported, "The Indian has as much right to his illusions as the adventists, or the theosophists, or the spiritualists, or the faith curists, or any other believers in any other creeds." But that progressive-sounding statement came on the heels of a lead paragraph that labeled the Ghost Dance "an epidemic" and the belief in an Indian messiah a "mental disease." Nevertheless, the paper at that point recommended leaving the Ghost Dancers alone.[54]

Soon, however, newspapers began sounding increasingly strident alarms. The *Omaha Bee* reported apprehension on the frontier because the government allowed Indians to own "the very best firearms to be obtained in the country." It stated that every male at the Lower Brulé and Crow Creek agencies had a Winchester rifle and a pair of pistols. It also mentioned an ominous and supposedly well-known charge that Indians who traded with whites invested every spare cent in cartridges, which they stockpiled for "future reference."[55]

According to the *Omaha Bee*, by November 1890 the Ghost Dance totally occupied the minds of the Sioux at the Cheyenne River Reservation and led them to abandon all sensible—according to U.S. norms—behavior in favor of performing the Ghost Dance and pondering the coming of the Indian messiah. "The Indians talk of nothing else—think of nothing else," the article said. In a revelation that must have disturbed much of the Christian United States, the story described the experience of an anonymous Cheyenne River Indian who went into a trance and spoke with the Holy Ghost. In the conversation, the entranced Indian learned that a messiah would soon arrive to wipe out all white people and return North America to its state prior to the arrival of whites. The resulting "fanaticism" led the Indians to give up work, farming, and school in favor of dancing the Ghost Dance day and night. The story erroneously attributed the Ghost Dance to Sitting Bull's "mesmeric powers" over his people, which he used to entice people into the new religion. Despite this article's alarmist tone, its concluding paragraph admitted there had been no "evidence of an outbreak" and conceded, "Sitting Bull urges upon the Indians the necessity of being peaceable, saying Christ does not wish the Indians to kill the whites, for he will remove them across the ocean."[56]

Like most other papers, the *Omaha Bee* displayed a degree of ambivalence toward the Ghost Dance. In the November 18 edition, for instance, a report filling an entire column of the front page described the Ghost Dance as originally a peaceful religion but explained that certain bearers of the message had added militant elements when they brought it to the plains. But stories in the adjacent column sent mixed signals. "The Settlers Alarmed" reported "depredatory bands of Indians armed to the teeth" and U.S. women and children moving to areas considered safe from attack. "No Troops Ordered Out" claimed that the army did not see fit to send troops into the field to address Indian relations. In "The Sioux Uneasy" the *Bee* explained that, according to army reports, some entire agencies were quiet; some at Standing Rock were "somewhat uneasy because of the supposed coming of their Messiah"; and at Pine Ridge, where the Oglalas had been "allowed to engage in ghost and other dances, there [was] much excitement but no probability of an outbreak."[57]

The next day, in a front-page article, the *Omaha Bee* misinterpreted the Ghost Dance. The writer argued that the feared Indian attack stemmed not from "the old spirit of aboriginal discontent at the encroachments of civilization, but by the teachings of a so-called Messiah. . . . The apparent effect of his gospel of peace has thus far been to make his followers thirsty for the blood of white men and to stimulate a concerted and threatening movement all along the border." Separating the Ghost Dance from the spread of white hegemony showed ignorance of epic proportions. Similar ignorance came in characterizing all Ghost Dancers as thirsting for white men's blood. Such characterizations were produced mostly, if not entirely, by whites. The writer's logic led to the conclusion that "authorities should not trust the treacherous Indians with precious human lives as long as they have numbers and arms sufficient to repeat the horrors of the old border days."[58] Despite the absence of a real threat from the Ghost Dance, media reports suggested increased tension and appear to have contributed to escalating anxiety.

Representatives of the Christian community had similarly mixed reactions to the Ghost Dance. In a November 19 interview in Sioux City, Iowa, the Episcopal bishop W. H. Hare opined that the Ghost Dance had already gone into decline and posed little or no threat. "[Ghost Dance] prophets have said that the quaking of the earth and the coming of the Messiah would occur at the next new moon, and when their predictions are not fulfilled the excitement will be allayed," the bishop said. Proving something of a prophet himself, he declared deploying troops among the Ghost Dance Indians a mistake certain to produce war.[59]

Protestant missionaries used twisted, perhaps self-deluding logic to call for halting the Ghost Dance. The argument, as expressed in *The Word Carrier,* reflected the interrelationship between religion and politics, at least as some missionaries understood it, and points out the degree to which they wished to accomplish cultural cleansing. They identified a clear link between religion and political life among Indians and viewed the U.S. government as bearing a responsibility to end religious dances. They pointed out that war dances and sun dances had been suppressed for political and humane reasons, respectively, and called for additional dances to be suppressed for moral purposes. Oddly, in calling for the eradication of these ceremonies they pointed not to the religion's ostensibly suspect nature but to its potential to yield riot and rebellion.[60] The missionaries showed cautious respect for

First Amendment rights, perhaps realizing their own ceremonies could, under certain circumstances, be threatened by government suppression. Perhaps they wished to capitalize on the logic set forth by the U.S. Supreme Court in *Reynolds v. United States.* Whatever their conclusion, the rhetoric employed to get them there betrayed their desire to eradicate Indian religion.

Some religious groups may have seen the Ghost Dance as a threatening competitor, especially when reports indicated it was spreading on the plains. In the last week of November 1890, a report from Lawrence, Kansas, showed the Ghost Dance spreading to tribes in Indian Territory (now Oklahoma). A Sioux, "acting as a missionary," had come to teach the religion to the Cheyennes and Arapahos, the Kiowas, the Comanches, and the Apaches. These tribes reportedly held joint Ghost Dances and were becoming "more restless and desperate as the time for the coming of the new Messiah" drew near. This news disturbed evangelical Protestants as they struggled to spread their faith in the West. It also disturbed federal officials as they pondered the government's ability to enforce order there. Shortly after alarming the nation about hysteria in Indian Territory, however, the press tried to pull back, hinting that initial reports may have been exaggerated. By mid-December newspapers were reporting that Indians in Oklahoma were "peaceably disposed" and that the Ghost Dances had "died out somewhat."[61]

Other religious groups attacked the Ghost Dance in its practitioners' own language. One of the earliest mentions of the Ghost Dance in *Iapi Oaye* appeared in November 1890. A front-page headline—"Messiya Itonśni," or "Lying Messiah"—framed a letter from Sam White Bird, a Christian convert writing from the Lower Brulé Agency. He tried to convince readers that the Indian messiah was a sham.[62] White Bird reported that as many as half the people at Rosebud believed in the Indian messiah, which, because he was a Christian, made him sad. Specifically, he referred to (and included in translation) six verses from Matthew warning against believing in false Christs. White Bird then implored his readers to remain true to the Bible and its followers, who are correct and good, and to resist the call of false prophets and their followers, who are misled and evil.[63] The paper initially responded to the Ghost Dance religion by trying to discredit it—with spiritual extortion via the threat of damnation—and to try to reinforce Christianity.

The Sioux Presbyterian minister Rev. Louis Mazawakinyanna (Iron Wing) was quoted in the same issue as saying that if people would go to church regularly, they would go to heaven. Mazawakinyanna indicated that a number of Sioux thought God had not been strong enough to guide them through their tribulations and had not served them well. But Mazawakinyanna kept trying to rally people to the real (i.e., Christian) God.[64]

Samuel Spaniard, a Sicangu/Brulé, reported that in the face of the rumors, he always remembered the teachings of the Bible. Spaniard characterized the notion of the Indian messiah (Wovoka) as a lie, although one clever enough that some people believed in him and did the Ghost Dance. In describing the dance, he emphasized the dancers' toppling over and then reviving and reported that any number of dancers would go from place to place to perform it. Spaniard called the dance a bad influence and confessed that he felt disheartened whenever he heard about it.[65]

John P. Williamson, the missionary at Santee now contributing to *Iapi Oaye,* fought the Ghost Dance by trying to discredit it. Williamson wrote an article teaching the signs that would announce the second coming of Jesus, not the Indian messiah. He countered the argument, made by some Ghost Dancers, that the biblical Jesus had come not for the Indians but only for the whites. To the contrary, Williamson wrote, Jesus told the twelve apostles to go through the world to teach all men. Williamson quoted from 1 John 2:2 and Isaiah 49:6, claiming that Jesus came for the "ikcewicaśta," or common man.[66] He further argued that the Bible (specifically, the book of Matthew) clearly states that the messiah will return from the East, not the West. Claims that the Indian messiah would come from the West, therefore, revealed any such individual as an impostor. Third, regarding the rumored resurrection of Indians, Williamson wrote that the dead would indeed rise, but only the Christian dead and only when Jesus returns.[67]

While Ghost Dance believers expected the resurrection during the coming spring, the missionary argued that no one can foretell the return of Jesus until God's heavenly trumpets announce the event. "But those who are not saved will not hear," Williamson stated, "Thus the ghost dance followers will not know." Finally, he attacked the "miracle" of the ghost dancers dying and coming back to life (fainting and reviving). "That is the work of the devil," Williamson observed. For good measure, he closed by quoting Matthew 24:23–26, which warns of false Christs and false prophets who will try to lead people astray.[68] This editorial typifies *Iapi Oaye*'s responses to the Ghost Dance. In a patient tone, using deliberate and at times seemingly interminable rhetoric, Williamson emphasized the importance of Christianity and the biblical proof that the Ghost Dance was the work of "wakanśica," the devil.

The popular press reflected dominant culture attitudes toward American Indian religion in general and the Ghost Dance in particular. In the *Omaha Bee* Charles Cressey denigrated the Ghost Dance and its followers, referring to the dance's message as superstition born of fantasy.[69] When viewed from the comfortable distance of more than a century hence, however, the line separating one person's superstition from another's religion seems remarkably thin. Cressey demeaned Indians and their beliefs and in the process justified actions to eradicate them and replace them with non-superstitious religion, as he understood it.

In mid-November President Benjamin Harrison ordered the War Department to suppress the threat of an outbreak among the Sioux and, as reported in the *Omaha Bee*, "use sanguinary measures to enforce submission if necessary." This marked a shift to military rule in Lakota country, and the motivation was clearly religious repression. The agent at Rosebud had already been taking action to discourage adherents to the Ghost Dance. Rosebud residents transported their own supplies from Valentine, Nebraska, to the reservation and got paid for doing that work. The agent, however, banned followers of the "new 'Messiah'" from this practice, thus singling out members of this religious group for economic reprisals.[70]

On November 19 the *Omaha Bee* reported that three troops of cavalry and one infantry company stood ready to travel to the vicinity of the Pine Ridge and Rosebud agencies to "try and prevent the Indians from dancing the ghost dance"; failing that, the paper added, the soldiers would "make ghosts of the Indians." On that date at Standing Rock, Agent McLaughlin wrote to the commissioner of Indian affairs to express his conviction that within his jurisdiction the Ghost Dance could be "broken up" using "reasonable means."[71] Regardless of the means they might use, McLaughlin's letter shows that the government and its agents were focused on the dance and stopping religious practices. Covering the troops' arrival at Rushville, Nebraska, on November 19, one reporter supported that assertion, writing that the soldiers' intended at all costs to suppress the Ghost Dance. All other options had failed to restore order, but soldiers would do it by stopping the dance.[72]

According to reports government officials substantiated the *Omaha Bee*'s comments. Sources supposedly close to Agent Daniel F. Royer, Special Agent James A. Cooper, and Brigadier General John R. Brooke said that Cooper recommended staving off trouble by capturing Ghost Dance leaders. As the triumvirate waited for instructions from the departments of the interior and war, they heard a report from an Indian source, presumably Lakota, that Ghost Dancers at Wounded Knee were performing the religion's ceremonies with guns strapped to their backs in expectation of a confrontation with the army.[73]

Newspaper reports further contributed to the hysterical atmosphere surrounding the Ghost Dance by labeling its devotees "the enemy" and by referring to Indians not subscribing to the Ghost Dance as "loyal."[74] Other reports included hyperbolic commentary: "The Indians are actually crazed with religious fanaticism and excitement at the ghost dances is of a most intense character."[75] The *Omaha Bee* reported that certain Ghost Dancers near Pine Ridge were conspiring to ambush U.S. Army troops. According to the allegations, Ghost Dancers would hold a dance in a natural amphitheater near the confluence of White Horse and Wounded Knee creeks hoping that troops would come to stop them. Other Indians would hide along the road to the site and ambush the troops as they arrived. Described under the headline "A Crisis Imminent," the allegations surely helped increase tension and suspicion among the white population and may also have contributed to heightened paranoia among government officials, from Indian agents to the military.[76] Other papers added to the hysterical atmosphere by reporting the Ghost Dance religion to be adding adherents daily, particularly "young bucks . . . eager for a fight."[77] Reports of the dance spreading throughout the Dakotas continued through December.[78]

According to the newspapers, the Lakotas were preparing for battle with the white race. Omaha's *Morning World-Herald* reported that the Lakotas were "in good shape for a fight," meaning they were well supplied with guns, ammunition, and food. The same story said that the Lakotas "expect[ed] the Messiah every day," lending an ominous tone to the news that they were ready for a fight.[79] In addition, reports from some "friendly" Indians indicated that the Ghost Dance had taken on militant characteristics that could have unpleasant consequences for whites. Plenty Bear, for example, supposedly told Agent Royer that more than 2,000 Indians were performing the Ghost Dance with "many warlike accompaniments" near Wounded Knee in late November. In the same story the reporter refers to certain Indian activities, such as burning white settlers' homes and stealing livestock, as "deviltry."[80]

Despite the preponderance of material condemning the Ghost Dance as dangerous, a few white observers saw no threat. One observer who attended a Ghost Dance with an interpreter concluded that the ceremony was almost strictly religious (apparently he was referring to reports and suspicions it was a war dance) and that at no time during the two or three hours he watched did he feel endangered. Some Indian accounts reinforced this observer's point. In November a contingent of forty-five Indians who had been working for Buffalo Bill's Wild West Show arrived at Pine Ridge, reportedly to visit relatives there. The acting commissioner of Indian affairs seized the opportunity, asking them to use their influence with their relatives and friends to prevent "an uprising or further fanatical demonstrations." The group included Black Elk, the medicine man of whom John Niehardt wrote and who converted to Catholicism, and Rocky Bear, said to be a friend and associate of Red Cloud. Rocky Bear expressed doubts about the seriousness of the Ghost Dance. "Our brothers at Pine Ridge seem crazy over this new religion or new teaching just as some white folks get crazy over religion," Rocky Bear is alleged to have told a reporter. "My people may get crazier than white people do, and if so I am very sorry. We here know that the day for the red man to fight against the paleface is far, far past."[81] These comments indicate that observers who did not see the Ghost Dance as a threat understood it as a fundamentally religious phenomenon.

Even some members of the military viewed the Ghost Dance as the Indians' way of dealing with great changes to their lives and saw little threat from the religion. One Captain Higgins, an aide-de-camp to General Nelson Miles, reportedly said the Ghost Dance would help Indians with "their inability to cope with the white man." In the same newspaper interview, Higgins mentioned that he knew of other tribes subscribing to similar beliefs over at least the previous decade. He saw the Ghost Dance as posing little danger to neighboring whites because its practitioners lacked the horses and resources to go on the offensive.[82]

As for the Ghost Dancers, some appeared defiant, at least according to press reports. Little Wound, identified as "the high priest of the ghost dancers" by Charles Cressey of the *Omaha Bee,* supposedly wrote a letter to Agent Royer asking why soldiers were coming to Pine Ridge. "We have done nothing," Cressey quoted Little Wound as having written. "Our dance is a religious dance, so we are going to dance until the spring. If we find then that Christ does not appear we will stop, but not in the meantime."[83]

In addition to creating a hysterical atmosphere in Nebraska and the Dakotas, the press fueled fears that the Ghost Dance would sweep the West. The *Omaha Morning World-Herald* reported a contingent of Poncas traveling west through Nebraska's Elkhorn River valley on their way to Pine Ridge to join the Ghost Dance. The paper subsequently retracted this report, saying that the Poncas and Santees in Nebraska had not adopted the Ghost Dance. Less than a week later the paper reported a "fierce battle" between the Northern Cheyennes and the U.S. Army. Although the story absolved the Ghost Dance of playing any role in the reported fighting, and General Miles denied the fight's existence in a separate story lower on the same page, the article nevertheless increased tension among readers. A report from New Mexico said that the Navajos had become "very insolent and overbearing and [were] holding large dances," adding, "It is believed that the Messiah craze has reached them." Word also came from Texas that the Comanches and Kiowas had joined the Cheyennes and Arapahos in their messianic expectations and that 3,000 Ghost Dancers had congregated on the Canadian River, where they were armed and well supplied with cattle. Ghost Dance reports continued to appear throughout December, some from as far away as California. The press regarded even traditional dances with suspicion, fearing that news of the Indian messiah and the Ghost Dance would turn other dances dangerous to whites and spread "hysteria" among tribes.[84]

When the press reported the Ghost Dance in Montana, it included details that must have disturbed American moral leaders. All the Indians there, so the report went, subscribed to the religion, even "the more intelligent half-breeds." Making matters worse, one of the most respected and feared Plains Indians, Sitting Bull, appeared to have masterminded the religion's spread to Montana. White Gut, described as one of Sitting Bull's lieutenants, had gone to the area on a mission. White Gut preached the Ghost Dance, denounced schools, and told Indians to arm themselves and prepare to meet other Indians, presumably Ghost Dancers, the next spring in the Black Hills. When U.S. authorities in Montana ordered White Gut and his two companions off the unnamed reservation, the Lakotas reportedly went north into Canada to convert Oglalas and Hunkpapas living there. The press labeled the Lakotas living in Canada "a bad lot" and linked them to the Custer fight and the Dakota Conflict of 1862, in Minnesota.

On hearing of the Ghost Dance, the Gros Ventres sent emissaries from Montana to Sitting Bull's camp to learn more, according to the press. Whatever these emissaries learned about the Ghost Dance, the press found the highlight of their trip to be the tale of Yellow Hawk. Yellow Hawk told of a dream in which he was commanded to commit suicide—with the promise of resurrection—as a test of his faith. Yellow Hawk complied with his dream, and his companions went on without him. When they reached Standing Rock, they found Yellow Hawk resurrected and waiting for them.[85] The press cast Sitting Bull as an ominous figure spreading a religion hostile to the United States, its people, and its goals throughout the West.

Meanwhile, the U.S. Army prepared itself for action in Lakota country, although the nature of the action seemed unclear at first. After arriving at Pine Ridge, the army's commanding officer reportedly awaited instructions from Washington telling him whether his troops should "interfere with the ghost dance—the stimulating factor of the new Christ Messiah craze."[86] Even as the army awaited orders, the press reported their beneficial influence. "Presence of Troops at Pine Ridge Having a Good Effect on Indians," declared a subheadline in the *Omaha Morning World-Herald*. The article reported, probably with unintended double entendre, that "all the residents of the agency [were] saved" by the troops' arrival. The *World-Herald* story also related the government plan to isolate the bad Indians and to use Indian police to stop the Ghost Dance—or failing that, to use military force.[87]

By November 21, it is alleged, army leaders at Pine Ridge had received orders "to separate the good and bad Indians . . . and to bring the peaceable ones into the agency's teepees." This would basically put the "good Indians" in something like protective custody while exposing the "bad Indians," those observing the Ghost Dance, to violence from the army. Although no fighting had yet occurred, the Indians involved with the Ghost Dance were referred to as "belligerents." According to the papers, the army would order the Indians to stop dancing and arrest those who refused. Those who refused arrest would be shot.[88] Senator Wilbur Fiske Sanders of Montana supported a similar plan. "If we are now to have a battle or war the Indians who are assembled ought first to be thoroughly sifted, if possible," Sanders said, "to the end that no Indians be destroyed who have not fully made up their minds to go upon the war path and accept the consequences of that rash act." Sanders also voiced his belief in a hierarchy of faiths. "I have never believed in the maxim, 'There is no good Indian but a dead Indian,'" a reporter quoted him as saying. "But I do not count a gray barbarian better than Christian children."[89] Sanders, like others in the government and among American society, felt that bad Indians were expendable and perhaps even deserved being destroyed, while Christians, Indian and non-Indian alike, should enjoy the protection of the law and the reign of the country.

Indian agents, too, did their best to separate the "good" Indians from the "bad," even using the former to suppress the latter. At the Yankton Agency in South Dakota, Agent E. W. Foster ordered William T. Selwyn, a full-blooded Yankton who had held a variety of government jobs at several Sioux agencies, to arrest a Ghost Dance adherent who had come to the area, apparently with evangelical purposes. The Ghost Dancer, Kuwapi, had journeyed from Rosebud to teach the religion. Like most if not all accounts of arrests of Ghost Dance adherents, this one mentions no specific charges.[90]

Barely had December arrived when General Miles told the media that he expected conflict with the Ghost Dancers. Miles said danger was imminent and traced the sources of Indian discontent to inadequate food supplies, "religious delusion and the innate disposition of the savage to go to war."[91] Furthermore, Miles referred to the Ghost Dance as "a religious delusion" in official correspondence, so he was not merely pandering to reporters.[92]

At this stage the Ghost Dancers clearly recognized the government's plan and showed an apparent awareness of the United States' reputation for protecting religious liberty. One Ghost Dancer explicitly mentioned freedom of religion while talking to whites visiting a ceremony in late November 1890. According to a press account of the conversation, the Ghost Dancer explained that the Lakotas were "simply holding religious services like the white man, the only difference being that they did not pass the hat." He also pointed out that "the government had no right to interfere with any man's religious worship."[93] Jack Red Cloud, son of the chief of the same name and reported in the press as a Ghost Dance "ring leader," made a similar statement to a reporter who asked him if he knew that by dancing he had been breaking agency orders for more than a month. According to the reporter, the younger Red Cloud replied that the Ghost Dance was a religious affair and that Indian Ghost Dancers should be treated no differently than whites practicing their religion would be.[94]

Newspapers further heightened excitement by exaggerating reports of Indian raids on non-Indian farmers and ranchers.[95] In addition, skirmishes occurred between Indians and their non-Indian neighbors. Ironically, at least in stories about early conflicts, the ranchers and farmers had no trouble protecting themselves. The *Omaha Morning World-Herald* published accounts warning that vigilante groups could do the country a favor by reducing the number of Indians.[96]

Reports of U.S. property damaged at the hands of Ghost Dancers began appearing in late November. The ranchers Scotty Phillips and Charles Waldren, "cattle kings on the late reservation lands," complained to South Dakota's governor that Lakotas had begun killing cattle by the score. They identified the cattle killers as members of Short Bull's camp, a group they described as "of the ugly, wilder class, who have the firmest sort of faith in the new Messiah craze."[97] Based on this information, South Dakota governor Arthur C. Mellette telegraphed General Miles asking the army to establish two new posts for security. The text of the telegram, which appeared in the press, described the Lakotas as "surly and defiant." It also reported that one unidentified Lakota recalled days when his people had "beat out the brains of children and drank women's blood" and predicted that the time was coming when they would do so again.[98] Now the Ghost Dance was being pictured as a threat even greater to American values than to Christianity. Ghost Dancers, at least according to the papers and probably to many of their readers, threatened capitalism, property, and white women and children.

Perceived threats to property and domestic tranquility led citizens of Dawes County, Nebraska, to petition the government for protection from its wards, the Indians. According to the petition, non-Indians living near the

Lakota reservations believed that since they paid the government for the land on which they lived, the government owed them peace, security, and the ability to prosper. "The frequent recurrence of threatened Indian outbreaks is a source of alarm," the document's authors wrote, "resulting in injury, loss and disaster to us, individually and collectively, retarding the further settlement and development of all the country bordering upon or adjacent to said reservation, thereby depreciating and jeopardizing our property, and virtually defrauding us of vested rights." The petitioners thus asked the government to disarm their Indian neighbors, to make it a crime to supply Indians with arms, and for good measure, to replace Indian horses with "oxen trained for the plow."[99] Dawes County's residents cared less about barbarism's threats to morality than they did about its threats to economic development.

On November 28, when the agent at Crow Creek heard of the Ghost Dance among Lower Brulés near the Rosebud Reservation, he sent Indian police and scouts to stop the ceremony. The Lower Brulé Indian police broke up the dance and jailed the leading participants. According to the news report, "Affairs were lively for a time but the police [were] too much for the new adherents of the Messiah craze."[100] The Lower Brulé agent reported that after initial attempts to suppress the religion failed and resulted in "hostility," he had twenty-two Indians arrested, seventeen of whom served eight-week sentences at Ft. Snelling, Minnesota. The agent proudly reported that "all other measures for quelling the disturbances that seemed likely to arise" were performed by agency officials, including Indian police, without aid of the War Department.[101]

Reports of property damage continued through the first weeks of December. According to one report, a small band of Sioux tried to stampede a horse herd near Buffalo Gap, South Dakota. The herd's owner and three or four other men went after the Sioux and killed four while suffering no injuries themselves. The same story reported that Indians robbed another rancher in the same county of $150, a gun, and some horses.[102]

A second story on that day related vague details of "numerous small bands of Indians" raiding farmers and ranchers. The raiders allegedly drove off horses, stole cattle, and broke into cabins from which they took clothing, food, and other property. In response, according to the report, a posse of twenty armed men set out for the site of the raids; another twenty ranchers were to join them. If no soldiers arrived to protect the Indians from this vigilante group, the report suggested, there would be "fewer Indians for the government to feed."[103]

Shortly after these incidents the U.S. Army placed itself between the

Lakotas and the ranchers.[104] This may have calmed the situation in South Dakota, but the press reported new problems related to the Ghost Dance in North Dakota. The press claimed that Indians it identified only as Sioux had camped near New Rockford and danced the Ghost Dance. "Their whoops could be plainly heard in the city," according to a story that appeared in an Omaha paper. The report also linked these Ghost Dancers with the theft of flour from a local mill and the deaths of cattle belonging to local non-Indian ranchers.[105] People following these events in the press saw one group of Ghost Dancers controlled only to see another flare-up of "heathenism" resulting in harassment of settlers in another region.

The *Omaha Bee* predicted a "dramatic close of the Messiah craze among the Indians" as it reported General Miles's plan to end the Ghost Dance. The story described the army's plan as an "immediate tightening of the great military cordon now surrounding the ghost dancers." Closer to the action, the *Rushville (Neb.) Standard* reacted more calmly to the Ghost Dance and reported that U.S. troops should have no trouble halting the "crazy dancing" without shedding blood.[106] According to these articles, the army clearly intended to bring order to the plains by ending the Ghost Dance. White settlers' security would come with the suppression of Indian religion.

To U.S. leaders, security in Lakota country focused on one key man: Sitting Bull. Rumors reported in the press provided both a foundation for government suspicions of Sitting Bull's role in the Ghost Dance and a possible justification for future military action. One scout—of unidentified background—was alleged to have speculated to an army captain that Sitting Bull wanted to assemble as large a force as possible for action in the spring of 1891. According to this line of thought, even if divine assistance failed to materialize that spring, contrary to the predictions of some Ghost Dancers, Sitting Bull would use his warriors to fight the United States and perhaps once again escape to Canada, where he might try to negotiate a new treaty with the United States. Another source speculated that although Sitting Bull had no plans to go to war, he would do so if provoked by trouble on other Lakota reservations or by a military attempt to arrest him.[107] Whether these reports were true is almost beside the point. Settlers in the Dakotas and representatives of the U.S. Army felt a near-paranoid fear that Sitting Bull would orchestrate an attack on U.S. citizens or flee beyond the government's control. The United States could not risk that.

To avert that risk and assert control, the U.S. government assembled an overwhelming force to face the Ghost Dancers. "A battery of Hotchkiss guns has been received in the city and tomorrow the artillery men and horses will arrive from Fort Meade." That sentence began a story in the *Omaha Morn-ing World-Herald* on December 15, the day Indian police killed Sitting Bull. That day's paper also reported that army officers had orders to "disarm Short Bull and Kicking Bear's braves at all hazards."[108]

Sometime in late November Agent McLaughlin had visited Sitting Bull's camp at Standing Rock to dissuade the Hunkpapa leader and his followers from practicing the Ghost Dance. According to McLaughlin, he tried to con-vince Sitting Bull that the Ghost Dance was nonsense, telling him, "Your preaching and practicing of this absurd Messiah doctrine is causing a great deal of uneasiness among the Indians of the reservation, and you should stop it at once."[109] Despite denigrating the Ghost Dance, McLaughlin referred to it as a religion and plotted strategies for its demise, such as starving its adherents into submission. As of mid-November 1890 McLaughlin believed he could arrest Sitting Bull and end the Ghost Dance at Standing Rock without violence.[110]

McLaughlin apparently met some success, for the press reported that the dance had ceased for the time being at Standing Rock. "The agent is very suc-cessful in winning the Indians away from the craze," the *Omaha Morning World-Herald* reported. Two days later another story in the *World-Herald* stated, "The only trouble at all probable is that the Messiah faction may at-tempt to compel other Indians to believe as they do."[111] These reports and McLaughlin's own records show not only the U.S. government's anti–Ghost Dance agenda but also the real possibility of using nonviolent means to achieve it. But the history of Lakota-U.S. relations and the palpable tension building in Lakota country and centered on the Ghost Dance combined to create an explosive atmosphere that would be ignited with tragic results.

The missionaries Elias Gilbert (a Christian Indian) and Mary Collins tried to convince Sitting Bull and his followers to stop observing the Ghost Dance, but with little success. They arrived at the camp as Sitting Bull was painting people to participate in a Ghost Dance. The missionaries implored him to stop and to cancel the dance, but Sitting Bull continued his preparations, say-ing nothing more than "O.K. [Ho]." Later, watching about one hundred of Sitting Bull's followers perform the Ghost Dance saddened Gilbert: "Those that know the Bible would not be helped by the Ghost Dance, I thought as I stood there." When he and Collins held Christian services near the encamp-ment, only two worshipers attended. Gilbert held Sitting Bull responsible for this, writing that the holy man had lost his good reputation and had saddened many people by adopting the Ghost Dance.[112]

Agent McLaughlin tried again to end the Ghost Dance among Sitting Bull's people. In December McLaughlin threatened to withhold government supplies from Lakotas at his agency who refused to abandon their religion. According to a report from McLaughlin to the commissioner of Indian affairs quoted extensively in the *Omaha Bee,* McLaughlin went to Sitting Bull's camp to convince the Lakotas to stop dancing. Although he did not try to stop the dance in progress when he arrived, McLaughlin had a long talk with Sitting Bull and a number of his followers, according to a report. The agent "assured them of what this absurd craze would lead to if these demoralizing dances and disregard of department orders were not soon discontinued." In case his logic did not appeal to the Lakotas, the agent declared that all Lakotas who renounced the Ghost Dance and consented to government terms could come to the agency, where, if they agreed to camp for "a few weeks," they would receive the supplies promised them by their treaty with the government. But "those selecting their medicine practices in violation of the department orders" would be unwelcome at the agency and would not receive treaty goods.[113]

This tactic apparently failed to produce the desired results, or perhaps McLaughlin grew impatient, for he ordered Standing Rock's ceska maza to arrest Sitting Bull shortly thereafter. McLaughlin gave explicit orders to the Indian police: "You must not let [Sitting Bull] escape under any circumstances."[114] These orders could be read as meaning the police should kill Sitting Bull if necessary. McLaughlin knew Sitting Bull's followers stayed near their beloved leader's cabin and would never allow a peaceful abduction of their holy man.

Early on the morning of December 15, 1890, after offering Christian prayers for success in arresting Sitting Bull, the ceska maza rode off from Lt. Bullhead's home toward Sitting Bull's camp. In his account of Sitting Bull's death, Lone Man, mentioned at the start of this chapter, referred to the holy man's followers as "ghost dancers." The dancers' religious affiliation stood foremost in his mind as their salient characteristic and reinforces the notion that the U.S. government and "progressive" Lakotas knew well that they had targeted a religious group.[115]

Strife within the Lakota community, however, complicated matters. When Bullhead and others had first considered joining the ceska maza soon after Indian police had been created, Lakotas opposed to the United States raided Bullhead's property. They broke windows on his cabin and killed his chickens, pigs, and dogs. When they caught Bullhead, they held him at gunpoint until he agreed not to join.[116] Many of the Indian police may have harbored bitter feelings toward Sitting Bull and his followers.

On arriving at the compound, the ceska maza knocked on Sitting Bull's door and entered his house when he invited them in. The police told Sitting Bull he was under arrest, and he agreed to go peacefully once he dressed for the icy drizzle outside. After dressing in the presence of the police, Sitting Bull started to leave with them. The arrest quickly turned chaotic. One of Sitting Bull's wives cried a keening call of farewell and grief, drawing attention to the arrest and probably heightening the anxiety of those in the house. One of Sitting Bull's followers, Mato Wawoyuspa (Bear That Catches), confronted the ceska maza, defied them to take Sitting Bull, and called on the chief's followers to protect their leader. Then one of Sitting Bull's sons entered the dialogue. "You always called yourself a brave chief," Crow Foot said to his father. "Now you are allowing yourself to be taken by the ceska maza." This remark caught the chief's attention. He paused a moment and stated, "Ho ca mni kte sni yelo" (then I will not go).[117]

By this time several people had made their ways to their leader's house and were protesting the arrest and taunting the ceska maza. The police briefly tried to change Sitting Bull's mind, but making no progress, two of them grabbed Sitting Bull and began to remove him forcibly from his home. Lt. Bullhead had Sitting Bull's right arm; Shavehead had his left arm; and Red Tomahawk, another policeman, followed close behind. They remembered McLaughlin's instructions when Bear That Catches drew a gun and shot Bullhead, wounding the policeman. Still holding Sitting Bull, whom the police knew to be unarmed because they had seen him dress, Bullhead shot the chief, hitting him in the chest. From behind, Red Tomahawk shot Sitting Bull in the head. Sitting Bull died immediately.[118]

In the ensuing melee the police killed seven more Ghost Dancers, and the Ghost Dancers shot and killed four police, including Bullhead, who died of his wounds within hours. When the surviving police discovered Crow Foot, the chief's teenaged son begged, "My uncles, do not kill me." The police asked the wounded Bullhead what to do. "Do what you like with him," the lieutenant replied. "He is one of them that has caused this trouble." Lone Man smashed the young man across the head with a rifle butt, sending Crow Foot reeling out of the house. There Lone Man and two others, tears falling from their eyes, shot Sitting Bull's progeny dead.[119]

Meanwhile, soldiers sent to reinforce the police arrived at the compound. Although the soldiers knew the police were in the compound, their first action on arriving was to begin firing artillery rounds into the camp. As the barrage continued, several cannon balls nearly hit Lone Man, who was waving a flag of truce. Eventually the soldiers ceased firing and rode into the compound to investigate. On seeing the situation, they congratulated the po-

lice for performing their duty. The next day Agent McLaughlin congratulated Lone Man, saying, "I feel proud of you for the very brave way you . . .
carried out your part in the fight with the Ghost Dancers."[120]

In the aftermath of Sitting Bull's death, the army surrounded his followers and arrested those they could. General Miles reportedly believed that Sitting Bull's death left the "hostile conspiracy" (the *Omaha Bee*'s words) without a head and that it would soon end. In another story, the press quoted Miles
as describing the Ghost Dance as a conspiracy more widespread and involving more Indians than had any other Indian action against non-Indians and
naming Tecumseh and Pontiac as examples dwarfed by the Ghost Dance phenomenon. Miles estimated that 30,000 Indians, including 6,000 warriors,
stood ready to attack non-Indians as part of the Ghost Dance conspiracy. Buffalo Bill Cody thought likewise. Cody believed Sitting Bull and "a few other
crafty leaders" were using the Ghost Dance to force the U.S. government to
provide overdue payments and increase rations to Indians. Protestant missionaries wrote that Sitting Bull "well deserved his death."[121]

Agent McLaughlin claimed that Sitting Bull brought his own death by
screaming orders to his followers to attack the Indian police who were arresting him. Although McLaughlin may have earnestly wished to avoid bloodshed, he probably was not entirely unhappy about Sitting Bull's death. Assessing the situation, McLaughlin wrote, "Sitting Bull's medicine had not
saved him, and the shot that killed him put a stop forever to the domination
of the ancient régime among the Sioux of the Standing Rock Reservation."[122]
For McLaughlin, Sitting Bull's death removed the last and greatest obstacle to
his task of "civilizing" the Lakotas.

Miles, Cody, and the missionaries who sanctioned Sitting Bull's murder
likely did not figure on certain consequences of Sitting Bull's death. For instance, they probably did not count on the event spreading the Ghost Dance
to bands previously not practicing the religion. Shortly after Sitting Bull's
death a report surfaced that his ghost had appeared and inspired a new Ghost
Dance among a band of Oohenunpa (Two Kettles) Lakotas who apparently
had not been practicing the religion before then. According to the report, the
Oohenunpas began a "wild ghost dance" after two men of the band reported
seeing a white figure one of them believed was Sitting Bull. The figure glided
from hilltop to hilltop, beckoning the observers to follow it toward the Bad-
lands. The Oohenunpas allegedly took this as a sign that Sitting Bull was
the Indian messiah and that he wanted them to join his followers. After hearing of this, the Oohenunpa band supposedly began to perform the Ghost

Dance.[123] White fears were further confirmed with reports of a new Ghost Dance on the previously peaceful ("obedient to the U.S. government" might be a better way to phrase it) Ft. Berthold Reservation in North Dakota.[124]

Arriving at Pine Ridge coincidentally with a new moon, as had been prophesied, a possible messiah spent a night with Mahpiyaluta (Red Cloud) before being chased from the reservation by authorities. The man, a peripatetic Iowan named A. C. Hopkins who was reported to have recently stirred a disturbance among Menominees in Wisconsin and who had undertaken a campaign to make the pansy the United States' national flower, claimed to be "Christ in a poetic way." With the approval of American Horse, a "progressive" Lakota, displeased U.S. authorities chased Hopkins from Pine Ridge and considered how to prove him an impostor. Other Lakotas, however, believed Hopkins might indeed be their messiah and sent messengers out to spread the word of his arrival. They suspected U.S. government agents had exiled their new religious leader.[125]

These Lakotas gave credence to Hopkins's appearance because, according to reports, several weeks earlier Short Bull had predicted that the messiah would make his next appearance at Pine Ridge. The apparent fulfillment of this prophecy imparted new momentum to the Ghost Dance and gave Short Bull enhanced standing among his followers—and perhaps among others who had been pondering the Ghost Dance but had not committed to it.[126] Although the U.S. Army probably did not drive off a savior, segments of the Lakota community believed the government had interfered with their religion.

Following Sitting Bull's murder, a contingent of about one hundred Indians, presumably Oglalas, went to meet with the Ghost Dancers in a last-ditch effort to convince them to quit dancing and report to the agency. The reporter Thomas Tibbles speculated that a few of the Ghost Dancers would come in but that fighting was inevitable.[127]

Although the government succeeded in eliminating Sitting Bull, as well as his son and several of his important followers, its tactics backfired. Instead of ending the Ghost Dance, Sitting Bull's death heightened the Ghost Dancers' fears of the government and its soldiers. Some from Sitting Bull's camp abandoned the religion, but most fled to join Big Foot's people, taking with them news of what had happened and what they could expect.

Some estimates indicate as many as a third of all Lakotas accepted the Ghost Dance at some time, and the religion had spread throughout Lakota country in the summer and fall of 1890. Although some Hunkpapas abandoned the religion on Sitting Bull's death, Miniconjous at the Cheyenne River

Reservation, Oglalas at Pine Ridge, and Sicangus at Rosebud continued to practice the Ghost Dance. As more Lakotas converted, the pressure from Indian agents to halt the dance increased. Agents and other whites feared what they perceived to be militant aspects of the dance, especially the supposedly bulletproof ghost shirts worn in the ceremony. By mid-November the army had responded to Indian agents' pleas for protection by mobilizing troops to occupy reservations considered dangerous and ordering Lakotas confined to their individual reservations.[128]

A Miniconjou named Big Foot (also known as Spotted Elk), led a Ghost Dance at Cheyenne River Reservation. On the day after Sitting Bull's death, the army ordered Colonel E. V. Sumner to arrest him.[129] When Sumner finally met with Big Foot on December 21, the latter had swelled his band's ranks with refugees from Sitting Bull's followers. After first threatening to take Big Foot and his people west to Fort Meade, Sumner agreed to allow Big Foot to surrender at Fort Bennett, to the east, which was closer to the reservation. When Big Foot's band lingered at its camp, Sumner sent a messenger to hurry them along. According to an Indian survivor, however, the messenger told the band that Sumner would arrest them and ship them to an ocean island. Heading south for Pine Ridge, the messenger reportedly said, held the band's best bet for remaining free.

On learning of the band's southward departure, the army gave chase. On December 28 a column of the Seventh Cavalry located Big Foot's band and ordered them to a camp the army had prepared on Wounded Knee Creek. The next morning, as the army disarmed the band, a scuffle broke out. An unexpected gunshot triggered a firefight between the few Lakotas who still had guns and the U.S. forces, which had surrounded the camp with soldiers and artillery.[130]

A Lakota version of the massacre's first shot says that during the disarmament process, a deaf Lakota held his rifle over his head stating that he had paid a lot of money for the gun, that it was his gun, and that no one would take it from him without offering him adequate compensation. Three sergeants approached the man and began struggling with him for the gun. In the fracas, the gun, pointed into the air at about a 45-degree angle, discharged and triggered a volley from the soldiers surrounding the Lakotas.[131]

According to some white civilian eyewitness accounts, neither the Lakotas nor the U.S. soldiers planned or expected a conflict at Wounded Knee; however, actions that morning quickly heightened tensions between the two groups. The interpreter Phillip Wells said that Col. Forsyth asked him to relay the colonel's reassurances to Big Foot: "He need have no fear in giving up his arms, as I wish to treat you [Big Foot and, presumably, his band] with nothing but kindness." When Big Foot responded that his people had no more weapons, Forsyth responded, "You are lying to me in return for all my kindness to you." The kindness to which Forsyth referred included assigning his physician to attend to Big Foot, who was ill, and providing the band with provisions. Clearly, however, the cavalry commander experienced some resentment toward Big Foot.

Meanwhile, according to Wells's account, a medicine man performed part of the Ghost Dance ceremony fairly quietly and almost to himself as the soldiers separated the Lakota men from the women and surrounded the men with the intention of disarming them. Wells reported that the medicine man addressed the young men of Big Foot's band, telling them that the soldiers' bullets would not harm them. At the medicine man's urging, five or six young Lakotas drew weapons they had concealed on their persons and fired on the American soldiers.[132]

Lakotas from Big Foot's band corroborate much of Wells's story. Elks Saw Him (Hehaka Wanyakapi), an Oglala Ghost Dancer from Hump's band, had recently joined Big Foot's band and claimed to have witnessed the massacre. According to Elks Saw Him, the Lakotas had no fear or suspicion of the soldiers until the morning of December 29 when troops separated the men from the women and the soldiers surrounding the men began to load their guns. He did not see who fired the shot that started the massacre.[133] Frog, one of Big Foot's brothers, confirmed the report that a medicine man was performing a Ghost Dance ritual and exhorted the young men of the band to resist the soldiers. According to Frog, the older men in the band surrendered their guns without question. He blamed the medicine man for inciting the tragedy. Help Them, another of Big Foot's band, supported much of what Frog said and corroborated Wells's report that the medicine man had assured the young Lakotas that the American soldiers' bullets would not harm them.[134]

The journalist Charles Allen claimed to have witnessed Big Foot's death, an event that, if his account is accurate, reflects extraordinarily poorly on the American soldiers. As Allen told Eli Ricker, Big Foot was lying on the ground when the shooting commenced; when he began to rise, an officer shot him in the back. Big Foot's daughter, having seen her father shot, ran to him. She, too, was shot in the back.[135]

Language used in reporting the massacre continued to reflect the attitude that Ghost Dancers were justifiably killed based on their amoral, un-Christian activities. Referring to Lakotas who had yet to surrender in Wounded Knee's aftermath, the *Omaha Bee* declared, "These devils have just one and only one alternative now, either to lay down their arms or be shot down carrying them."[136] Stories in Omaha's *Morning World-Herald* used similar language: "The soldiers are shooting the Indians down wherever found, no quarter being given by any one." As for the massacre's origins, the earliest reports indicated that the Lakotas had attacked the army. "It could only have been insanity which prompted such a deed," declared the *Morning World-Herald* in words similar to those the press had used in describing the lunacy of Indians believing in their own messiah. The *World-Herald*'s story reassured its readers, writing, "It is doubted that if before night either a buck or a squaw out of all of Big Foot's band will be left to tell the tale of this day's treachery."[137]

Based on interviews with John Shangreau, an Indian scout who witnessed the massacre, Eli Ricker speculated that the men of the Seventh Cavalry had their unit's debacle at the Little Bighorn in the backs of their minds and perhaps were already feeling tense when the shot at Wounded Knee surprised them. Despite having no order to fire, the soldiers did so nonetheless, and in hunting down and killing women and children, they showed a "deficiency in discipline" by acting "in the spirit of total destruction—soldiers beyond all command eagerly and irregularly pursuing women and children upon the hills and shooting them to death without remorse or mercy." Shangreau reported that an officer remarked to him, "Scout, we've got our revenge now." Shangreau asked, "What revenge?" The officer replied, "Why, don't you know, the Custer massacre?" Ricker concluded that the soldiers "did not seem capable of the Christian impulse to spare life in cases where it ought not to be taken."[138]

Another Indian scout working for the U.S. Army, Man Above, told a similar tale. According to Man Above, U.S. officers had told the scouts that the troops would kill Big Foot's band when they could because they were in the Custer battle. One survivor of the Custer battle told Man Above that if they found Big Foot's band, they were going to disarm them, and if the Lakotas got angry about it, they would all be killed.[139]

Some of the top officers apparently held similar views. Major T. L. Williams of the First Nebraska National Guard alleged that after the massacre, while under arrest pending court-martial proceedings, Col. Forsyth of the Seventh Cavalry told him that "he was ordered to disarm Big Foot's band; not to let any of them get away; and that none of them got away." Forsyth complained that he had been arrested for carrying out orders issued by General Miles.[140]

Following the Wounded Knee massacre, reports circulated of a general Indian war, possibly lasting through the summer. Non-Indians read that the

Lakotas were now suspicious of the United States and its soldiers, fearing that they had come to take the Lakotas' remaining lands by force. Non-Indians also read that those Lakotas still armed would likely refuse to surrender their weapons. Making matters worse, reports indicated that Mahpiyaluhta (Red Cloud) had turned his sympathies from the United States to the Ghost Dancers. This likely incited considerable anxiety in the U.S. population, for Mahpiyaluhta had been one of the Lakotas' most successful war leaders. His return to resistance boded ill for peace on the plains.[141]

Army investigations affirmed the brutal nature of the all-out attack on the Ghost Dancers of Big Foot's camp. One group of bodies that drew attention in the government's investigation of the massacre contained a woman and three children, a boy about eight to ten years old and two girls about five to seven years old. Cavalry gunned them down at close range—close enough to kill all four with six shots and close enough that the gunshots burned the clothing and flesh of every victim.[142]

From Pine Ridge Robert White filed a Dakota-language story for *Iapi Oaye* that explained the massacre in stark terms. White wrote that about two hundred Lakota Ghost Dancers died because of their dancing. "They were not permitted (or encouraged) to do the dance," according to White. "But they did not listen and, thus, they died." In February the paper maintained the same hard line, although it urged that those widowed or orphaned by Wounded Knee should be consoled. But, the article warned, the survivors should heed Jesus' teachings and go to church, for otherwise their souls would be in peril.[143]

Another Lakota convert to Christianity, Paul Crow Eagle (Kangiwabli), speculated that the true cause of Wounded Knee was not the Ghost Dance at all but political divisiveness among the Lakotas in deciding whether to adopt white ways. Many traditionalists, of course, followed Sitting Bull and adopted the Ghost Dance in hopes of regaining the past. Crow Eagle recognized that the fighting continued after Wounded Knee and that given the scarcity of buffalo, the Lakotas needed to unite to help each other. Part of that, he writes, would involve adopting Christianity. "God made the earth and man," he wrote. "The Ghost Dancers are all gone and the Christian Indians do not believe in the Ghost Dance."[144]

In *The Word Carrier, Iapi Oaye*'s English-language counterpart, Protestant missionaries perversely argued that tragic as Wounded Knee was, it might have done the Lakotas some good. While acknowledging that the tragedy looked increasingly worse as more information came to light, the paper noted "a providential aspect" to the affair. In the grand scheme, the disaster was a "blessing" to the rebellious Lakotas, who needed to feel consequences for their actions to instill fear that would keep them from committing further folly.[145] Some representatives of the Christian community, then, applauded the government's brutal suppression of the Ghost Dance.

Ghost Dancers not killed at Wounded Knee faced incarceration and exile. According to one of the U.S. Army's Indian scouts, about a week after the massacre he accompanied prisoners—Ghost Dance leaders including Kicking Bear and Short Bull and about twenty others—to Chicago's Ft. Sheridan for confinement. From there many were shipped to Europe to travel with Buffalo Bill's Wild West Show. Of course, that also meant they were conveniently kept off the reservation and away from their people for a substantial period of time. Furthermore, touring with the Wild West Show probably meant the exiled Ghost Dancers were forced to convert, at least nominally, to Christianity. A stipulation in Cody's contract for Indians touring with the show required them to "be of the same religious faith," meaning Christian. To support this conversion, Cody hired a representative of that faith to travel with the show.[146]

Less than a year after the event, Gen. Nelson Miles, the commanding U.S. officer, described Wounded Knee as "wholesale massacre" and wrote, "I have never heard of a more brutal, cold-blooded massacre than that at Wounded Knee." He claimed his plan for a peaceful disarmament of the Lakotas would have worked had it not been for "stupidity and criminal neglect of duty" by his subordinate, Col. Forsyth of the Seventh Cavalry. In the days after Wounded Knee, Forsyth allegedly led his unit into a situation in which it was nearly trapped by Lakotas and, had it not been for the timely arrival of buffalo soldiers of the Ninth Cavalry, might have met a fate similar to its predecessors' at the Little Bighorn. Despite his reaction to the massacre, Miles praised the soldiers who had "given their lives in the cause of good government" and who helped in "suppressing one of the most threatening Indian outbreaks." Miles's comments provided further evidence of the government's view of the Ghost Dance as a dangerous phenomenon to be halted. Miles referred to the Ghost Dance as a widespread "disaffection . . . involving many tribes . . . , [a] conspiracy . . . to produce a general uprising of all the Indians."[147]

Although the government recognized the Ghost Dance as a source of danger, General Miles wrote off the "uprising" by citing a simplistic cause. Analyzing the events in Lakota country, Miles is reported to have said, "It is simply a matter of more or less beef." He condensed the cultural implications of Lakota history through 1890 into this simple prescription: "Give the Indian the beef he is entitled to and we will have peace."[148] This type of cultural misunderstanding lay behind the disaster at Wounded Knee.

Colonel Forsyth's misconduct as commander of the Seventh Cavalry led to his removal from command. General Miles charged that Forsyth's arrangement of troops and artillery led the soldiers to kill a number of their own in cross fire. Miles also expressed displeasure with the killing of so many Lakota women and children.[149]

Meanwhile, Pine Ridge remained under military rule. After Wounded Knee General Miles suggested to his superiors in Washington, D.C., that the Indian agencies experiencing the Ghost Dance be placed under military control. Just more than a week after the massacre, it is reported, Miles received a telegram from Washington approving his suggestion. Charles G. Penney, a captain in the Sixth Infantry, acted as agent at least until September 1891. Despite the massacre of Big Foot's band, Penney reported lingering Ghost Dance sentiment. "There is a considerable number of very conservative Indians, medicine men and others, who still insist upon a revival of the Messiah craze and the ghost dancing," Penney reported. "However quiet and peaceful these Indians may appear to be, it is by no means a fact that permanent peace has been established." To the east, the army ruled Rosebud through July 31, 1891.[150]

Despite the massacre, word of tribes practicing Ghost Dancing continued to surface. Kickapoos in Kansas began a Ghost Dance the day before Wounded Knee and continued it through the week of the massacre. Readers may have been skeptical of this news, since an earlier report of the Kickapoos practicing the religion turned out to be false. Reports also surfaced of several tribes—Bannocks in Idaho, Shoshones in Nevada, and Mesquakies in Iowa—holding Ghost Dances in early January. In the case of the Bannocks, local U.S. officials feared the dance's implications and called for militia and federal troops, whereas news from Nevada indicated that violence was unlikely unless the government tried to stop the Shoshones from dancing. The Bannocks' knowledge of the Paiute and Shoshone languages had made them mediators between Wovoka and the Plains tribes to the east, and they played an important role in the religion's spread. They continued in this role through the 1890s.[151]

Some whites celebrated the Wounded Knee massacre for ending outward expressions of the Ghost Dance among the Lakotas, but the massacre devastated the Lakotas emotionally, and at least some remained faithful enough to the new religion to keep it alive secretly. Contemporary observers noted that the Lakotas were "downcast and apathetic" after the incident. According to reports, they expressed frustration with the futility of trying to adopt white ways, feeling their efforts at change were met with murder. Sixteen years after the massacre, moreover, one observer noted, "Indians are dancing the ghost dance everywhere here [presumably southwest South Dakota, indicating Lakotas] under a different name."[152]

Despite the brutal force employed against the Lakota Ghost Dancers, adherents among other Plains tribes attempted to observe the religion, and the U.S. government continued to suppress it. Perhaps because of the brutal murders of the Lakotas, as well as other factors, the government had an easier time controlling and eventually ending the religion among other tribes. Indian agents arrested Ghost Dance prophets among the Otos and Pawnees. The agent in charge of the Otos and Missouris "found it necessary to institute rigid discipline" to eliminate the dance. The agent arrested Buffalo Black, the Oto Ghost Dance prophet, and sent him to a Wichita jail "for safe-keeping." When this failed to produce the desired effect of ending the Oto Ghost Dance, the agent threatened to cut off the tribe's rations. With this, the agent reported that he had succeeded in getting the Otos to "entirely quit the dance." Contemporary observers noted that since the Otos and Missouris numbered only 362 members, officials had a rather easy time suppressing the religion among them.[153]

Government officials took the same course with the Pawnees. The Ghost Dance came to the Pawnees in the fall of 1891. Frank White, a Pawnee who had visited Ghost Dancers among the Comanches and Wichitas, brought the doctrine and songs home that year and in the fall began teaching both among the Pawnees. As the Pawnee Ghost Dance prophet, White organized Ghost Dances throughout that winter. By February 1892 an estimated two-thirds of the tribe had accepted his version of the Ghost Dance. Believing the Indian millennium to be imminent, many of these Pawnees stopped working and devoted their attention to Ghost Dance ceremonies, to the dismay of the government agent. The agent did his best to convince the Pawnees that their messiah to come was a fiction. He also asserted that the U.S. government would endure and would not tolerate the Ghost Dance. Despite government attempts to prevent the dance, Pawnees conducted ceremonies secretly. On learning that White continued to organize Ghost Dances, the agent and a deputy U.S. marshal arrested him. A U.S. commissioner ordered White to appear in district court on the charge of inciting Indians to an insurrection. White spent about ten days in jail before the court heard his case. According to the Pawnees' agent, the judge gave White a stern talking to and sent him back to the reservation, where the Ghost Dance ceased and the community returned to prosperity and serenity.[154]

The foregoing, however, does not tell the whole story. White's arrest and confinement came at a critical time, for the federal government was pushing the Pawnees to accept its allotment policy (breaking up tribally held lands for individual ownership). Many of the Pawnees opposed to allotment had been participating in White's Ghost Dances. According to reports, in White's absence these Pawnees were told they would be allowed to continue practicing the Ghost Dance if they accepted allotments. Following their faith (which would, they believed, soon restore their lands), many accepted. The agents continued their efforts to snuff the Ghost Dance, but it survived through 1900. At the turn of the century one Pawnee religious leader felt discouraged by certain Pawnee youths whose interest in the Ghost Dance steered them away from the older religion he was trying to teach them. As had believers in other tribes, Pawnee Ghost Dancers hoped their current conditions would be swept away and older, better times restored to them. The Pawnees further resembled believers in other tribes in adding elements of their culture—namely, the hand game—to the Ghost Dance. They thus produced a hybrid four-day Ghost Dance hand-game ceremony.[155]

The Kiowas splintered over the Ghost Dance. In 1888 a prophecy similar to Wovoka's surfaced among them. The Kiowa prophet Paingya told Kiowas that a whirlwind would remove whites from the earth and a great fire would then destroy all traces of them. When neither event happened at an appointed time, the Kiowas lost faith in Paingya, although many welcomed Wovoka's message when the Ghost Dance came to the Kiowas in 1890.[156]

Among the Kiowas the United States found a valuable ally in its fight against the Ghost Dance, a young man named Apiatan, or Wooden Lance. Shortly after the Ghost Dance won its first adherents among the Kiowas in the summer of 1890, Apiatan received an invitation to visit Sioux country. He accepted, partly to visit relatives among the Sioux and partly to learn more about the Ghost Dance. Because it promised reunion with deceased relatives, the religion intrigued Apiatan, who had recently seen one of his children die. After a brief visit at Pine Ridge in the late summer or fall of 1890, Apiatan extended his journey to Nevada so he could meet Wovoka. That meeting disappointed Apiatan greatly. Expecting an omniscient, crucifixion-scarred Wovoka, Apiatan found instead an unscarred prophet who had to ask what the young Kiowa wanted. Apiatan's faith crumbled. His heart fell further when he learned that he could not visit his deceased child. Furthermore, Wovoka allegedly told Apiatan some Ghost Dancers, particularly the Sioux, had twisted his peaceful message and caused trouble. Apiatan, Wovoka said, should return home and urge the Kiowas to abandon the Ghost Dance.[157]

Apiatan left for home saddened and disillusioned. One report said that he stopped at the Bannock Agency in Idaho to mail a letter home reporting that Wovoka was a fraud. Some Kiowas doubted the letter's authenticity, however, since it was delivered by a white man. When Apiatan returned home in mid-February 1891, he addressed a gathering of Kiowas, Comanches, Caddos, Wichitas, and Arapahos. He told them to forget about the Ghost Dance. Some Kiowas took Apiatan's advice. Other Kiowas, as well as Caddos, Wichitas, and other tribes, doubted Apiatan's story and believed that whites had paid him to lie to the Indians about his visit to Wovoka.[158]

Some Kiowas tried to revive the Ghost Dance between 1891 and 1894 only to face continued harassment from their agent. By 1894, however, the agent gave permission for a Ghost Dance. That September a four-day ceremony drew several thousand dancers from several tribes.[159] The Kiowa Afraid of Bears, too, did not forget the Ghost Dance. In fact, he reinterpreted the dance for the Kiowas, creating a new ceremony, the Feather Dance, which writers have referred to synonymously with the Ghost Dance. Many of the dance rituals and songs of the Feather Dance closely followed the directions a Ghost Dance apostle gave the Kiowas.[160]

The U.S. government fought the Feather Dance among the Kiowas. Government pressure eventually took the form of withholding tribal rations and lease rentals from allotments until, in 1916, the Kiowas signed an agreement to abandon the dance. From that point until at least the 1970s, the Kiowas did not hold an official Feather Dance. In 1892 Apiatan received a medal bearing President Benjamin Harrison's likeness and a new house "for his services in reporting against the dance." Back in Lakota country, the agent at Rosebud reflected that "Indians have learned that it is dangerous to oppose by force, the law of the Great Father."[161]

Not all Plains tribes accepted the Ghost Dance, and one of their stories may be instructive. The Comanches ultimately rejected the ceremony for a combination of reasons. One possibility rests with U.S. government officials in Oklahoma who were perhaps more enlightened than their counterparts in South Dakota. One officer saw the Ghost Dance as a step toward converting Comanches to Christianity. Another compared it to "an old-fashioned Methodist or Baptist church meeting." Why not, they speculated, let the ceremony run its course? They observed Ghost Dance ceremonies closely but did not interfere with them. Another possible explanation stems from Quanah Parker, the most prominent and powerful Comanche leader. Unlike his Hunkpapa Lakota counterpart, Sitting Bull, Parker opposed the Ghost Dance. By this time Parker had chosen peaceful accommodation with the United States and was making a living in the market economy.[162] Perhaps competent government officials and a less volatile Lakota leadership could have averted disaster.

Such ideas probably occurred to James Mooney when he investigated the Ghost Dance and the massacre at Wounded Knee for the government and concluded, "the Sioux outbreak of 1890 was due entirely to local grievances, recent or long standing." The Ghost Dance religion, he decided, played only a peripheral role in the events and had little or no direct influence on the massacre. To defend this conclusion, Mooney pointed out that despite the religion's spread across much of the West, no other Ghost Dance–related violence occurred. In a development more notable than that of the Comanches, the Paiutes—the tribe that produced the Ghost Dance prophet Wovoka—experienced "never the slightest trouble."[163]

Certainly the Lakotas had a long list of grievances against the U.S. government. But the Ghost Dance religion embodied more than just a response to hard times. It fit within Lakota spirituality. Even before this religion appeared to assume some militant characteristics, the U.S. government identified the Lakotas as the most dangerous and warlike tribe in the United States, and it undertook a campaign to silence the religion's adherents. They happened to include some of the Lakotas' most formidable political leaders as well.

Furthermore, such an analysis underscores the problem of cross-cultural understanding. Although U.S. society tries to separate religious elements from political and economic elements, Lakota society does not recognize such a separation. As the previous discussion indicates, that separation is more cosmetic than real. Whatever political and economic issues fed conflicts between the citizens and government of the United States and the Lakotas, the record shows strong religious attitudes informed policies, thoughts, and actions by missionaries, soldiers, politicians, and citizens at large. Lakotas view their economic and political experiences as part of a unified stream of events understood in terms that include religious paradigms. Perhaps U.S. officials recognized this and saw the Ghost Dance as an opportunity to capture and silence some of the most vocal and troublesome opponents of civilization, leaders such as Hump and Sitting Bull. The military action against the Lakotas was in essence the result of the government officials' policy. Among the Lakotas, the U.S. government pursued a program of cultural obliteration that included assassinating religious-political leaders and brought about the ruthless, vicious murders of hundreds of Ghost Dancers. Attitudes expressed by civil and religious leaders indicate that on the Great Plains, native peoples would follow precepts of American Christian civilization . . . or else.

As the nineteenth century drew to a close, the U.S. government had firmly shown its dominance in the West. The soldiers it sent to confront the Ghost Dance went to confront other problems, too, such as property destruction, and operated in an atmosphere poisoned by prejudice and Custer's defeat. Not only did the nation control the territory; it had shoved the values of the region's people into a mold favored by a Christian government. Just as it had forced the Mormons to comply politically and culturally, it had done the same to many Ghost Dancers. Even though the Ghost Dance survived throughout the 1890s, it had been virtually eliminated among the practitioners deemed most dangerous to the United States. Furthermore, the United States had shown that it would stop at almost nothing to impose Christian ideals on its peoples, even in that portion of the country best known for its freedom, liberty, and opportunity. As the nation entered the twentieth century, there could be no doubt that the United States had re-created the West in the image of its Christian mainstream, and not necessarily of religious freedom and tolerance.

★

4 Uncle Sam and the Sinful Messiah

We see [David Koresh's] departure as a sign from God. It was a loss to
the world . . . but we know the world will be getting a second chance.
He's doing the work right now.

—Janet McBean, Branch Davidian

ON APRIL 19, 1993, at about 6 A.M., an agent of the Federal Bureau of Investigation (FBI) telephoned David Koresh to warn him and his heavily armed
Branch Davidian followers that within minutes agents in armored vehicles
would begin gassing the building in which they were barricaded. Koresh, considered a messiah by many Branch Davidians, and more than seventy of his
followers had been holed up in the building at the compound they called
Mount Carmel, near Waco, Texas, for fifty-one days. Since February 28 the
Branch Davidians had held off the hundreds of local, state, and federal law-
enforcement officers surrounding them. By April 19 the FBI's patience had
disappeared, and the agency took decisive action to end the standoff.

Moments after the warning call, which promised the Branch Davidians
that the gas attack "was not an assault," armored vehicles began punching
holes through Mount Carmel's walls and injecting gas into the building
through nozzles attached to their rams. The Branch Davidians fired on the
armored vehicles. The FBI had authorization to gas the entire building. Off
and on for the next six hours, the armored vehicles ripped holes in Mount
Carmel and sprayed gas inside, while four Bradley fighting vehicles fired "ferret rounds"—canisters containing gas—into the building.[1]

As the tank-like vehicles punched holes through Mount Carmel's walls,
they may have trapped Branch Davidians inside. Although FBI agents assured the inhabitants of safe passage, announcing over loudspeakers, "We
are facilitating you leaving the compound by enlarging the door," the ram-
ming action collapsed a stairwell in a major escape route that the FBI had
hoped the women and children would use to get away from the gas. The at-

tack also collapsed a stairway near the front door, blocking that exit. Other windows and another stairwell remained accessible.[2]

Shortly after noon at least three fires started simultaneously inside the building and spread rapidly. At 12:16 the first Davidian to escape the flames left Mount Carmel. Between 12:20 and 12:30 seven more fled from the flames. Around 12:25 the FBI agents closest to Mount Carmel reported "systematic" gunfire inside. Many agents believed that the inhabitants were killing one another, ending their own lives, or both. The last of nine survivors emerged shortly after 3 P.M. Inside Mount Carmel seventy-four Branch Davidians had died, including twenty-one children aged thirteen or younger. Some died from the fire; others, including David Koresh, died of gunshot wounds, some probably self-inflicted. Some, perhaps many, went to their deaths believing that they had brought about "the new heaven and the new earth" described in the biblical book of Revelation (21:1).[3]

More than a century after the massacre at Wounded Knee, the U.S. government again found itself at odds with a religious group in the West. This time, in central Texas, another branch of the federal government replaced the army as the tool of enforcement. As had been the case in Utah and in South Dakota, a complex cluster of issues surrounded the conflict between the government and the Branch Davidians, some of which appear remarkably similar to those involved in Utah and South Dakota. Again, politics and religion intertwined and led to a disaster. Again, people acting on their best principles committed a great evil. Again, one might question the extent to which the United States would tolerate an armed, isolationist religious group led by a prophet receiving directions from God, practicing a communal lifestyle, and engaging in a form of plural marriage. The rhetoric used to describe the Branch Davidians bore striking similarities to that used in the nineteenth century to describe Mormons and Ghost Dancers. The results, too, looked alarmingly familiar, at least when compared to Wounded Knee: nearly an entire religious group perished violently in the conflict. Although the FBI agents surrounding the Branch Davidians did not act as the Seventh Cavalry had in South Dakota—the FBI claimed, probably correctly, that the Davidians had killed themselves either with fire or gunshots—the fact remains that they played an important role in the deaths of the Branch Davidians. Near the dawn of the twenty-first century the Branch Davidians learned what the Mormons and the Ghost Dancers had learned in the nineteenth: the West had limits when it came to religious freedom. American society still did not tolerate barbarians in the garden.

The Branch Davidians trace their roots to the Seventh-day Adventist

Church, from which they splintered. Victor Houteff, a Bulgarian immigrant with a third-grade education, led the split. After converting to Seventh-day Adventism in 1918, when he was thirty-two and living in Los Angeles, Houteff began developing two concepts considered heretical by the church. Houteff believed his divinely appointed mission was to purify the church from within and to gather 144,000 "servants of God" who would be saved at the Second Coming. He also believed that biblical prophets taught that the Kingdom of God would be a literal kingdom on earth centered in Palestine.

When Houteff began teaching these ideas in his Seventh-day Adventist church in 1929, some listened with interest, but the elders disapproved and prohibited him from further teaching. He nevertheless published his ideas in two volumes titled *The Shepherd's Rod* and attracted followers who became known collectively as the Shepherd's Rod and who spread Houteff's message. By 1934 Seventh-day Adventist officials had lost patience with Houteff and removed him from the church rolls. He gathered his followers and continued teaching.

Houteff moved the group to Texas, near Waco, in 1935. There they established a commune they called Mount Carmel and sought self-sufficiency. In 1942 the group adopted the name Davidian Seventh-day Adventists. After Houteff died in 1955, his wife, Florence, took over the group and moved them to a 941-acre tract near Elk, Texas, nine miles east of Waco. The remaining members dubbed it New Mount Carmel. In 1959 Florence Houteff predicted that the world would end and that the Kingdom of God would begin during Passover. More than nine hundred followers from around the country gathered at Mount Carmel to greet the millennium. When it did not happen, many became disillusioned and left, including Florence Houteff.

During the 1960s various factions fought for control of Mount Carmel. Eventually the property fell to Ben and Lois Roden. Ben Roden claimed leadership of the group based on a revelation he reported receiving: he was the "Branch" mentioned in the book of Zechariah (6:12), and he had been ordered to build a theocratic kingdom in preparation for Christ's return. After Ben Roden died in 1978, Lois took the reins based on her revelation that the Holy Spirit was a feminine figure. While Lois Roden traveled frequently to spread her message, her son, George, attempted to assume his father's mantle as leader of the Branch Davidians. Unfortunately for George, his mother had settled on someone else to assume the group's leadership, a recent member with an impressive knowledge of scripture and deep sincerity and with whom she, at sixty-seven, may have had an affair. That newcomer was Vernon Wayne Howell. Lois Roden took young Howell under her wing and gave him a venue for preaching his message. By 1984 he had become a charismatic speaker who so impressed Roden that she dubbed him "a messenger from God."[4]

In 1959, the same year the Davidian Seventh-day Adventists reached their nadir, Bonny Clark, fifteen and unmarried, gave birth to a son in Houston, Texas. The boy, Vernon, took the last name of his father, Bobby Howell, then a young carpenter whom Vernon would not meet until twenty-four years later.[5]

By the time he reached twelve, Vernon Howell had developed passions for music and the Bible. Howell quenched his desire for music by learning to play the guitar, and before he turned thirteen he had memorized most of the New Testament. As he worked out his own scriptural interpretations, though, parents of other youngsters began forbidding them to associate with Howell. He dropped out of high school in 1977 and worked intermittently as a produce picker and a carpenter. While attending a Seventh-day Adventist church in Tyler, Texas, the then twenty-one-year-old Howell experienced what he took to be a message from God telling him that he should make the fifteen-year-old preacher's daughter his wife. The preacher and his wife objected and forbade their daughter from associating with Howell. Sometime after that incident, on a Sabbath when the pastor asked for individual testimony at the end of a service, Howell ignored the convention of speaking from the pews, strode to the pulpit, and began an emotional speech. Howell went on at length, until other church members removed him from the pulpit. Shortly thereafter the church disfellowshipped Howell. With his spiritual quest in Tyler abruptly ended, Howell took to the road, landing at Mount Carmel Center, home of the Branch Davidians.[6]

At Mount Carmel Howell quickly became an enemy of George Roden, and the two embarked on a bizarre struggle for control of the commune. Roden gained full control of Mount Carmel in 1985, renamed it Rodenville, and expelled all dissidents. Meanwhile, traveling in Israel, Howell received what he termed a definitive revelation charging him with a mission as a messianic "Cyrus," the Persian king who conquered Babylon and allowed the Jews to return to Jerusalem. Howell returned to the Waco area to lead the expelled dissident group, which steadily increased membership. In 1986 Howell revealed to followers that his mission would involve his taking more than one wife. The struggle between Howell and Roden intensified in November 1987 when Roden disinterred the corpse of a Davidian dead for twenty years and challenged Howell to a contest to see who could resurrect her. Howell, perceiving an opportunity, tried to get the McLennan County sheriff to arrest Roden for corpse violation. The sheriff told Howell he would need evidence.

Howell took seven loyal followers, armed them, and attempted to take the body from Mount Carmel. Instead, a forty-five-minute gunfight ensued, and it ended only because armed deputies got the drop on Howell before he and his followers could finish off the pinned-down Roden. Howell faced attempted murder charges, but a hung jury led the judge to declare a mistrial. Within six months, however, Roden too faced murder charges, from an unrelated incident. He used an insanity plea to beat the charge, but it landed him in a state hospital indefinitely. In Roden's absence, Howell took control of Mount Carmel.

In 1990 Howell changed his name to suit his definitive revelation. Taking inspiration from his revelation that he was to set in motion end-time events prophesied in many Bible passages, he adopted the name *David Koresh* to signify his role as God's chosen one (*David* for the Hebrew king and *Koresh* for King Cyrus, who defeated the Babylonians, a group symbolizing unbelievers for Koresh). Thus Vernon Howell became David Koresh.[7]

Koresh drew followers who believed that he alone could open the seven seals mentioned in Revelation. The Davidians believed that when Koresh opened the seals—a process he understood to involve interpreting the entire Bible, especially prophetic writings, and directing events revealed there—he would unleash catastrophic events that would destroy humankind and propel him and his followers into heaven. Koresh considered himself to be "the Lamb," who according to Revelation (e.g., 5:6) will open the seals. Many Bible scholars believe the Lamb symbolizes Christ, a belief Koresh apparently shared. "If the Bible is true," Koresh told one reporter, "then I'm Christ." In this incarnation, however, Christ—like other mortals—would be sinful, and because of that, Koresh offered a new path to salvation.[8] Koresh did not merely offer a new path to salvation, however; he convinced followers that they needed him to achieve it. According to one former Davidian, the group came to believe Koresh over the Bible.[9]

A brief note on terminology illustrates how confusion and controversy surrounded Koresh and his followers. The key rests in Revelation's question "Who is worthy to open the scroll and break its seals?" (5:2). The text identifies a figure known as the Lamb, who alone can open the seven seals locking a mysterious book. Traditional Christianity understood this figure to be Jesus of Nazareth. But Koresh claimed to be the Lamb, the one who could break the seven seals. This produced considerable confusion, especially among mainstream Christians who assumed that Koresh claimed to be Jesus Christ. According to biblical scholars who studied his writings, however, he made a substantially different claim. Koresh did claim to be a "christ," but this term derives from a Greek word, *christos,* meaning "anointed one"; it refers to the use of oil in Hebrew coronation ceremonies. The ancient Hebrew word for "anointed one" is *mashiah,* which gives us the term *messiah.* Koresh and his followers believed that prophets foretold of a christ in addition to Jesus of Nazareth, one who would appear at the end of time to break the seven seals. Koresh claimed to be this latter-day Christ. Koresh taught that scripture said this messiah—Koresh himself—would be sinful, thus explaining some of his behavior and the title of an exposé in the Waco newspaper, "The Sinful Messiah." He also claimed to speak the words of God, although he did not claim to be God.[10]

The Revelation of St. John, a book steeped in symbolism and vivid imagery of grotesque monsters and bloody battles between good and evil, has inspired considerable study—and controversy—because it supposedly contains clues about when and how Jesus will return and how the world will end. John Alsup, a professor of New Testament studies at the Austin (Texas) Presbyterian Theological Seminary, argues that Revelation "has a rocky road of interpretations." Written in an era of intense persecution of Christians, Revelation's underlying meaning, Alsup says, is that however difficult life becomes, it will improve. Another professor of religious studies, Robert Fastiggi of St. Edward's University, argues that four main schools of interpreting Revelation have emerged. The first portrays Revelation as a mysterious puzzle pointing to events in the past or future. According to the second, Revelation applied to the era in which it written but has little relevance today. The third holds that Revelation metaphorically presents the spiritual battle waged in the lives of Christians and their church. The fourth characterizes the work as a symbolic depiction of the end of the world.[11]

In the United States popular belief in the end of human history as described in the Bible seemed to reach new heights as the twentieth century drew to a close. According to a 1983 Gallup poll, 62 percent of those polled had "no doubts" that Jesus would return to the earth. In 1980, 40 percent of American respondents told Gallup they believed the Bible to be "the actual Word of God, . . . to be taken literally word for word," while 45 percent believed the Bible to be divinely inspired. In 1988, 80 percent said they expected to appear before God on Judgment Day. Further, these ranks appeared to be swelling during the century's final decades. Prophecy believers tend to be more heavily concentrated among the "evangelical" or "fundamentalist" Protestant sectors, whose membership grew dramatically during the 1970s and 1980s as the "more liberal, so-called mainstream denominations" lost members.[12]

The intellectual historian Paul Boyer visualizes the population of prophecy believers as existing in concentric rings grouped by depth of conviction. Boyer populates the center with a core group who devote significant portions of their energies to thinking about prophecy. He places in the next ring a larger population of believers who have only a fuzzy understanding of biblical eschatology but who firmly believe that the Bible contains clues about the future. These millions of Americans, Boyer argues, are "susceptible to popularizers who confidently weave Bible passages into highly imaginative end-time scenarios, or who promulgate particular schemes of prophetic interpretations." Cities in the Southwest and Far West—Dallas, Los Angeles, Tulsa, and Oklahoma City—have particularly high concentrations of prophecy believers.[13] This description certainly fits the Branch Davidians, many of whom came from Texas or who were recruited in the Los Angeles area. Jan Jarboe, a senior editor at *Texas Monthly,* took a more cynical view of those who cast their lots with Koresh, describing them as people who feel so empty, afraid, and disillusioned that they will do almost anything to achieve a sense of security.[14] Whatever the explanation (and these certainly do not exhaust the possibilities), David Koresh tapped into these currents to create a religiously based community centered on him and his message. As it had for Houteff before him, the West offered David Koresh an opportunity for success. The region and this community housed there also offered answers or hope to those who chose to follow Koresh.

In some ways the hope behind this community reflected themes from the West's past. Koresh's use of Revelation as a base for spiritual and secular power has its roots in dispensationalism, a school of thought dating to nineteenth-century Scotland, according to Bob Patterson, a professor of religion at Baylor University. Dispensationalists believe that the seven churches mentioned in Revelation (1:11) symbolize seven church *ages,* with the last representing the present age, that of the apostate church. Conditions on earth will deteriorate so far, dispensationalists believe, that Christ will return. Branch Davidians, it was alleged, believed a christ had come in the form of David Koresh. Mainstream Seventh-day Adventists, the denomination in which Koresh was raised and to which the Branch Davidians trace their roots, do not accept this interpretation. Instead, Seventh-day Adventists, along with most other Protestant denominations, believe that Jesus Christ opened six of the seals after he ascended to heaven. "[David Koresh's] concept of Revelation is foreign to the teaching of Seventh-day Adventists," according to Cyril Miller, president of the Southwestern Union Conference of Seventh-day Adventists at the time of the 1993 Mount Carmel crisis. Miller added, "Persons like [Koresh] are victims of their own hallucinations."[15] Those following such hopes for salvation can be compared to explorers who sailed west seeking wealth or settlers who traveled west for land or basically anyone who went west seeking opportunity of any sort.

However deluded Koresh and his followers may have appeared to outside observers, Boyer places them squarely in a long tradition of American Christianity. In this respect they might appear to have been as well grounded in reality (or the hype surrounding the myth of the West) as others who headed west. Boyer argues that "millions of Americans, perhaps even a majority," share Koresh's alienation and core doctrines. Beliefs related to Koresh's "Americanization of prophecy" date to the New England Puritans. In 1697 Samuel Sewell of Massachusetts proposed that America might be "the seat of the Divine Metropolis" in the Millennium. During the 1740s preachers of the Great Awakening, including Jonathan Edwards, speculated that the Millennium would begin in America. Just before the Civil War, in 1859, the Reverend Fountain Pitts of Tennessee preached a sermon in the U.S. Capitol in which he claimed the Book of Daniel foretold the events of July 4, 1776.[16]

The Branch Davidian experience also reflects an American theme of cults appearing and facing hostile public reaction. Boyer writes that the First Amendment created a uniquely "laissez-faire religious culture" in the United States that made it fertile ground for "spiritual innovation and radicalism." America's religious culture helped spawn Seventh-day Adventists, Mormons, Perfectionists, Jehovah's Witnesses, and Christian Scientists, to name a few, all of which were denounced as "dangerous radicals and a grave threat to orthodoxy and social order" in language similar to that used against the Branch Davidians in the late twentieth century.[17]

Study of prophecies and the end of the world—eschatology—fascinates many groups within Christianity. But their obsession with the last book of the New Testament, the Revelation of St. John, separated Koresh and the Branch Davidians from mainstream Christianity. Former Branch Davidians said that Koresh's teachings came almost exclusively from either Revelation or the Old Testament. A former member, Marc Breault, explained, "The whole movement was focused on the end of the world; nothing else was really that important." In Koresh's teachings much of the New Testament had become obsolete because, in his opinion, so few people were living up to its lessons. God responded to the world's sordidness by anointing Koresh.[18]

While waiting for the end of time, Koresh and the Davidians set about building a heavenly community on earth. Women in the group, married and single alike, became the House of David, or Koresh's wives. The children they produced with him would help Koresh and his male followers rule the earth after slaying the unbelievers. The group's men, named the Mighty Men after a verse in the Song of Solomon about the men who guarded King Solomon's bed, would meet their perfect mates—crafted from their own ribs—in heaven.[19] According to a former member, Koresh viewed marriage as glorified adultery and thus reordered it. Koresh annulled all his followers' marriages, explained that *all* women belonged to him (in his capacity as the Lamb of Revelation), and hoarded women as a miser hoards money, according to the news reports. Then Koresh segregated living quarters by gender. At one point men and women mixed only for Bible study, and Koresh chastised husbands who tried to maintain contact with their wives. According to reports, Koresh's collection of "wives," or females with whom he had sex, grew to fifteen, some as young as fourteen years old. Other reports say he arranged marriages between Davidians with U.S. citizenship and those from other countries who wished to remain in the United States after their visas expired.[20]

The Branch Davidians depended on Koresh for more than spiritual guidance. In addition to ordering their sex lives, Koresh regulated dress and diet at Mount Carmel. According to one elderly couple who joined the group, Koresh allowed members to eat oranges and bananas but forbade apples—the thin skin, he said, allowed poisons to enter the fruit. He inspected people's living quarters to see that they followed his wishes. When one family bought french fries against his wishes, he ejected them from the group. News reports also alleged that Koresh controlled his followers' credit cards and property and demanded they "tithe" to him 100 percent of their incomes. One couple, acting on Koresh's request, bought him a home in Pomona, California, valued at $100,000 and a van worth $10,000. Another couple, retired civil servants, sold their home in Hawaii and gave Koresh the proceeds, more than half a million dollars. After completing their trek from Hawaii to Mount Carmel, the couple sold their van and used the money to buy a red Camaro per God's directions—relayed through Koresh.[21]

The way Koresh and his followers treated children at Mount Carmel gives perhaps the best reason for vilifying them. In the view of Dr. Bruce Perry, an associate professor of psychiatry at the Baylor College of Medicine, and no doubt of mainstream society in general, the family structure of the Branch Davidians had broken down. Perry examined children who had lived at Mount Carmel and found that when he asked them to draw a picture of their families, they often drew clusters of their favorite people. The children had been taught to consider Koresh their father; those who were not his biological children or those whom he had not "adopted," however, were called "bastards."[22]

Kiri Jewell, a former Davidian who was twelve years old in March 1993, has provided the most compelling accounts of a child's life at Mount Carmel. Jewell said she was paddled for not learning a Bible lesson quickly enough. Koresh taught Davidians, including children, the best way to commit suicide—by putting a gun in one's mouth and shooting. Jewell also reported that Koresh had sex with girls as young as twelve and that her own mother was grooming her to become one of Koresh's "wives." Koresh gave such girls a Star of David medallion to wear.[23] As much as these revelations might have shocked the public, her full story, not told until two years later, made them seem like child's play.

Mental health experts consulted by law enforcement and the media during the Branch Davidian siege tended to diagnose Koresh as mentally ill. The New York psychiatrist Alexander Deutsch, who had studied cult leaders, said self-proclaimed messiahs such as Koresh may be mentally ill, con artists, or both. "I think we're dealing with some sort of perversion of the religious instinct," Deutsch told the media.[24] Deutsch apparently gave no thought to the possibility that Koresh was sane and believed he communicated with God. Such reactions to Koresh show that just as unusual religious movements, such as Mormonism and the Ghost Dance, had elicited suspicious responses from mainstream society in the nineteenth century, they continued to do so in the late twentieth century. By then, however, science had provided a new vocabulary for denouncing fringe religious leaders.

Some psychiatrists speculated that Koresh might be suffering from Jerusalem syndrome, the tendency among some visitors to the Holy Land to proclaim they are figures from the Bible or, perhaps, on a mission from God. Jews experiencing the syndrome might believe themselves to be Abraham or King David, for example, while Christians might believe themselves to be Jesus, one of his disciples, or the Virgin Mary. Dr. Eli Witztum, a Jerusalem psychiatrist who treats the disorder, speculated that Koresh's visit to Jerusalem several years before the 1993 standoff intensified his messianic self-image. Many of Witztum's patients have a history of such episodes prior to visiting the Holy Land, but traveling to the site of their religions' origins exacerbates their condition. Witztum explains, "They become so inspired or affected, depending on how you look at it, that they just snap."[25] Although Witztum spoke in terms of mental health, his comments show a tolerance for religious diversity and an acceptance of religion not often apparent among law-enforcement officials or mental-health professionals in the United States. Living in Jerusalem, where Jews, Moslems, and Christians share close quarters and violent conditions, may have contributed to his attitude; those in the

United States, where religious diversity is considerably less pressing, may feel little or no need to consider such things.

The conflict between Branch Davidian beliefs and practices and those of mainstream society eventually stirred interest in the Waco community, particularly at the local newspaper, the *Waco Tribune-Herald*. As good newspeople tend to do, the staff members envisioned themselves as protectors of the community, so they followed the rumors they heard about Koresh and Mount Carmel and set out to provoke action against the Branch Davidians with a seven-part exposé titled "The Sinful Messiah." The rhetoric employed in the series reveals another facet of mainstream society's reaction to the Branch Davidians. In the first installment the *Tribune-Herald* introduced its readers to David Koresh with the following thumbnail sketch: "He has dimples, claims a ninth-grade education, married his legal wife when she was 14, enjoys a beer now and then, plays a mean guitar, reportedly packs a 9mm Glock and keeps an arsenal of military assault rifles, and willingly admits that he is a sinner without equal."[26] The *Tribune-Herald*'s series not only introduced Waco-area readers to Koresh but also served as a quick reference for the horde of media representatives that descended on Waco within days of its publication. Because the "Sinful Messiah" series played such an influential role in shaping the world's image of Koresh and his Branch Davidian followers, it deserves careful attention.

The *Tribune-Herald* reporters Mark England and Darlene McCormick investigated the Branch Davidians for eight months while preparing the series, which was intended "to warn the community about Vernon Howell."[27] They relied heavily on former Branch Davidians and anticult experts for information, which contributed to the series' consistently hostile tone toward the group. In fairness, if the various allegations against Koresh are proved true, he and the Branch Davidians deserved the hostility. The paper also showed disrespect for the Branch Davidians by referring to Koresh as Vernon Wayne Howell, despite the fact he had legally changed his name two years before the series appeared. The *Tribune-Herald* justified this policy by claiming that most area residents knew Koresh by his previous name. The paper, not to mention government officials and the rest of the media, also used the pejorative term *cult* to describe the people following Koresh's teachings and living at Mount Carmel. The political scientist Michael Barkun, however, argues that the term *cult* has become virtually meaningless, "little more than a label slapped on religious groups regarded as too exotic, marginal or dangerous."[28] Indeed, one might reasonably say that in the late twentieth century *cult* carried many of the same connotations that *babarian* did in the nineteenth.

The first installment of the "Sinful Messiah" series, which appeared on the front page, identified the Branch Davidians as an international assemblage of miscreants. Members did in fact come from Australia, England, New Zealand, Canada, and throughout the United States. According to the newspaper, they had come to the seventy-seven-acre Mount Carmel community to support and follow the teachings of a man who abused children psychologically and physically, boasted of having sex with underage girls in the group, claimed the divine right to take every man's wife, and had at least fifteen wives.[29]

As the series unfolded, the *Tribune-Herald* based entire segments on interviews with anticult activists identified as "experts." One such story, "Experts: Branch Davidians Dangerous, Destructive Cult," relied on information supplied by Rick Ross, a cult deprogrammer, and Priscilla Coates, a ten-year Cult Awareness Network volunteer. Within months of the "Sinful Messiah" series' appearance, however, authorities in Washington State arrested Ross on charges of unlawfully imprisoning a man he failed to deprogram. *Tribune-Herald* reporters wrote that "the Gospel According to Vernon Howell is a dangerous, volatile swerve out of the mainstream," basing this assertion on their interviews with the cult experts. Ross described Koresh as "the absolute authoritarian leader" of the Davidians who "control[ed] everything and everyone in that compound, period." Koresh's powers of control were so great, according to one ex-Davidian interviewed for the story, that the group could recruit anyone. "I don't care who you are," he told reporters, "you could be the strongest person in the world."[30]

Focusing on Koresh, the "Sinful Messiah" series vilified him while absolving most of his followers of any responsibility for accepting his teachings. A sentence from the second installment illustrates this point: "Lurking behind the Branch Davidians' blind faith in Vernon Howell was the acknowledgment that a ninth-grade dropout was keeping them spellbound."[31] Other articles appearing in the *Tribune-Herald*'s coverage of the Branch Davidians referred to Koresh as a "doomsday prophet," "a deranged, violent megalomaniac with a messiah complex," "a classic sociopath," and a "false prophet." A writer for the *Christian Century* described Koresh as having a "twisted notion of himself as a messiah" and as being a "religious fanatic." *Time* called him "the mad messiah of Waco."[32] The media saw and portrayed a sinister David Koresh casting a spell over his followers, whom he induced to follow him without questioning their actions or his motives.

In all, the *Tribune-Herald* painted a picture of Koresh as a religious Svengali who held a mysterious, seemingly irresistible power over his followers.

Some individuals who had no trouble resisting Koresh, though, cast doubt on this portrayal. For example, the Waco-area rock-and-roll singer Jimbo Ward felt no compulsion to follow Koresh. Ward jammed with Koresh, who played electric guitar and hoped to use rock songs to spread his theology. Ward told a reporter for the *Tribune-Herald*, "When [Koresh] was around us, he was a rock 'n' roll wannabe rather than a Jesus Christ wannabe."[33] In addition, Koresh tried to convert Jason Collins, a singer. When Koresh started proselytizing at a nightclub, Collins responded, "'Hey, man, I just like to drink my beer and hang out, and that's what I'm going to do.'"[34] Another Waco-area musician, the drummer Shannon Bright, became interested in Koresh's message after jamming with Koresh, whom he called "an excellent guitarist" and "one of the nicest guys I ever met." While exploring Koresh's teachings, Bright spent much of his free time at Mount Carmel. He said people could pass freely in and out of Mount Carmel and disputed allegations that Koresh manipulated people by so overwhelming them with scripture that they gave up thinking for themselves and simply accepted what Koresh said. Despite Koresh's skill and the appeal of his teachings, Bright harbored doubts and stopped visiting Mount Carmel. Neither Ward, Collins, nor Bright had trouble resisting Koresh's call to religion.

Others who heard Koresh "harmonize" the Bible did not resist. Livingstone Fagan first heard Koresh teach in 1988 while Fagan was a Seventh-day Adventist seminary student in Great Britain. In the course of one three-hour lesson, Fagan said, "I had perceived more significant biblical truths than I had done, the entire eight years I had been involved with organized religion." On completing his studies, Fagan traveled to the United States and visited Mount Carmel, where he eventually returned to live. Fagan said that at Mount Carmel, "designed of heaven," he and other Branch Davidians "were able to hear God's word, while blocking out the artificial noise of humanity." When outsiders charged that the Davidians were "brainwashed," Fagan responded, "No, the truth is, it is the world that is brainwashed." Jaime Castillo wrote in a similar vein, praising Koresh for his ability to bring scripture to life.[35] Although some listeners could not quite buy Koresh's message, those who heard in his words the works of an astounding teacher became his loyal followers.

Still another opinion came from a Waco physician who had treated Koresh and other Branch Davidians in his office fifteen or twenty times during the three years preceding the raid. "He is a very gentle man," the physician, who requested anonymity, told the *Tribune-Herald*. "He is very intelligent and very articulate. They make him sound like a ruthless killer, and that's just absurd."[36] David Koresh obviously inspired a variety of opinions, some sharply conflicting with others, but by 1992 the idiosyncrasies practiced by Koresh and his followers at Mount Carmel were drawing increasing attention from the outside world.

Perhaps more than any other idiosyncrasy, the Branch Davidians' proclivity for arming themselves alarmed outsiders; in fact, it led to their demise. Koresh taught that the government, particularly federal law-enforcement agents, represented "Assyrians" or "Babylonians" bent on destroying the true believers—the Branch Davidians. Koresh preached that law-enforcement agents planned to kill him and his followers, thereby initiating Armageddon, as early as 1985. Even children among the Branch Davidians knew that "bad guys" would kill Koresh and the Davidians. After this conflict Koresh would be resurrected and "chop the heads off the bad guys, and they would burn in hell." Then the children would go to heaven with their parents. Sometime between March and September 1992, one or more members of the Branch Davidian community saw local law-enforcement agents practicing special weapons and tactics (SWAT) training near Mount Carmel. To Koresh, this proved his point. He responded by calling Branch Davidians living in California and Great Britain to come to Mount Carmel and by beginning a massive arms buildup for the impending apocalyptic battle.[37] Some sources indicate that the Davidians engaged in weapons trade for profit, too. Unbeknownst to the outside world, as of February 28, 1993, the Davidians' arsenal included fifty-nine handguns; twelve shotguns; ninety-four rifles, including two .50-caliber Barrett rifles capable of hitting targets more than a mile away; forty-five machine guns; 1.8 million rounds of ammunition; hand grenade parts; and semiautomatic assault rifles that they had modified to increase their rates of fire. The "Sinful Messiah" series alleged that the Davidians "could be manufacturing . . . a type of machine gun." After neighbors complained about the Davidians firing what sounded like automatic weapons, members of the group voluntarily contacted the McLennan County Sheriff's Department to report the modifications, which appear to have been legal.[38]

Much as the Mormons and Ghost Dancers had before them, the Branch Davidians saw a need to arm themselves for self-defense, although their weapons cache could be considered inventory as well as an arsenal. The Mormon Nauvoo Legion represented a substantial force in its day, as did Lakota warriors, and now, at least in terms of armaments, so did the Branch Davidians. Although they faced little if any harassment from their mainstream neighbors, their religious beliefs told them to prepare for a government attack. When it came, like Mormons awaiting the Utah Expedition, the Branch Davidians were prepared. As had happened in the Utah War and the military response to the Ghost Dance, the government sent an overwhelming force into a provocative situation. Much as is the case regarding Wounded Knee, the world may never learn who fired the first shot at Mount Carmel; sadly, the result proved nearly as tragic.

Around the same time that *Waco Tribune-Herald* reporters began investigating the Branch Davidians, the Bureau of Alcohol, Tobacco, and Firearms (BATF) initiated its own inquiry. In May 1992 a United Parcel Service delivery driver had told the McLennan County Sheriff's Department about suspicious shipments of firearms, grenade casings, and "substantial amounts" of black powder. The sheriff's department asked the BATF to investigate. Because the Branch Davidians, "a potentially volatile group with strong professed religious beliefs," might have possessed large quantities of arms and explosives, the BATF designated the case "sensitive" and "significant," ensuring that it would receive special attention.[39]

Early in that investigation a BATF agent inspected the records of a gun dealer linked to Koresh. According to some accounts, the dealer phoned Koresh during the inspection and told him that the agent was asking questions about his purchases. Koresh then told the dealer to invite the agent to Mount Carmel to look at the guns for himself. When the dealer relayed the invitation to the agent, however, the agent refused the invitation and angrily berated the dealer for having called Koresh.[40]

Like the *Tribune-Herald*, the BATF concluded that Koresh held a mysterious power over his followers. The agent performing the initial investigation, Davey Aguilera, reported in December 1992 that all Mount Carmel's residents were "fiercely loyal to Koresh and devoted to his religious teachings." Agent Robert Rodriguez, who infiltrated Mount Carmel feigning interest in Koresh's teaching and who attended at least four Bible study sessions there, said many of the Davidians seemed intelligent but completely under Koresh's sway. Koresh's hypnotic powers proved almost too powerful for even Rodriguez, who said that being able to leave Mount Carmel as he pleased probably saved him. Had he been unable to escape Koresh's unrelenting Bible studies, he suggested, he might have become a Branch Davidian when Koresh invited him to join the group. Fellow agents kept a close eye on Rodriguez, reminding him from time to time that Koresh's teachings were just his interpretations. "[The other agents] would talk to me, bring me back," Rodriguez told the *Tribune-Herald*.[41]

The investigation led the BATF to conclude that Koresh and his followers were manufacturing weapons illegally at Mount Carmel. It also prompted the BATF to focus on Koresh, "because of his propensity toward violence and *his ability to control others.*" The initial BATF report on the Branch Davidians emphasized that several members had given Koresh all their assets and that they all "permitted" him to have sex with any woman in the cult. These behaviors, coupled with allegations that Koresh physically and sexually abused children, "showed Koresh to have set up a world of his own, where legal prohibitions were disregarded freely."[42] As had happened with other groups, sexual relationships dictated by religious belief produced significant behaviors that set the Branch Davidians apart from mainstream America and contributed to the government's justification for action against them.

At the end of January 1993 the BATF began planning how it would serve search and arrest warrants on Koresh and the Branch Davidians. For several reasons the agents in charge opted for what law-enforcement officials call a "dynamic entry." To people outside law-enforcement circles, especially people on the receiving end of a dynamic entry, the procedure appears remarkably like an attack. Part of the BATF's stated rationale for making a forced entry into Mount Carmel was the belief that Koresh rarely left the residence, so that if agents were to serve the warrant, they would have to serve it there. Almost as soon as the BATF explanation hit the media, area residents said it was mistaken. "To say that he never leaves that place is ridiculous," Margaret Jones, one of Koresh's friends, told the *Tribune-Herald.* According to Jones, "Everybody and their dog" saw Koresh and many other Davidians away from Mount Carmel. Jones conceded that "Jesus with a 9 mm is not particularly enticing," but she added, "I don't like to see the federal agents lying about the situation, either."[43] Later investigations of the raid would show that the agents had indeed lied about this and other elements of their investigation of Koresh and the Branch Davidians.

BATF planners also believed they had to surprise the Branch Davidians and execute the warrants before those inside the compound could arm themselves to resist. In other words, the BATF knew quite well that Koresh preached a religious message involving an apocalyptic battle with law enforcement and probably had the armaments to make it happen. He once told his followers, "You can't die for God if you can't kill for God." Agents also remembered Koresh's gunfight with George Roden, which they held as an indicator of his potential response to being served with federal warrants. The BATF, then, found itself in the awkward position of having to enforce federal law on a group it knew to be not only armed but religiously motivated and potentially dangerous.

The planned dynamic entry called for one detachment of agents to climb onto Mount Carmel's roof and enter the arms room and Koresh's room through separate windows. Those agents would create a diversion by using "flashbangs," grenades that produce a loud explosion and flash of light but no fragments, while other agents would enter the front door and secure the rest of Mount Carmel. Unlike the typical dynamic entry, which begins before sunrise, the BATF action against the Branch Davidians was scheduled to begin at 10 A.M., when, the planners hoped, most of the male Branch Davidians would be working on a construction project and therefore a long way from the group's weapons.[44]

The BATF attacked Mount Carmel at 9:55 A.M. on February 28, according to the account in the *Tribune-Herald*. Despite knowing that they had lost the element of surprise—a television news camera operator covering the event asked directions to Mount Carmel from a motorist who happened to be a Branch Davidian—the BATF went ahead with the raid. With three helicopters circling on the horizon, two cattle trucks holding about one hundred BATF agents pulled into the property. At least one agent had prepared for the raid with a prayer, asking God to protect him and to look after his wife and three sons. As the trucks approached the residence, the helicopters closed, one hovering near the building. Agents piled out of the trucks, throwing concussion grenades and shouting "Come out!" The Branch Davidians answered with a hail of gunfire, reported to be from automatic weapons. Agents hunkered down for what would be a forty-five-minute firefight, followed by more sporadic shooting. Four agents died, as did at least two Branch Davidians, and twenty more agents and at least three Branch Davidians suffered wounds in the battle. It marked the deadliest day in BATF history. As for the Branch Davidians' hostile response to the raid, Koresh later explained to his attorney: "I don't care who they are. Nobody is going to come to my home, with my babies around, shaking guns around, without a gun back in their face. That's just the American way."[45] The siege was on.

For the next fifty-one days the U.S. government would make a massive show of force against the Branch Davidians. Within a day of the raid, the FBI took over from the BATF. More than 700 law-enforcement personnel took part, with 250 to 300 FBI agents present at any given time. The FBI agents enjoyed the support of BATF agents, U.S. Customs officials, Waco police, personnel from the McLennan County Sheriff's Office, Texas Rangers, the Texas Department of Public Safety, the U.S. Army, and the Texas National Guard. The government also sent nine Bradley fighting vehicles, five combat engineer vehicles, a tank retrieval vehicle, and two Abrams tanks. Reporters also swarmed to the scene. According to estimates, by midafternoon on the day of the raid some sixty reporters and camera crews from at least seventeen television stations and the Cable News Network had arrived to cover the event.[46]

From the beginning Koresh tried to tell the government that the raid was about theology. In a 911 call made during the first hours of the raid, a frantic Koresh told Larry Lynch of the McLennan County Sheriff's Department that he had been teaching his followers for years that such an event would occur. Later in the same conversation Koresh told Lynch, "Theology is life and death," adding that the Davidians would "serve God first." Koresh put the raid and standoff in perspective for the Branch Davidians, telling them that both constituted part of the apocalyptic struggle with the government that he had been predicting for years. Others in Mount Carmel, steeped in Koresh's teachings, believed the BATF had come to kill them.[47] From day one it should have been clear to authorities that this would not be a typical negotiating task.

Negotiations appeared to be on the brink of ending the standoff when Koresh promised to surrender on March 2 if authorities would allow him to broadcast an hour-long sermon on several radio stations. At the last moment, however, Koresh told authorities that he had received a message from God instructing him to wait. He later added that he would not leave Mount Carmel until God told him to do so.[48]

The FBI's objective in the siege was to get all the Branch Davidians, particularly the children, to leave Mount Carmel without further injuries or deaths. On the day it took charge of the siege, the FBI contacted Dr. Park Dietz, a clinical professor of psychiatry and biobehavioral sciences at the UCLA School of Medicine. The FBI asked Dietz, a longtime bureau consultant, to develop a personality profile of Koresh. Dietz concluded that Koresh's psychopathology included an antisocial, narcissistic personality that enabled him to become a "master of manipulation." Koresh also suffered from a "system of grandiose delusions, in which Koresh saw himself as a prophet of God, uniquely equipped to interpret the Bible." Overall, Dietz concluded, the twin problems of grandiosity and delusions of persecution alternately fueled Koresh's actions. Dietz predicted that while the grandiosity prevailed, as it did early in the siege, Koresh would be friendly with negotiators, which he was; if the balance shifted to persecution, however, Koresh would withdraw from communications, make more accusations against outsiders, and become more dangerous. Consequently, Dietz and Pete Smerick, an FBI criminal investigative analyst, developed a profile that recommended negotiators acknowledge Koresh's worldview, particularly the "conspiracy" against the Davidians and their right to defend themselves against it. Dietz and Smerick also recommended that negotiators suggest to Koresh that he could win in court if he surrendered and would not go to prison.[49]

Smerick and fellow FBI psychological profiler Mark Young followed the Dietz-Smerick analysis with a novel strategy for dealing with Koresh. Smerick and Young recommended that FBI avoid its standard practice of increasing tactical pressure on Koresh and the Davidians, which would likely increase their fear and paranoia, and instead simply back off. This, they hoped, would demonstrate that the government had no intention of fighting an apocalyptic battle with the Davidians, thus undermining Koresh's influence among his followers. Any FBI attack, they feared, would result in a fight to the death by the Branch Davidians. Smerick feared FBI commanders wanted to treat Koresh "not as a negotiation partner, but rather as a 'psychotic criminal' who needed to be caught and punished."[50] The Smerick-Young memo went largely unheeded.

Early in the siege government negotiators grew frustrated with Koresh's focus on religious matters, seemingly often to the exclusion of resolving the conflict at hand. Bob Ricks, a spokesperson for the FBI, complained that after government offers, Koresh often went into "a discussion of Scripture." Before the siege was a week old, negotiators found themselves on the receiving end of a four-hour sermon from Koresh. They also heard complaints from Wayne Martin, a Harvard-educated lawyer and Branch Davidian, that America's political system was in decay and in conflict with God's law and that God had chosen Koresh to rule over his kingdom on earth. Martin told the negotiators they and America were witnessing the birth of a new nation founded on the seven seals (i.e., explaining the Bible, especially prophecies, and using the information to effect the culmination of history). Furthermore, Martin told the agents they were enemies of the seven seals and would go to hell if they caused "aggression." Also during that first week, Koresh told negotiators he was Christ. The negotiators remained calm, even complimenting Koresh on his knowledge of the Bible, and urged him to come out. Koresh, meanwhile, tried to convert the negotiators to his religion. It would prove a tall challenge, though, considering that one religious expert accused the FBI agents of knowing so little about the Bible that some thought the seven seals were "seagoing creatures with whiskers."[51]

In an effort to remedy that situation and to understand Koresh, FBI agents studied the seven seals in Revelation, the core of Koresh's teachings; they also studied Isaiah for information about the name *David Koresh*. When Congress held hearings on the Branch Davidian episode two years after its conclusion, Rep. John Conyers Jr., of Michigan, asked the FBI negotiator

James Cavanaugh about the degree to which he and other negotiators recognized that they were dealing with a religious group subscribing to beliefs outside the mainstream. Cavanaugh replied that he and other negotiators respected the Branch Davidians' religious beliefs but not their right to have hand grenades and submachine guns and to shoot federal agents.[52] Nonetheless, while religion was clearly important to Koresh, the respect federal negotiators felt for Branch Davidian beliefs remains difficult to ascertain.

Meanwhile, Steve Schneider, one of Koresh's top lieutenants, began mentioning to negotiators a theme that would recur several times in discussions with the FBI: fire. On March 13 Schneider claimed the government wanted to kill the Davidians and burn Mount Carmel. Exactly two weeks later, in response to a vague FBI threat to take "additional action" if the Davidians did not send out at least ten people, Schneider said they did not fear the FBI: "You can burn us down, kill us, whatever."[53]

Law-enforcement agents soon grew frustrated with theological discussions and tried to steer the talks toward a settlement. The FBI increased pressure on the Davidians through psychological harassment such as shining bright spotlights on Mount Carmel through much of the night to deprive inhabitants of sleep. The FBI spokesman Richard Swenson showed the increasing frustration among government agents when he said, "We're not here to be converted. . . . We want to talk about substantive issues." Most in the FBI believed that agents had spent enough time listening to Koresh's religious doctrines. By trying to limit religious discussions and increasing pressure on the compound's residents, the FBI attempted to show the Davidians that federal agents were "in control of the situation."[54] Understandable as this might be, it indicates that the FBI missed the point of discussing anything with Koresh, whose life revolved around religion. In Koresh's view, when he discussed the seven seals with federal agents, he was discussing substantive issues, arguably the most substantive issues he could conceive—the end of the world and eternal salvation.

As the siege and negotiations continued, it became apparent that the Branch Davidians who left the compound—and presumably Koresh's influence—remained true to their beliefs, casting doubt on the notion that they were unthinking dupes under Koresh's spell. After Livingstone Fagan, a now high-ranking Branch Davidian who had helped recruit members in Britain, left Mount Carmel on March 23, he commented that the siege was "working out fine" and on "God's schedule."[55] Another Branch Davidian who left Mount Carmel during the siege, Gladys Ottman, told her son that she continued to believe Koresh was the new Christ and that only he could open the seven seals. She also said she had not wanted to leave Mount Carmel but had been "chosen by God to leave."[56] Branch Davidian Rita Riddle said the siege excited group members because they could see Koresh's prophecies unfolding before their eyes.[57] These Branch Davidians did not abandon their beliefs on gaining their freedom. It is of course possible that Koresh still held sway over them, but it is possible, too, that they were not brainwashed at all but rather were exercising free will in following his teachings, as they had all along.

One Branch Davidian suggested that more members would have left Mount Carmel if not for fear and mistrust of the FBI. Clive Doyle said the group feared the FBI agents, who bared their buttocks at Branch Davidians from tanks, cut off their electricity, and harassed them with bright lights and loud music. They also mistrusted the FBI, whose negotiators told them they could keep their Bibles when they came out, because Branch Davidians remaining inside Mount Carmel saw agents confiscate departing coreligionists' belongings, including Bibles. Branch Davidians also feared that FBI agents were eager to retaliate for the deaths of the four BATF agents killed on February 28.[58]

Meanwhile, at least some in the FBI had concluded they had to deal with Koresh and his theology, whose vision of apocalyptic violence could be extremely dangerous to the people inside Mount Carmel. According to Bob Ricks, the special agent in charge of the FBI's Oklahoma City office, the agents operated under the assumption that Koresh believed himself to be God, and it was their job to prove to him he was not. Ricks considered this an extremely difficult task, which suggests the ease with which agents could have become frustrated dealing with Koresh and his follower.[59] They considered Koresh delusional and his followers dupes. At the same time, this assumption shows that at least some FBI agents realized they were dealing with a man and a group heavily influenced by strong religious beliefs. Finally, it raises a central question: given that some agents believed Koresh saw potential benefit in having some of his followers killed, why would the FBI attempt to oust the Branch Davidians from Mount Carmel with aggressive tactics?

The siege appeared to be taking a turn on Friday, April 9, when a Branch Davidian delivered a letter to the FBI. Supposedly the letter recounted a revelation Koresh had received from God—perhaps the long-awaited sign from God required before the Davidians could surrender. Transcribed by the Branch Davidian Judy Schneider, the letter was addressed to "friends" and signed "Yahweh Koresh," which David Koresh claimed to be God's true name. An FBI spokesman described the "threatening" letter as containing "messages of a powerful, angry God, empowering his chosen people to punish and harm those who oppose them." Quoting the Bible, the letter compared the government to Babylon and suggested that the Branch Davidians would fight it: "I have laid a snare for thee, and thou art also taken, O Babylon, and thou wast not aware; thou art found, and also caught, because thou hast striven against the Lord." FBI experts concluded from the letter that Koresh "was possibly a functioning, paranoid-type psychotic" who had no intention of surrendering.[60]

Instead of being a sign of imminent surrender, the letter appears to be a justification for the standoff and further evidence that Koresh and his followers viewed the event in religious terms. It also put Koresh and his followers in a position similar to the Mormons, since both groups believed in ongoing revelation from God. Furthermore, it indicates that the Davidians did not wish to compromise with "Babylon," which to them meant the U.S. government.

The following day, April 10, Koresh sent out a second threatening letter. This letter contained many characteristics of the first: Koresh had dictated the contents as a revelation, it was signed "Yahweh Koresh," it cited Bible verses, and it threatened the destruction of federal forces by fire or other means. A former Branch Davidian interpreted the letter as a sign that Koresh expected to conquer the federal forces and that he had no intention of ending the standoff soon or peacefully.[61]

Evidence indicates that by April 14, when Koresh promised yet another surrender scenario, the FBI's patience had been stretched near its breaking point. Using the attorney Dick DeGuerin as his intermediary, Koresh announced that he would lead his people from Mount Carmel after completing a book-length manuscript on the seven seals. Bob Ricks compared the situation to the *Peanuts* cartoon scenario in which Lucy, holding a football for Charlie Brown to kick, repeatedly pulls it away at the last second, frustrating his attempt to kick the ball; the comparison indicates Ricks' growing frustration with Koresh. Ricks listed three other times during the siege when the Branch Davidians appeared to have fixed a point for ending the siege, only to renege on their promise. According to Ricks, Koresh had completed explaining the first seal, a task that took three days and produced about thirty pages of handwritten text. Extrapolating for the remainder of the seals, Ricks estimated a finished product of about two hundred pages would not be completed until about May 4.[62]

DeGuerin constituted a valuable ally in this situation. FBI officials had become convinced that Koresh was a con man and a liar. DeGuerin, the first attorney the FBI allowed to speak personally with any Branch Davidians, met with Koresh several times during the final stages of the standoff, believed him to be sane, and told authorities that Koresh truly wanted to discuss the Bible and to explain his beliefs. The FBI wrote off Koresh's rambling sermons as "Bible babble" despite DeGuerin's professions of his client's lucidity. Nevertheless, FBI officials hoped that allowing DeGuerin to meet with Koresh would hasten the Branch Davidians' surrender. As DeGuerin undertook the task of calming his client's fears and mistrust of the federal government, both DeGuerin and an FBI spokesman told the media that no deadlines had been placed on the negotiation process.[63]

If Koresh wrote at the pace estimated by Ricks, the standoff would have ended in just more than two weeks. But disbelief and frustration plagued the FBI. In Washington, D.C., in fact, on the very afternoon Koresh announced his new precondition for surrender, FBI Director William Sessions briefed Attorney General Janet Reno on the pros and cons of using tear gas to flush the Branch Davidians from Mount Carmel. Reno, who had taken her oath of office just a few weeks earlier, on March 12, faced an extraordinarily difficult situation.[64]

FBI agents had proposed the assault plan to Reno two days earlier. "We had run out of other plans," an FBI official told a *Time* reporter. This suggests the FBI did not consider more waiting an option. Reno asked hundreds of questions of the FBI planners. She studied the plan for days and then grilled army special forces experts about it. FBI officials told Reno that the longer the siege lasted, the worse conditions would be for children inside Mount Carmel. Finally, with assurances that the gas would be nonlethal and would cause no long-term harm to the children, Reno approved the attack on April 17. Justifying her decision, Reno explained, "Short of allowing David Koresh to go free, he is not coming out voluntarily."[65] Reno's decision guaranteed her prediction.

Armored vehicles began removing cars and trucks near the compound on Sunday, April 18, to clear the grounds for the next day's assault. The FBI warned the Branch Davidians to stay inside while the armored vehicles cleared the cars, including Koresh's Chevy Camaro. Inside Mount Carmel adults held children up to the windows. Looking at one window, an FBI sniper saw a cardboard sign, decorated with images of fire, that read, "Flames Await."[66]

As the siege and its attendant negotiations dragged on, the people of Waco reacted in a variety of ways to the events at Mount Carmel. Waco-area residents found themselves suddenly immersed in a circus of reporters and law-enforcement agents obsessed with their Mount Carmel neighbors, whom they had previously considered merely eccentric but now viewed as ominously dangerous. Some believed the government had overstepped its bounds, but most closed ranks behind mainstream religious and social values and supported the actions of the federal agents.[67]

Texas has historically offered a variety of religious experiences, thanks largely to its location. Catholic Mexico wanted settlers so badly for remote, sparsely settled Texas that it agreed to forgo religious requirements, such as mandatory mass attendance, to draw them. Of the hundreds of colonists Stephen Austin brought to Texas in the early 1820s, no more than 10 percent became practicing Catholics. As Austin and his settlers thrived on Catholic tolerance, born of necessity though it was, they refused to extend benevolence to the region's original inhabitants. Austin called the natives "universal enemies to man" and believed they could be subdued only through extermination.[68]

The pendulum of tolerance had traveled toward understanding by mid-century, again out of necessity. Waco's founders built the city with a measure of tolerance that quickly spawned a diversity of Christian denominations. Jacob de Cordova, a Jew who could read and write Hebrew and had some training in Jewish religious law, founded Waco in the late 1840s. At about the same time voters in Harris County elected him to the Texas state legislature, perhaps reflecting a liberal attitude toward religion in young Texas. De Cordova showed his tolerance and perhaps his eagerness to attract settlers to his new community on the Brazos River by donating land to Waco for city parks, schools, and other public uses, as well as giving land to a variety of denominations. Most of the latter donations were used as sites for Christian churches. Waco's Jewish community held its services in rented rooms, stores, or homes until 1879, when it organized a formal congregation, Rodef Sholom, and bought a building.[69]

Before the century turned, though, Waco's religious tolerance appeared to have run thin. On April Fool's Day in 1898 an angry Baptist gunned down the journalist William Cowper Brann, who had made a habit of criticizing religious hypocrisy, especially when it occurred at Baylor University. Brann's demise could be traced to commentary about Baylor's president, who had offered a young Brazilian woman a Baylor education in exchange for her domestic labor. While employed at the president's home, the woman became pregnant. When the baby was born, Brann called the child a "beautiful three-pound Baylor diploma." Enraged at this insult, Baylor students stormed the offices of Brann's *Iconoclast,* the monthly in which he had published his remarks, and threatened to hang or to tar and feather Brann if he did not apologize. Sensibly, he apologized. Later remarks earned Brann further enmity of the Baylor community. The president of the board of trustees horsewhipped him. Then, on April 1, 1898, the father of a Baylor coed, still irate over the episode, shot Brann in the back as he walked down a Waco street. Brann returned fire. Both men died within hours.[70]

Whatever their predecessors had thought about various religious groups, the Texans living nearest Mount Carmel registered surprise that the Branch Davidians had caused such a fuss. Their reaction lent credence to the West's reputation for tolerance and reflected westerners' suspicions of the federal government. The proprietor of a store in nearby Elk said the Davidians had never caused him any problems before the raid. One of his customers saw merit to each side's case in the standoff. "I think the sneak attack was wrong," Kenneth Ellis told a reporter, adding, "This is America. They should have given them a chance to surrender." Another Elk business owner shared that sentiment. Dennis Moore, a tavern keeper, believed the Davidians were justified in protecting their property. Moore also disagreed with labeling the Davidians a cult. "We always referred to it as a religious commune, not a cult," he said. Moore then predicted, "The federal people are going to go in and murder what's left over there [at Mount Carmel]." Another area resident condemned the raid in a letter to the editor printed in the *Waco Tribune-Herald*. William Murray, of Moody, Texas, wrote, "The raid on the so-called 'cult' in Elk was precisely staged by the feds for maximum media impact, designed to fill us with fear and condition us to support more get-tough tax dollars as well as a new round of restrictive laws and ordinances."[71] These westerners felt their religiously eccentric neighbors had the rights to do as they pleased as long as they did not bother anyone and to defend their property from aggressors, even if— perhaps *especially* if—the aggressors happened to be the government, which might impose its will even more harshly than it already had.

The raid and siege also drew protests from the Libertarian Party, which saw the government's action as infringing on basic constitutional liberties. The national Libertarian Party has long advocated abolishing the BATF. Protesters carried signs reading, "Is Your Church ATF-Approved?" "Is Your Church Next?" and "Freedom of religion is for all beliefs." About one week into the standoff, Gary Johnson, spokesperson for the Libertarian Party of Texas, told the *Waco Tribune-Herald* that cults were no exception to the freedom of worship. Furthermore, he emphasized the right to bear arms as a last resort for resisting tyranny. Libertarian protesters in Dallas felt the Branch Davidian raid exposed a government agency run amok, charging that it was part of a "mi-

nority cleaning" campaign. "[The BATF] pick[s] on people who are not easy
to defend," charged Honey Dodge, a Libertarian protesting in Dallas. Dodge
added, "These people are not necessarily my favorite kind of people, but this
is where they'll start."[72]

But most central Texas residents reacted to the events differently. In
Waco, a city the *Tribune-Herald* called "mainstream in its Protestantism,"
the people "struggled with disbelief . . . that a fanatic named Vernon Howell chose to live out his confusing and self-destructive prophecy so nearby."
Part of the town's struggle saw mainstream Protestant Waco close ranks to
support those who had come to exorcise its demon. A hospital gave shelter
to reporters. A pizza parlor sent free food to law-enforcement officers. A
company sent free cellular phones to officials involved in the siege. And a
Baptist group gathered pastors to comfort the injured and bereaved.[73]

Waco's mainstream political and religious communities had united to
pray for an end to the siege. St. Paul's Episcopal Church held prayer vigils
every day at 5:30 P.M. to seek a peaceful end. At least eight other Waco churches
scheduled prayer vigils, too, many of them daily.[74] Other Waco ministers later
organized a "service of unity," hoping to use spiritual means to end the standoff.[75] Mayor Bob Sheehy wrote a letter to all Waco churches asking them to
pray for a quick resolution to the standoff at Mount Carmel. At Waco's First
Baptist Church, Kent Starr, chairman of the deacons, prayed for the families
of the slain agents and asked God to be with the Davidians and to guide the
conflict to a peaceful end. At Central Christian Church, Pastor Jerry Deffenbaugh told his congregation, "When congregations or religious groups wave
the flag of being independent, they often end up doing crazy things. If you are
not accountable to a larger body or fellowship, then perversion can easily set
in."[76] Mainstream Waco sent a clear message that first Sunday after the initial raid: religious freedom extends only as far as the mainstream deems fit.
Practices beyond those bounds are "crazy," amounting to "perversion," and
will be dealt with accordingly. Furthermore, Deffenbaugh's comment reflects
an age-old American tension between independence and control. The nation's early political leaders worried about demagogues seducing the witless
masses and feared the consequences of too much democracy. In the late-
twentieth-century culture wars, mainstream leaders worried about demagogues draping their crazy perversions under the protective cover of independence.

Mainstream attitudes could also be seen in an outpouring of economic
support for law enforcement. Within a week of the initial incident, local hospitality rose to the challenge of supporting the 600 law-enforcement officers

who had converged on Waco. McLennan County commissioner Ray Meadows organized a food drive to gather canned and other prepared food for the officers. Organizers planned to add collections to donations made by the Waco Restaurant Association. "I just feel like our law enforcement people need to know the county residents are behind them," Meadows said of his effort.[77] During the siege's first month, Michna's Bar-B-Que had donated 1,050 plate lunches to law-enforcement officers and journalists, the McLennan County Extension Service fed the agents beans and cornbread, high school home economics classes baked 325 dozen cookies during one week, and Church's Chicken donated 450 meals on a single day. Local gyms let agents work out for free, and a dry cleaner donated several thousand dollars in services to agents. Grocery stores, other restaurants, and retail stores also donated food to federal forces in the standoff. A representative of the Waco Restaurant Association estimated that members donated $60,000 worth of products to support the siege.[78] Mainstream Waco quickly closed ranks to support law enforcement as it confronted the eccentric religious group just outside the city.

Some of Waco's local hospitality came from a Salvation Army canteen set up near Mount Carmel to provide food and beverages for the press and law-enforcement officers. Two Salvation Army volunteers who identified themselves as good Christians questioned Koresh's religious beliefs. One, Donald Whittington, told a reporter, "I don't care who he says he is, Vernon Howell is not a Christian." Roy McClish, the other, added, "[Koresh] said he's in there waiting for a message from God before he comes out. I've got news for him. He's never going to hear from God." McClish perhaps would have been surprised to know that Whittington had told the reporter that he volunteered at the canteen because, he said, "God wants me to do it."[79] One lesson that might be drawn from this exchange is that God communicates with people but not with the likes of Koresh.

A Waco Baptist preacher expressed sentiments similar to those of the Salvation Army volunteers when he condemned Koresh's use of religious language to gain power for himself. The writer, the Reverend Dan Bagby, pastor of the Seventh and James Baptist Church in Waco, pointed out that not all people who use religious language are deeply religious. Bagby went on to accuse Koresh of not being religious, of manipulating religion for his own ends. He also charged that were Koresh to claim to be Jesus Christ, it would show him to be either mentally unstable or a charlatan who deceived people to gain a following. Bagby sympathized with Koresh's followers, who he felt had surrendered "their right to independent thinking . . . , their right to think, [and] then their selfhood" to Koresh's manipulative, destructive use of religious language. He added that those in Waco following mainstream religions rejected "religious rituals that manipulate, control, abuse, or destroy."[80] Bagby refused to recognize that the Davidians exercised independent thought in following Koresh and that even mainstream religions manipulate their followers' behavior through rituals and creeds. He also missed the distinction Koresh made between himself as a christ and Jesus Christ.

Paralleling Libertarians and government critics, virulent opponents of the Branch Davidians also voiced their feelings about the Mount Carmel standoff and how to end it quickly. Jim Denton, of Elm Mott, Texas, wrote that the taxpayers had tired of seeing millions of dollars spent on the standoff with the "criminal cult." If the Davidians refused to surrender, Denton suggested, the government should "burn them to the ground." The Waco-area landowner Dawn Bryant painted her sentiment about the situation on the window of her pickup truck: "Kill Koresh."[81]

Away from Waco the siege drew vocal support for the Branch Davidians, according to an informal study by Rowland Nethaway, the *Waco Tribune-Herald*'s senior editor. Early in the siege Nethaway wrote a column pondering why a religious cult would settle near Waco, stockpile arms, and fight the federal government. When newspapers around the country reprinted the column, it elicited support for the Branch Davidians that surprised Nethaway. In fact, no one who responded supported the government's position. According to Nethaway, the typical response criticized the government for coming onto the Branch Davidians' property and trying to take their guns. Furthermore, respondents told Nethaway that were they in a similar situation, they would respond as the Branch Davidians had. The law-enforcement agents got what they deserved, according to the respondents. Interestingly, none of these letters supported the Branch Davidians' theology; rather, the writers were clearly reacting to perceived breaches of the Branch Davidians' Second Amendment rights. Nethaway and the siege had struck a chord with these individualists, who continued to write to Nethaway for weeks. Some compared the Branch Davidians to the American colonists who fended off the tyrannical government of Great Britain. Others, however spuriously, compared the Branch Davidians to the rugged individuals who defended the Alamo from a tyrannical federal government in Mexico.[82] The initial raid and siege showed that some U.S. citizens believe the people have good reason to mistrust the government and need weapons to defend themselves from bureaucrats run amok. Responses to the situation also showed the complexity of the relevant issues, which mixed religion, law enforcement, and politics, to name the most obvious.

In a column written about six weeks into the standoff, Nethaway again pondered the situation's meaning. He concluded it revealed "differing views citizens have over what it means to be an American." Specifically, Nethaway wrote, "The 45-minute Sunday morning shoot-out at the religious cult's Mount Carmel compound—Ranch Apocalypse—touched on practically every issue our Founding Fathers put into those original amendments. Religion, speech, guns, assembly, security of homes, personal security, search and seizure—it's all there, and more."[83] Nethaway believed that had local authorities acted on previous complaints regarding child abuse, sexual molestation of children, statutory rape, polygamy, and bogus marriages, the public would not have protested. But the federal government's heavy-handed tactics, combined with the BATF's postraid dishonesty, made the public suspicious about the government's use of force and its justification thereof. If the Mount Carmel episode prompted debate about the relationship between individual liberties and government responsibilities, perhaps some good might come of it, Nethaway suggested.[84]

Some pundits perceived the standoff as part of a violent mythos associated with Texas, which has witnessed events such as President John F. Kennedy's assassination in Dallas, a deadly sniper attack at the University of Texas, and as recently as 1991, a rampage by a gunman who killed nearly two dozen diners at a Killeen cafeteria. Sharon Jenkins, an associate professor of psychology at the University of North Texas at the time of the siege, said, "Texas builds a myth around these kinds of individuals." According to Jenkins, the report that Koresh smiled defiantly at BATF agents before slamming Mount Carmel's front door in their faces fits into that myth. Jenkins said, "There is some part of that myth that romanticizes slamming the door in the face of the law and smiling." A British journalist who came to Waco to cover the Branch Davidian siege said he was drawn by this myth and the state's "Wild West image." American violence in general, he told a reporter, is "just beyond the understanding of people in western Europe."[85] In *The New Republic* the columnist Leon Wieseltier wrote, tongue in cheek: "Who exactly were the Davidians bothering? The administration says they were hoarding guns. How un-American and how un-Texan."[86] In Washington, D.C., the columnist R. Emmett Tyrell Jr. asked rhetorically, "If Americans cannot live the life of the rugged—albeit somewhat loony—individualist in the vast reaches of the great West, where can they live normal American lives?"[87] As if to support these opinions, some Texans suggested that the FBI end the siege as the Mexican forces had ended the siege at the Alamo—by playing the march "Deguello," which signaled "no quarter," over the loudspeakers set up at Mount Carmel and ordering a final, decisive assault on the group.[88] The siege at Mount Carmel struck a responsive chord with many Americans who objected to the government's apparent trampling on cherished liberties. These citizens appeared especially concerned that this attack happened in the American West, where they expected the flame of those freedoms to burn brightest.

Elsewhere, more "cult experts" predicted that Branch Davidians leaving Mount Carmel would find it difficult to return to "normal" life. Dr. J. Douglas Crowder, a psychiatrist and professor of psychiatry at University of Texas Southwestern Medical School, told the *Waco Tribune-Herald* that those exiting Mount Carmel would need "intensive therapy" to lead normal lives. Branch Davidians leaving the group would likely be overwhelmed after having had Koresh make most of their decisions, according to Crowder. He also opined that they would have to face the fact that "they have been wrong for a substantial period of time." To face that challenge, he suggested, they would need emotional support from mainstream religious leaders, mental-health professionals, and family and friends. An emeritus professor of psychology at the University of California at Berkeley expressed similar opinions, noting, "The whole group of them really needs help in understanding how it was that they followed this guy . . . , how they were duped, why they did not leave at any point."[89] Closer to the siege, Robert Sloan, a professor of religion at Baylor University, determined that Koresh read Bible prophecies with the understanding that they applied directly to him. Sloan seemed to find this problematic: "How you psychologically deal with somebody like that I don't know."[90] To the keepers of mainstream society, the Branch Davidians were the helpless pawns of a deluded sociopath, not willing members of a true religious group.

As the siege dragged on, law-enforcement officials became impatient with the lack of progress and with Koresh's broken promises to leave Mount Carmel. On April 19, fifty-one days after the BATF action, they proceeded with the "gas insertion" (to use law-enforcement parlance) that precipitated the fire. Whether started by Branch Davidians or by the federal attack, the intense fire burned Branch Davidians beyond recognition; many incinerated to dust.[91] Gunshot wounds killed a number of Davidians inside the compound, including Koresh, who had been shot between the eyes.[92]

FBI agents thought the gas attack would stimulate the maternal instincts of women inside Mount Carmel, leading them to bring their children out to save them. "Unfortunately," said Bob Ricks, "they bunkered down the children, the best we can tell, and they allowed those children to go up in flames with them." Investigators excavating the Mount Carmel rubble discovered that Ricks's assessment was accurate. They found the remains of many children clutched in their mothers' arms. The FBI had not been paying attention to those voices that said the Branch Davidians feared the government and expected to be killed by its agents. Branch Davidian mothers could not be expected to run to FBI agents for safety. In fact, one woman ran from the burning compound, saw the agents, and ran back into the building.[93]

Even though the Branch Davidians had time to prepare for the gas attack, they did not have enough gas masks for everyone. Most of those with masks were men; some women had masks, but most children did not. Access to the storm shelter—a buried school bus—was cut off by the combat engineering vehicles (CEVs, which are tanks modified with ramrods), but it would have been a poor shelter, because it was one of the first areas gassed, according to the Davidian Clive Doyle, who survived the attack. Then, too, Branch Davidians feared that anyone leaving the shelter of Mount Carmel would be shot by FBI snipers. Those in the parts of the building attacked with ferret rounds had to concentrate on dodging them as they came through windows and walls "like rockets."[94]

The gas attack complicated evacuation further because of the torment it caused its victims. Doyle said the gas burned his skin like acid. Some tried to wipe off the gas with wet cloths, which intensified the burning. Once the fire started, it spread so quickly that many who wished to escape may have been prevented from doing so by the thick, black smoke and the burning, blinding effects of the gas. The gas used by the FBI causes severe burning in the eyes with copious tears and involuntary eye closing. It can also cause shortness of breath, intense nausea, retching, and abdominal cramps. In addition to these physical symptoms, panic complicated the situation inside the building. A chemist estimated that the FBI used about two to four times the amount of gas necessary to incapacitate people in a building the size of Mount Carmel.[95]

As for the origin of the fire, the government and surviving Branch Davidians offered different explanations. According to the official government explanation, Branch Davidians set three or more fires simultaneously at different locations within Mount Carmel. In separate interviews with their attorneys, however, six survivors gave consistent accounts that differed from the government's version. They claimed that when the tank rammed holes in the building's walls, it also ruptured a propane tank and toppled lanterns, which spilled fuel and sparks into the flammable materials scattered throughout the house. They also charged that the FBI gas attack had two other deadly consequences. First, it forced many Branch Davidians away from windows and doors. Had that not been the case, they said, more people could have escaped the fire. Second, it led many to don gas masks, which clouded with soot, smoke, and sweat, making it difficult to see exit routes.[96]

President Bill Clinton issued a statement supporting federal law-enforcement tactics the day after the fire. Clinton called Koresh "dangerous, irrational, and probably insane" and charged that he had engaged in activities violating federal law and "common standards of decency." The president also placed responsibility for the Davidians' deaths solely on Koresh's shoulders. As the president closed his prepared remarks, he pointed to the Branch Davidian tragedy as an instructive example, saying, "I hope very much that others who will be tempted to join cults and to become involved with people like David Koresh will be deterred by the horrible scenes they have seen over the last seven weeks."[97]

Clinton's remarks both recall responses by nineteenth-century mainstream leaders to Mormonism and the Ghost Dance, although they were couched in different language and a milder tone, and show religion's influence. Clinton, a Southern Baptist, met regularly with spiritual advisers, most from Protestant denominations. These advisers often provided spiritual counsel but also offered opinions on policy matters, most notably the abortion issue. The Reverend Rex Horne, pastor of Immanuel Baptist Church in Little Rock, Arkansas, which Clinton attended while governor of Arkansas, spoke on the telephone with the president for fifteen minutes every Saturday night when Clinton was in Washington. Clinton also met monthly with Rev. Bill Hybels, senior pastor of the Willow Creek Community Church in South Barrington, Illinois. During their hour-long meetings the men prayed and discussed politics.[98] Perhaps, then, it is not surprising to find him reacting to the Branch Davidian disaster by saying, essentially, that followers of false prophets get their just desserts.

Years later, in his memoir *My Life,* Clinton reflected regretfully on the episode. He recalled that Reno had come to him the night of April 18 seeking his counsel on the FBI's plan to storm the property. The two wrestled with concerns about FBI reports of Koresh sexually abusing children, the possibility of mass suicide, and the issue of keeping so many FBI resources committed to the standoff for so long. Clinton had faced a similar situation when he governed Arkansas. In that case, he said, he denied an FBI request to raid an armed compound in favor of a prolonged blockade. That standoff ended with no lives lost. Despite that experience, Clinton writes, he ignored his instinct and told Reno to proceed with the raid if she thought it offered the best solution. The deadly result taught him to follow his gut when his instincts conflicted with advice. The experience also prompted him, when interviewing Louis Freeh as a prospective FBI director, to ask whether he would have succumbed to pressure to storm the property rather than keeping agents waiting. Clinton writes that Freeh impressed him by responding that the agents "get paid to wait."[99]

As for the new attorney general, evidence does not show that religion played as strong a role in her actions as it apparently did in shaping Clinton's comments. Why did Janet Reno approve the gas attack rather than wait for Koresh to finish his manuscript or pursue another strategy? *Newsweek* suggested that FBI agents overwhelmed the new attorney general, who was still living out of boxes. As a Reno confidante put it, "Fifty-two guys in blue suits from the FBI show up with a bunch of charts and tell you to do it their way, so you do." The same *Newsweek* analysis explained that Reno held off the FBI "cowboys" for a few days that April, "But then she caved."[100] Although this explanation may hold a grain of truth, it does not do justice to Reno.

Reno explained in congressional hearings that a perceived impasse in negotiations and concern for the welfare of the children inside Mount Carmel had moved her to act. FBI officials convinced her that Koresh would not surrender, and she believed "a dangerous situation was becoming more dangerous, especially for the children." Moreover, she said, FBI negotiators had told her that nobody else would voluntarily leave the compound. This, however, points up more inconsistencies in the government's handling of the situation. The FBI's chief negotiator, Byron Sage, made contradictory reports. The Justice Department's report supports Reno's story, quoting Sage as having said further negotiations would have been fruitless. When Sage testified before the congressional committee, however, he reported that he had never given up hope.

Reno further muddied the waters by testifying that she would have gladly waited a year for Koresh and his followers to exit Mount Carmel peacefully. But, she said, Koresh had lied to officials from the beginning and on several topics, leading them to believe he had no intention of surrendering. This does not jibe, however, with the *Time* report that two days before the attack, Koresh had, for the first time, claimed to have received the sign from God he had been awaiting.[101] Sadly, however much Reno wished to protect Branch Davidian children, the government, through its psychological warfare on the group (including techniques to cause sleep deprivation), inflicted tremendous suffering on those children and ultimately contributed to their deaths.

In concluding remarks at the congressional hearings concerning the tragedy, Congressman Bill McCollum of Florida, chairman of the House Subcommittee on Crime and co-chair of the hearings, took Reno and the FBI to task. McCollum faulted Reno for not speaking directly with FBI officials on the scene and with Koresh's lawyer; had those conversations occurred, he believed, they would have given her a more accurate picture of the events unfolding in the final days of the siege and might have revealed progress in the negotiations. He also criticized Reno for not appreciating "the nature of the people in the compound and their religious tenets and total subservience to Koresh." This knowledge, he believed, would have helped her to understand that the gas attack would not flush out the women and children. To the contrary, he argued, Reno might have seen that the women would hunker down, pray, and consider it "their destiny and perhaps their salvation to die there together." Despite the heavy criticism, Reno's willingness to accept full responsibility boosted her reputation. In October 1993 *Newsweek* called her "by far the most popular member of Clinton's cabinet, a near folk hero ever since she assumed responsibility for the Waco disaster."[102] Mainstream America, hungry for law, order, and morality and ravenous for a responsible figure in Washington, admired the new attorney general.

The surviving Branch Davidians—about forty remained after the fire—reacted differently to news of the fire. In a telephone interview from jail, Brad Branch told Cable News Network, "This is a systematic assassination by the FBI to eliminate all of the crime scene, now they're finishing off the job, destroying the crime scene." In the immediate aftermath Annetta Richards harbored doubts about whether Koresh actually perished in the flames. If he did, she expected his resurrection, partly because the events at Mount Carmel had proved that Koresh had hit the mark with his prophecies. "My faith in the word is more firm because I have seen prophesies David has taught us have been fulfilled," Richards told a newspaper reporter days after the fire.[103]

More than a month after the fire, others believed God and Koresh were planning a return to resume building an earthly kingdom. Janet McBean, a California-based Davidian, viewed Koresh's death as a sign from God. She expected to wait a short time and then be reunited with Koresh to resume their task.[104] Some Branch Davidians remained believers as long as a year after the fire. Renos Avraam, one of two Davidians convicted for aiding and abetting voluntary manslaughter, expected Koresh to return, putting skeptics to shame. At that point, Avraam believed, the world would see Koresh was no charlatan. In fact, he predicted Koresh's second coming would be a majestic, glorious event and that Koresh would "be like a ghost rider in the sky."[105] The raid, siege, and fire had the unexpected effect of strengthening some in their faith. To the most dedicated Branch Davidians, Koresh remained their leader.

Livingstone Fagan used his time in prison to write his version of the Mount Carmel tragedy, which he posted on the Internet. In addition to explaining Koresh's teachings on the seven seals, Fagan used the document to defend the

Branch Davidians and to attack the U.S. government's tactics in dealing with them. Fagan pointed to government breaches of the Davidians' First and Fourth Amendment rights. He claimed that the BATF "unlawfully challenged" the group's right to practice religion "under the guise of serving a search warrant." Fagan also wrote, "I don't believe it takes much intelligence to conclude that approximately 100 fully armed agents, 3 military styled helicopters, plus all that hardware that came against us, constitutes unreasonable search and seizure." Like Fagan, Jaime Castillo, also jailed for his role at Mount Carmel, used the Internet to post his reasons for following Koresh.[106]

Others associated with the Branch Davidians attacked the government's actions. Koresh's attorney, Dick DeGuerin, called the FBI's assault "senseless" and "aggressive." DeGuerin added, "I think that could have only been seen by those inside as the Apocalypse coming upon them." Biased as DeGuerin might have been, his reading of the situation probably best describes how the Branch Davidians interpreted the FBI's actions on April 19. As it happened, the raid may have been even more destructive than the body count and material destruction indicated. Four months after the fire federal officials confirmed that a computer disk had been retrieved from the rubble of Mount Carmel but refused to comment on its contents. Ruth Ottman, who escaped the April 19 inferno, claimed the disk contained Koresh's writings on the seven seals—the work that Koresh claimed in April he must complete as a condition for surrender and that the FBI doubted he was actually writing, contributing to its decision to mount the gas attack. In fact, the disk did contain Koresh's writings, which religious scholars have described as a coherent and organized commentary on biblical passages.[107] The disk and its contents appear to show that DeGuerin had good reason to trust Koresh to bring his people out of Mount Carmel, as he had indicated he would. The Branch Davidians who perished in the April 19 fire clearly played a large role in their own demise, but the government contributed to their actions by attacking Mount Carmel, thus initiating a chain of events that precluded Koresh from finishing these writings. What might have become important spiritual literature perished in the fire.

The Branch Davidian children who survived the fire found themselves under state care while their parents tried to satisfy officials that they were fit to them. State child-care officials said they were trying to walk a fine line between respecting the Davidians' religious beliefs and ensuring the children's safety. Davidian parents seeking to regain custody of their children had to satisfy state officials that they had "firm ties to reality." Sheila Martin, who lost her husband and three children in the fire, had to explain her emotionless reaction. Martin replied that she would see her family again on the day of resurrection. According to Jesse Guardiola, a supervisor for Texas Child Protective Services in Waco, Martin "modified [her answer] from waiting on the resurrection of David Koresh to how it is in the Bible." Guardiola further explained, "It is not our intent to judge their religious beliefs or values. But in looking at social norms, we have to decide, 'Are they with us or not?' If they are off on a philosophy at odds with social norms, it will be a concern for us."[108] In effect, Texas officials told surviving Davidian parents to modify their religious beliefs—to forsake their barbarian ways—and participate in the "social norm" or face losing custody of their children.

After the fire the *Waco Tribune-Herald* continued to vilify Koresh, depicting him in a biographical article as suffering a split personality. *Tribune-Herald* reporters concluded that Koresh led a "double life," sometimes as Vernon Howell, "eager-to-please small-town boy," sometimes as David Koresh, "calculating cult leader." The paper produced no such story about the federal agents who raided Mount Carmel; it did not portray them as churchgoing family men who earned a living donning bullet-proof vests and making heavily armed assaults on other humans to protect society. It did report, however, that before the February 28 raid at least one BATF agent prayed to God, asking protection for himself and his family.[109] This is not to say that societies do not need law-enforcement officials, or to preclude the possibility that those at Mount Carmel provided a needed service, but merely to point out that the media emphasized perceived incongruities in Koresh's life, the life of the "freak," while overlooking possible incongruities in the lives of "normal" BATF agents. A national news organization honored the *Tribune-Herald*'s "Sinful Messiah" series with an award for public service. In September 1993 the Associated Press Managing Editors, an association of news executives, honored Mark England and Darlene McCormick for their work on the series by giving them its annual public-service award for newspapers with a circulation of less than 50,000. At the heart of that series lay not just weapons allegations but also the Branch Davidians' social "abnormalities," particularly regarding family structure.[110] The Branch Davidians offended England's—and mainstream society's—sensibilities regarding family relationships. For fighting those evils, England and McCormick received one of their profession's highest honors. In this instance, evidence seems to indicate they did, in fact, ferret out a threat to society. But the episode raises important questions about the actions that the Constitution protects and the manner in which unconstitutional actions should be addressed. What if there had been no automatic weapons at Mount Carmel? What if allegations of child abuse and statutory rape had proved false?

In the months following the fire, Waco's mainstream spiritual leaders did their best to help their followers deal with the tragedy. Some organized an ecumenical prayer service for April 20 at Central Presbyterian Church in the hopes of helping community members begin dealing with the events. More than one hundred people attended the service, including Texas Governor Ann Richards, a Waco native. Others, like Norman Klein, rabbi of Waco's Temple Rodef Sholom, responded in print. Klein berated the news media because they "took Koresh's 'religious' ramblings seriously." He labeled Koresh a "cult leader," called the Branch Davidians "brainwashed," and defined "true religious leaders" as those who "empower their congregants and listeners to follow their own spiritual direction."[111]

In addition, the public now learned that BATF spokespeople had lied about elements of the agency's failed raid on February 28. In the week following the fire, previously sealed affidavits now made public indicated that raid organizers knew that Koresh and the Branch Davidians had been tipped off about the raid. In the days following the raid, however, BATF officials had staunchly denied that they knew the raid's secrecy and element of surprise had been compromised. On April 1, for example, the BATF's chief of intelligence told a CBS television reporter that the agency would not have proceeded with the raid had it known this. The Treasury Department fired two BATF agents, Phil Chojnacki and Charles Sarabyn, for proceeding with the raid. Chojnacki and Sarabyn had denied any awareness that the Branch Davidians knew the raid was coming, denials later shown to be lies. They also tried to conceal other misjudgments related to the raid. Oddly, the Treasury Department later reinstated both men, expunged their records, and awarded back pay and benefits for the time they were off duty.[112]

The government's next step in its response to the Branch Davidians came in early August when a federal grand jury handed down sweeping indictments for twelve surviving Davidians, charging them with murder, conspiracy to murder, and weapons violations. The August indictments replaced several others that had been filed between April and June.[113]

The government continued its use of overwhelming force in the trials of the Branch Davidians, according to one of the defense attorneys. Gary Coker, who defended Koresh in 1988 on an attempted murder charge stemming from the shootout with George Roden, called the 1994 Branch Davidian proceedings "a David and Goliath trial," with the government playing the role of Goliath. The government lent an unspecified number of BATF and FBI agents to the prosecutors to help prepare the case, according to the *Waco Tribune-Herald*. Coker characterized federal preparations as "almost embarrassing," charging that agents had gone so far as to check the defendants' credit histo-

ries. Most defense attorneys involved, he said, had taken the cases on a pro-
bono basis. "They're supposed to compete with hundreds of government investigators and several crime labs?" Coker asked rhetorically.[114]

The government based its case against the Branch Davidians on their
religious beliefs. Court records indicated that prosecutors would argue that
the group had spent years preparing for a showdown, which Koresh had
prophesied the government would win. After going to heaven, according to
the prosecutors' version of the prophecy, the Branch Davidians would return to earth to slaughter the unbelievers. The Baylor Law Professor Brian
Serr said that the government's case rested on Koresh's prophecy and his followers' complete belief in it.[115]

Attorneys associated with the defense viewed the trial as an assessment
of government actions. The nationally known attorney Gerry Spence, whom
defense lawyers had contacted for advice, said, "The theme in this case is
when the government is out of control, the people have to take control." Dick
DeGuerin, who had met with Koresh during the standoff and assembled the
defense team but who did not participate in the trial, agreed with Spence,
saying, "The real issue is the massive use of force to attack people in their
homes by the government."[116] DeGuerin further defended his client's actions, arguing that none of the activities at Mount Carmel constituted abuse.
Instead, he offered, the Branch Davidians lived a lifestyle outside accepted
norms. DeGuerin asked, "At what point does a society have a right to step in
and say you have to raise your family our way?" He continued: "It's apply-
ing Yuppie values to people who choose to live differently. These were lov-
ing families."[117]

After the six-week trial, Texas, the United States, and much of the world
waited in suspense for the jury's verdict. The jury acquitted eleven defendants
of the murder and conspiracy to murder charges. Kathryn Schroeder, the
twelfth indicted Branch Davidian, pleaded guilty to a lesser charge (forcibly
resisting federal officers) and testified against the remaining defendants. Because the Branch Davidians had scrambled to respond to the BATF raid, even
with forty-five minutes' warning, the jury did not believe the group had engaged in a conspiracy to kill federal officers. The jury, however, convicted five
Branch Davidians of voluntary manslaughter and two on weapons charges.
It further convicted six Davidians of using and carrying a firearm in relation
to the commission of a crime of violence, but U.S. District Court Judge Wal-
ter S. Smith Jr. set aside those convictions, dropping the weapons charge because it required a conviction on the conspiracy charge. That left four Branch
Davidians acquitted on all counts. Defense attorneys called the verdict a wake-

up call for law enforcement gone awry. Prosecutors claimed victory in obtaining the manslaughter convictions as justice for the slain officers.[118] But that would not end the Branch Davidians' journey through the legal system.

Prosecutors almost immediately asked Judge Smith to reinstate the charge he had thrown out. Eight days later Smith complied. At sentencing, despite a plea for leniency from the jury forewoman, Smith gave almost all the defendants the harshest sentences possible. Five Branch Davidians received forty-year sentences, thirty years for using or carrying a weapon during a violent crime and ten years for aiding and abetting voluntary manslaughter; three received fifteen-year sentences, ten years for aiding and abetting Koresh in the possession of machine guns and five years for conspiracy to manufacture and possess machine guns; and one received a five-year sentence on the weapons charge Smith had reinstated. One last defendant, who had plea bargained for a lighter sentence, received three years. The jury forewoman, who believed Smith had overlooked the jury's acquittal on the conspiracy charge because he often referred to the defendants as "co-conspirators," wept.[119]

What did the Branch Davidian tragedy mean to America? To editors at the *Waco Tribune-Herald,* it meant "major changes needed to be made in the way law enforcement agencies handle people who have beliefs outside of mainstream America." The editors feared that "Rambo-style assaults by law enforcement agencies" seriously hurt the government's credibility with law-abiding Americans. Officials further eroded public trust in the government by lying to cover their mistakes. The final important lesson taught by the Branch Davidian tragedy was "the need to keep law enforcement as local as possible." County and state agencies had opportunities to settle the conflicts at Mount Carmel well before they got out of hand but failed to seize them.

At the same time, national public-opinion polls conducted shortly after the fire showed "an overwhelming majority of Americans found no fault with the way law-enforcement authorities had brought the standoff to a head."[120] The *Waco Tribune-Herald* had previously dedicated itself to exposing the problems at Mount Carmel and portrayed Koresh with hostility and his followers as pitiable dupes; that it could later make the conclusions it did shows compassion. It also reveals the age-old western desire to keep the government, particularly the federal government, out of local affairs. The public-opinion poll reveals a great divide in America on fundamental issues: the right to practice religion freely, the right to bear arms, and the right to protection from unreasonable search and seizure. Just as millions lauded law-enforcement agents for their tough stand, millions of others criticized them for trampling basic rights.

To surviving Branch Davidians, the tragedy meant a substantial portion of their religious brethren had been wiped out while those who remained were depicted as freaks and murderers. When called to testify in congressional hearings, Clive Doyle, who escaped the fire at Mount Carmel, defended his colleagues, arguing they fired on agents in self-defense. Doyle also pointed out that all eleven Branch Davidians who went to trial had been acquitted of conspiracy and murder charges, yet President Clinton and others continued to refer to them as murderers. If the Branch Davidians were murderers, Doyle contended, then so were the federal agents who killed Branch Davidians.[121]

To Kiri Jewell, as she progressed through her teenage years, it meant reliving the horrors she had experienced at Koresh's hands. With the tragedy remaining a topic of debate, militia groups claimed that no proof existed that Koresh had sexually abused underage girls or planned an armed conflict with the U.S. government. Jewell, upset, decided to fight those opinions by retelling her story in graphic detail to Congress, which had convened hearings on the tragedy. Jewell testified that Koresh had sex with her in a motel room when she was ten years old. She also said Koresh taught that the group would fight, and lose, a battle with the federal government. Koresh called the government "Babylon," she said, and there was never a time when the Branch Davidians did not expect to be killed by "the Feds." Koresh and the Branch Davidians also spread word among themselves, including children such as Jewell, that if it became necessary to commit suicide during the battle with Babylon, the best method was "to put the gun in your mouth, back to the soft spot above your throat, before pulling the trigger." When people testifying before and after Jewell argued that the actions against Mount Carmel endangered the country's religious freedoms, Kiri's father, David Jewell, seethed, saying, "Koresh's religion was a disease."[122]

For people holding antigovernment views, the 1993 tragedy strengthened their convictions. Its most grotesquely dramatic aftershock was the major role it played in motivating Timothy McVeigh's bombing of the Alfred P. Murrah Federal Building in Oklahoma City. McVeigh, a former army sergeant and veteran of the Gulf War who held antigovernment views, reportedly grew furious over the events at Mount Carmel. He traveled to Waco to protest during the siege and was videotaped distributing bumper stickers that read, "Is Your Church ATF-Approved?" He detonated the Oklahoma City bomb on April 19, 1995, the second anniversary of the Mount Carmel fire.[123]

There can be no doubt that the BATF had reason to suspect illegal firearms activity at Mount Carmel. The BATF's response to that suspicion, however, raises serious questions, as does the FBI's handling of the standoff. Why did agents treat the Branch Davidians as they did? Did religion play a role? What lessons can this episode teach about liberty and faith in the West?

Disgruntled BATF agents suggested that the agency's culture led it to act as it did. Agent Sandra Hernandez, who had filed a sexual harassment complaint against the BATF, blamed a "John Wayne mentality" for the botched raid on Mount Carmel, although she did not participate in it. This echoes the characterization of the FBI as "cowboys" made by a confidante of Janet Reno's. Larry Stewart, the supervisor of the BATF Atlanta arson and bombing investigation squad and a lead plaintiff in a racial discrimination lawsuit filed by fifteen black agents, blamed inept management. Whatever the merits of the complaints by Hernandez and Stewart, they indicate turmoil within BATF and an agency culture that, if hostile to women and racial minorities, could easily have been hostile to a religious minority such as the Branch Davidians.[124] This also shows how the myths of the West, in this case that of cowboys, continued to operate in the minds of Americans.

As for the FBI, its tactical and negotiating arms worked at cross-purposes when dealing with the Branch Davidians. While the negotiators spent endless hours on the phone talking with Koresh and his lieutenants, the tactical forces grew impatient waiting for something—anything—to happen. Their efforts to intimidate the Branch Davidians undermined the negotiators' work. A sniper on the FBI's Hostage Rescue Team, Special Agent Christopher Whitcomb, left a detailed account that grants insight to at least one viewpoint. In his memoir *Cold Zero: Inside the FBI Hostage Rescue Team,* Whitcomb comments on the event from the perspective of a man who had Koresh in the crosshairs of a sight mounted on a high-powered rifle that he called "The Truth." Whitcomb and other government agents at the siege had devoted themselves to an occupation that is part profession, part cause. They were willing to sacrifice their lives to help people and to serve their country.

As the siege approached Easter, Whitcomb reflected on Easters past, times for family outings and celebrations of "the beauty of one man's remarkable sacrifice." Although that Easter in Waco might have meant little more for Whitcomb than another day on an undesirable assignment, he marked time's passing by noting a mainstream Christian holiday. He also viewed Koresh as someone who manipulated religion, describing him as "a salesman" and "a bullshit artist" comparable to "a time-share pimp, selling chunks of salvation." Whitcomb imagined Koresh luring prospective converts to a weekend at Ranch Apocalypse to hear his spiel and then convincing them to sign away their souls. On the night of April 18, the eve of the fateful engagement,

Whitcomb wrote of the members of his team, "Everyone climbed into their sleeping bags full of the anticipation children feel on Christmas Eve."[125] Whitcomb thus showed keen awareness of religion and how an enforcer of mainstream law and order conceived his mission outside Waco.

Both negotiators and tactical forces knew they faced people dominated by their religious beliefs, yet each FBI team downplayed those beliefs, probably because they differed radically from mainstream values and promoted activities regarded as barbaric, if not criminal, by most Americans. The political scientist Michael Barkun argued that the most damaging mistake made by government officials was not taking the Branch Davidians' religious beliefs seriously. Instead, they assumed the group to be deluded fanatics with no grasp of reality. In fact, Barkun contended, the Branch Davidians' religious beliefs were their reality. Those inside Mount Carmel could thus entertain no other reality, so that the two cultures, Branch Davidian and law-enforcement agents of mainstream U.S. society, ended up talking past each other. This state of affairs also strongly suggested the Branch Davidians would act according to their reality, which they would not negotiate. As the millennium drew near, Barkun predicted, more groups like the Branch Davidians would appear, and he warned that U.S. society should be prepared to deal with them.[126]

The historian Paul Boyer agrees. As the century came to an end, prophecy belief not only survived but continued to expand. Boyer contends that many people, alienated by a secular world that tells its history as "a mere recital of facts, signifying nothing," find comfort in a worldview in which all events are part of a unified stream leading to a definite destination—the end of the world and Jesus' return.[127] That desire presented nothing new in the West. Both Mormons and Ghost Dancers had viewed themselves as living lives and practicing ceremonies geared toward achieving salvation. Mormons found rich meaning in plural marriage and practicing the Word of Wisdom. Ghost Dancers likewise found purpose and spirituality in their ceremonies. As groups with similar beliefs emerge, they and the government, should it have to deal with them, should pay attention to what happened in 1993 near Waco.

Mainstream America, as represented by residents of Waco, closed ranks in condemning the Branch Davidians as freaks. According to media reports, most central Texans wished to avoid violence at Mount Carmel but supported the actions of law-enforcement officers as they sought to bring this marginal religious group to heel. Mainstream clergy and politicians joined forces in Waco to lead prayer vigils—presumably to a deity unsympathetic to the Branch Davidians' approach to theology—for a peaceful end to the confrontation outside town. Civic groups, businesses, and citizens showed their support for law enforcement by feeding officers and trying to make them feel at home during the long standoff.

Others, a presumably smaller albeit vocal group, objected to federal actions. These individualists, represented by Libertarians, militia types, and others, condemned what they viewed as a high-handed federal attack on fundamental liberties outlined in the Bill of Rights: free speech, freedom of religion, the right to bear arms, and the right to be free from unreasonable searches and seizures. They saw a government, represented largely by two law-enforcement agencies, acting with blatant disregard for bedrock American values. The government aggravated their criticisms by firing and then rehiring with back pay and benefits the two agents deemed responsible for the botched BATF raid that initiated the standoff.

A surviving Branch Davidian who lived near Mount Carmel in the years after the siege and sold answers to tourists' frequently asked questions about the group and the tragedy summarized the feelings of Branch Davidian sympathizers in the answer to "Question No. 32": "What Really Happened Here?" The answer suggests three related themes: "an end-time event" occurred, God provided a lesson on the "destruction of nations," and "the government ran amok and killed innocent people." Commenting in *The Nation,* David Corn concluded, "For nonbelievers, the choice is limited."[128]

Some saw in the Branch Davidian tragedy a microcosm of the mythic American West, which in turn represented the true America. In Texas, perhaps more western than any other state, they saw gun-toting religious radicals faced down by an even more heavily armed state in a conflict resolved in epic violence. It showed mainstream society, which cannot be labeled entirely secular, demarcating limits of religious tolerance. It exposed human frailties in the bureaucracy of justice. It fit the myth of the West and at the same time demonstrated its shortcomings.

Ultimately, the attack on April 19, however unintentionally, drove the Branch Davidians to kill themselves. They probably believed that the apocalyptic battle Koresh had promised for years had finally arrived and that they were on their way to the millennium. If so, perhaps the American West delivered on its promise. Even if they had not experienced unfettered freedom to practice their religion and bear arms, they had found their Promised Land. In a region that had swung from tolerating diversity in the form of non-Catholic settlers to blanket hostility to Indians and deadly outrage over an insult to Baptists, the Branch Davidians enjoyed years of peaceful coexistence capped by two months of crushing intolerance.

★

5   Uncle Sam's Land

Despotism may govern without faith, but liberty cannot. Religion is
much more necessary in the republic which they set forth in glowing
colors than in the monarchy which they attack; it is more needed in
democratic republics than in any others. How is it possible that society
should escape destruction if the moral tie is not strengthened in
proportion as the political tie is relaxed? And what can be done with a
people who are their own masters if they are not submissive to the
Deity?

—Alexis de Tocqueville, *Democracy in America*

ON MARCH 27, 1997, the world learned that thirty-nine members of a group
called Heaven's Gate had committed suicide in a million-dollar mansion in
Rancho Santa Fe, California. The group's founder, Marshall Herff Applewhite,
started to follow in the footsteps of his Presbyterian minister father, but ended
up abandoning his ministerial studies to study music. Applewhite taught
music and directed an Episcopal church choir in Houston in the early 1970s
before transforming into a "cult leader with beliefs in aliens and Armageddon." Those beliefs included the idea that a member of "the Kingdom of
Heaven (or what some might call two aliens from space)" took over his body
in the early 1970s. By the mid-1990s Applewhite and his followers were spreading their beliefs through lectures and on the Internet (the group supported
itself in part by designing Web sites).[1]

In 1995 the group began building a settlement on a forty-acre site near
Manzano, New Mexico, about sixty miles southeast of Albuquerque. So many
alternative groups holding bizarre beliefs lived in that area that many residents took Heaven's Gate to be normal in comparison. In April 1996, just ten
months after buying the property, the group sold it and went to California.
Before leaving, Heaven's Gate members tried to convince Jim Thorsen, the
site's current owner, to join them. Thorsen, active in New Mexico paramilitary groups, agreed with some of their ideas, particularly that "there was

great oppression coming against the religious people" of the United States and that there had been "a great falling away [presumably from true Christianity] and persecution." He disagreed, however, with certain tenets of the group's theology, particularly its conception of Jesus.[2]

In March 1997 the group interpreted the comet Hale-Bopp's blazing appearance in the heavens as the sign that a spaceship—trailing the comet—had come to rescue their souls from their earthly containers (bodies) and take them to "'Their World'—in the literal heavens." There, at the "next level," they would join the beings that had sent Jesus, whom they believed to have been an extraterrestrial also known as "the Captain." Heaven's Gate members believed evil humans killed the Captain before he could teach others how to enter the Kingdom of God. Humans then corrupted his teachings into a "watered-down Country Club religion." When Hale-Bopp appeared, Heaven's Gate members, dressed alike in androgynous black clothes and wearing buzz haircuts, voluntarily and in an orderly manner ingested a mix of phenobarbital and alcohol, slipped plastic bags over their heads, and died. They apparently hoped to free their souls to join the spaceship, which would take them to the kingdom of God.[3]

Religious groups such as Heaven's Gate, whose practices conflict with mainstream American beliefs, continue to find a home in the American West, which still boasts open spaces and a population of liberty-loving individualists. Mostly, everyone gets along well enough, but the three glaring and tragic exceptions discussed here reveal a cultural battleground where three powerful forces—the mythic West, religious belief, and the federal government—have mixed with volatile and deadly results. Nineteenth-century Mormonism, the Lakota Ghost Dance, and David Koresh's Branch Davidianism stretched the limits of mainstream America's tolerance to the breaking point and in so doing offer insights into religion's role in the history of the American West and the region's relationship to the rest of the country.

For Mormons, the West had multiple meanings. Moving west in search of a suitable environment for their unique vision dominated their nineteenth-century history. Joseph Smith and his followers encountered extreme and religiously based opposition from mainstream society that drove them ever westward in search of religious freedom and a site for their Zion. The Saints who followed Brigham Young discovered that sought-after space outside the United States but soon found themselves back within U.S. political boundaries. Their subsequent relations with the federal government reinforced a theme long acknowledged in western history: the crucial role that the government has played in the West.

The Saints took advantage of the West's environment to begin building the kingdom of God on earth, or their version of the Puritans' city on a hill, but that quickly put them at odds with the rest of the nation. Their numerical strength and distance from U.S. power allowed them to gain strength enough to challenge federal supremacy in the West, at least temporarily. But their theocratic system, practice of plural marriage, and ability and willingness to harass and maybe even stop overland traffic to the West Coast, among other things, threatened the nation's republican values, which carried their own religious freight. As the government sought to incorporate the West into the nation, it not only established political and economic institutions in the region but also introduced and reinforced cultural institutions there. The United States could not tolerate the threat of complete Mormon independence in the West, and its response to events in Utah during the 1850s might be considered a preview to the Civil War. The Utah Expedition and the massacre at Mountain Meadows might be seen as products of political and economic differences, but even those carried religious connotations, obviously on the Mormon side and more subtly on the U.S. side. For the rest of the nineteenth century, the Radical Republican spirit of reconstruction touched the West as it did the South, as is demonstrated by the decades-long crusade to ensure that Utah Territory adopted a traditional, monogamous family structure before it was granted statehood. Just as the Civil War's victors sought to remake southern society, they sought to remake western society in a protracted campaign against the "twin relics of barbarism." In this less violent culture war waged through the legal system, religion again motivated both sides. In *Reynolds v. United States,* the Edmunds Act, and especially the Edmunds-Tucker Act, one can find a church-state link buttressing a social order based on a New Testament model of marriage and opposing marriage based on other religious beliefs.[4]

For the Saints, the West held the opportunity to create their kingdom of God on earth, and for a while they achieved it in all its glory. By the time of statehood, however, interaction with the federal government had changed Mormonism and Mormon Utah. Utah remains to this day a stronghold for the Saints, described by Sydney E. Ahlstrom as "an American subculture," but the Saints achieved acceptance only after making their behavior conform to the dictates of mainstream culture as purveyed by the federal government.[5] That is, they had to abandon "barbaric" polygamy and become "civilized."

But this story of religion in the West does not end in 1890 with the Woodruff Manifesto or in 1896 with Utah's admission to the union under a state constitution banning plural marriage. The story has continued through the twentieth and into the twenty-first century. In 2004, as the nation debated same-sex marriage at home and dealt with extremist Islam at home and abroad, a new chapter in the tale of Mormonism and polygamy in the West was being written in Texas. When the LDS church renounced plural marriage in 1890, not all members accepted the change. Communities of polygamists continued to exist, notably on the Utah-Arizona border. The Fundamentalist Church of Jesus Christ of Latter-day Saints, based in the twin cities of Hilldale, Utah, and Colorado City, Arizona, constituted about 80 percent of those towns' populations. A church trust owned most of the land, and church members dominated all levels of local government and ran most of the businesses. At least some members consider the group's spiritual leader, Warren Jeffs, to be a prophet and God's representative on earth who arranges marriages based on revelation. According to reports, members believe that men must have at least three wives to achieve the greatest reward in heaven.

As had been the case for nineteenth-century Mormons and twentieth-century Branch Davidians, former group members leveled shocking allegations against the group and its leader. Allegations against Jeffs included charges of forcing young girls into marriages, child abuse, and homosexual rape. As these allegations were stirring concern and scrutiny in Arizona and Utah, one of Jeffs's associates bought a 1,600-acre ranch outside Eldorado, the seat of Schleicher County, Texas. Church officials said the property would be used as a hunting retreat, but after aerial photographs revealed substantial construction, it became clear the group had bigger plans. By August 2004 the property housed a cement plant, three three-story log cabins, two dormitory-style buildings, a meeting hall, a barn, a communal garden the size of a football field, and a network of roads. In addition to being concerned about plural marriage and losing control of local government, some neighboring Eldoradans feared a second coming of David Koresh. An Eldoradan named Thelma Bosmans told a reporter, "I don't think they're here to be our friends, and I wouldn't trust them as far as I could throw them." Bosmans also suggested that some of her neighbors interpreted the polygamists' arrival as a sign from God: "Most of the people I talk to are like, 'We believe in God, and we believe that God has sent them here for a reason: to wake us up from our apathy or to vote and be more alert,' or something like that."[6]

Whatever faults Eldoradans perceived in their new neighbors, some granted them at least grudging respect for their industry and efficiency. The Texas attorney general contacted Utah state officials to discuss allegations against the group but planned no action unless contacted by local officials. For the time being an uneasy coexistence settled on Schleicher County, and a western pattern seemed to be repeating itself. As a reporter for the *Dallas Morning News* put it, "The people of Eldorado struggle with whether their beliefs in independence and freedom from government persecution are more important than their religious convictions."[7]

Reaching conclusions about what the West meant to Lakota Ghost Dancers presents a more difficult problem, for what could "the West" have meant to them? They certainly did not understand the West in the same way as U.S. citizens and immigrants from abroad. To Ghost Dancers their home occupied the center of their universe, not the West of anything. The Ghost Dance came to them from the west, but that is incidental. Nonetheless, they occupied the West of America's imagination. In this conception, the West represented an area of opportunity for the United States, which after the Civil War bent itself on spreading its Christian civilization to its western territories, remaking the West in the image of the United States that had finally emerged from the East.

In 1890, with the Mormon conflict in the Great Basin nearing conclusion, the United States clashed with a new threat to its cultural hegemony, a flare-up of tribalism in the form of the Ghost Dance. Civilization programs dominated U.S. Indian policy during the late nineteenth century. The U.S. government tried to work changes on American Indian societies much as had it tried to change Mormon society, but on a grander scale. Mainstream Americans did not want the Indians to modify their beliefs and practices; they wanted wholesale abandonment. The government and its agents adopted a variety of coercive measures to effect this change. The people who drafted U.S. Indian policy were generally of the same stripe as those who drafted U.S. Mormon policy. On top of that, however, American Indians faced a more aggressive Americanizing mission because the government often delegated Indian affairs to Christian denominations competing for Indian converts. As the government tried to forge an American West, the Ghost Dance movement challenged the American mission. To be sure, one must consider concerns about law and order on and near the Lakota reservations, but the army's massacre of the Lakota Ghost Dancers vividly illustrated to native peoples that they should be very careful negotiating their coexistence with the United States.

In a sense, the Branch Davidians, too, emerged from the West, although the movement's founders traveled east from California to establish Mount Carmel in Texas. Like the Mormons, the Branch Davidians sought to isolate themselves from meddling neighbors to establish what they believed was a righteous religious community preparing for the millennium. They found the physical and social space to do so in Texas, a state with a mythology of rugged individualism capable of rivaling the entire region's. Strong grassroots support for property rights and the right to bear arms reinforced the myth.

As had Mormons, the Branch Davidians found a temporary refuge in the

West. From Mount Carmel's founding in 1935 until 1993, the group experienced the West as Ferenc Szasz described it, a haven for individualists. Texans seemed willing to tolerate eccentrics. Even in the aftermath of the BATF raid, a number of Waco-area residents sympathized publicly with the way the Branch Davidians responded to the raid—by defending their property against an intruder. That the intruder appeared in the form of the U.S. government and challenged individual rights to own weapons and to be secure in one's property contributed to their sympathy. These Texans found little concern in the allegations of a weapons stockpile, child abuse, or reordered marriage practices. As long as the Branch Davidians remained on their property and did not bother the neighbors, these Texans believed the group should be left alone.

When things changed in 1993, the Branch Davidians occupied the nation's attention because of a fluke, an investigation stemming from a poorly packaged hand grenade. The nation had not been wrestling with the Branch Davidian question, as it had been during the nineteenth century with the Mormon question and the Indian question. The government had not pursued Branch Davidian policy. But when the group's activities and beliefs came to light, the U.S. government stepped in to enforce the laws and to protect mainstream values. Overly aggressive methods and bad luck combined to bring death and destruction. In an evaluation of the relationship between the Branch Davidians and the outside world, the situation's considerable religious underpinnings quickly present themselves. Despite the significant difference in time, the rhetoric surrounding the Branch Davidian tragedy sounded remarkably similar to that of the other episodes considered here. Apparently the majority of central Texans quickly united in support of federal agents and mainstream values. The myth of the West remains strong there, but most Texans easily and quickly sided with law, order, and morality as represented by federal agents. The Branch Davidians inside Mount Carmel found themselves under attack not only for their alleged illegal activities but also for their religious beliefs. As had been the case for Mormons and Ghost Dancers, activities and religious beliefs went hand in hand.

The contradiction inherent within the West as a place—a home—for liberty and freedom was exposed by the pressures of religious exceptionalism. Within certain bounds, exceptional religion and religious diversity flourish in the United States. In his massive history of American religion, Sydney Ahlstrom writes, "The sheer multifariousness of the American religious heritage is the central problem of any historian who would undertake the general synoptic task." But the overwhelming majority of that diversity arose because the United States has been home to "virtually every surviving heresy and schism in Christian history." The key to understanding American religious history, according to Ahlstrom, lies in recognizing "the degree to which American civilization is a New World extension of Christendom." Catherine L. Albanese, another historian of religion, also acknowledges "the overall Protestant character of the United States." With these conclusions both scholars echo the observation recorded in the 1830s by Alexis de Tocqueville: "There is no country in the world where the Christian religion retains a greater influence over the souls of men than in America."[8] While the United States enjoys a degree of religious diversity, that diversity occurs mostly within a narrow spectrum of religious possibilities. Groups falling outside that spectrum and occupying the realm of religious exceptionalism can expect conflict with the mainstream. Nineteenth-century Mormons, Ghost Dancers, and twentieth-century Branch Davidians experienced that phenomenon with explosive force.

Mormons, Ghost Dancers, and Branch Davidians shared a number of religious beliefs that stretched mainstream tolerance to the breaking point. For example, they believed that Christianity had suffered a great apostasy, a falling away from true religion. Mormons believe that the true Christian church perished shortly after Jesus Christ died, only to be reestablished by Joseph Smith. Ghost Dancers worried they had lost favor with supernatural forces and began the Ghost Dance in an attempt to regain it. Branch Davidians believed humanity had strayed and that the only road to salvation lay in David Koresh's interpretation of the seven seals, which would usher them, alone, into heaven. In the cases of the Mormons and the Branch Davidians, this dim view of other Christians contributed to the groups' tendencies to isolate themselves from "unbelievers." As for the Ghost Dancers, Lakota society lent itself to Ghost Dancers' congregating separately from nonbelievers.

All three groups believe or believed in ongoing, direct revelation, whether the recipient be the president of the Mormon Church, Ghost Dancers, or David Koresh. Furthermore, in the two biblically based groups, Mormons and Branch Davidians, the prophet took precedence over the Bible. Where the prophet's word conflicted with written scripture, the prophet prevailed. This created potential conflict between divine order and law, republicanism, and social mores. Many Americans hold a belief, bordering on sacred, that individuals can be trusted to make responsible, informed, and independent decisions. Brigham Young and the Mormons, Lakota Ghost Dance leaders and their followers, and David Koresh and the Branch Davidians subverted that faith and threatened mainstream values. The leaders of each group claimed to speak for a higher authority in one form or another and enjoyed a loyalty from their followers that superseded loyalty to the United States. If God directs actions contrary to human rule, how should the believers behave? How much deviance from human rule can earthly authorities tolerate? The exceptional religious groups discussed here pushed the U.S. government's tolerance to its limits.

To one degree or another, each group perceived the U.S. government as its enemy. Both Mormons and Branch Davidians sometimes referred to Washington as Babylon. Despite Mormon pleas for protection from their persecutors in Missouri, the federal government averted its eyes as Missourians harassed, killed, and threatened to exterminate the Latter-day Saints. Once the Saints established their kingdom of God on earth in the Great Basin, beyond the reach of state and local governments that had proven hostile, Washington bureaucrats and their appointees resumed what Mormons would have perceived as harassment. Ghost Dancers, a subculture of Lakota society, viewed the U.S. government and whites as enemies, if not as sources of evil, the eradication of which would dramatically improve life for Lakotas and other Native Americans. David Koresh taught his followers that the U.S. government would engage the Branch Davidians in an apocalyptic battle, ultimately killing many Branch Davidians but at the same time setting in motion events leading to their salvation. As each group conflicted with the government from its residence in the West, it perceived the government as limiting its hopes for building a divine kingdom or sacred place in the West, the mythic land of cultural and religious freedoms.

Each group also believed in and practiced, to varying degrees, plural marriage. Nineteenth-century Mormon prophets told their people that God directed it. The practice would speed the journey of souls through their earthly phase and into the afterlife. The Ghost Dance belief said little, if anything, about plural marriage, but Lakota society practiced it as something of a welfare tool. In a society where husbands and fathers might easily perish while hunting or waging war, widows or orphans could marry an able-bodied man even if he already had a wife. At Mount Carmel David Koresh told his followers that all women in the group belonged to him, regardless of their marital status when they joined the Branch Davidians. Koresh fathered children with a number of the women, children who were to help him rule after Armageddon. These marriage relations did not fit the rule of mainstream America, and neither did the family arrangements. Marriage typically involves a sacred obligation and a civil contract regulated by law and is an institution widely believed to be the foundation on which society is built. In his *Reynolds v. United States* opinion, Chief Justice Morrison R. Waite acknowledged this and cited Francis Lieber, a Columbia University professor, who argued that polygamy leads to despotism and is incompatible with civilization and republican government. Groups practicing alternative marriage forms in the East, such as the Kingdom of Matthias and the Oneidans, faced censure from their mainstream neighbors, who ultimately forced the groups back into mainstream practices. In the West, especially the sparsely settled, remote nineteenth-century West, the federal government assumed that task. Worries about the foundations of civilization did not drive the government's relationship with the Branch Davidians in the twentieth-century West, but concerns about domestic relations, including marriage, contributed to its actions.[9]

The media played a remarkably similar role in all three cases, acting as watchdogs for mainstream values. They vilified each group, stirring mainstream sentiment against the "deviants" or "barbarians." Newspapers made much of Mormon polygamy, perhaps to titillate or shock readers in the East. Some even-handed treatments appeared, as in the case of the anonymous correspondent "Utah," but newspapers generally emphasized those Mormon practices found shocking by the mainstream. Ghost Dancers received similar coverage in an era of sensational journalism. Newspaper reports focused on the "false messiah" and capitalized on the fear of an Indian outbreak in the West. The Branch Davidians felt similar effects from the media spotlight, which shined most intensely on Koresh's reordering of marriage and allegations of illegal sexual practices and child abuse. In all three cases, the media judged the groups by Judeo-Christian standards and championed the tenets of Judeo-Christian civilization. Although that particular phrasing did not appear in reportage of the Branch Davidian tragedy, many articles implicitly stated as much, and other pieces, most notably those contributed to the *Waco Tribune-Herald* by local clergy members, explicitly did so.

The mainstream perceived each group as a body of weak-minded, superstitious sheep following a devious leader who exercised mind control over his flock. By the late twentieth century mainstream society had a well-developed mental-health profession that could marshal scientific evidence to assess David Koresh's state of mind. This development raises an interesting question: how might the treatment of Mormons and Ghost Dancers have differed had they paraded into history in the late twentieth century instead of the mid-nineteenth? Or conversely, how might Koresh and the Branch Davidians have been received had they existed in the nineteenth century rather than the late twentieth? Given the record of newspapers and government officials labeling Brigham Young and Ghost Dance leaders as charlatans and liars, Koresh probably would have received a similar label. All three groups would testify that religious freedom in the United States has limits, the testing of which can be perilous.

Finally, the federal government's use of force deserves consideration. Each episode shows how the government or its representatives can run amok even when pursuing legitimate ends. Those wielding federal force, particularly in the nineteenth century, inherited from Congregationalists, Presbyterians, and Baptists a vision of the United States as a Christian republic created in preparation for the millennium. That worldview sanctioned church-state collaboration in spreading liberty, just government, and pure Christianity as embodied in American churches. President James Buchanan certainly had the power to appoint a new governor and territorial officials for Utah. Nonetheless, his decision to use a significant portion of the U.S. Army to achieve that end, doing so while Congress was in recess and without giving notice to the people or officials of Utah, raises questions about the propriety of his methods. The heavy-handed response to the Ghost Dance reflects similar impropriety and the power wielded by panicky Indian agents and army officers wishing to rid themselves of a nemesis—and an obstacle to civilization—in the person of Sitting Bull. Even worse, the indiscriminate slaughter of Big Foot's band of Ghost Dancers shows the danger of poorly disciplined or misguided federal agents, especially those bearing arms. In twentieth-century Texas that scenario repeated itself in the Branch Davidian tragedy. The BATF had good reason to investigate the weapons activities of the Branch Davidians, but the manner in which it did so led to unnecessary and tragic bloodshed. The FBI's tactics produced worse results. Using armored vehicles to break down doors and punch through walls to insert tear gas would appear threatening under any circumstances, let alone to an insular group that for years had been conditioned to expect a deadly, apocalyptic battle with federal law-enforcement agents. No evidence suggests the government intended to kill Ghost Dancers or Branch Davidians, but the highly charged atmosphere surrounding those situations contributed to avoidable tragedies. Granting that each incident provided the federal government with legitimate, legal grounds to act against these groups, completely understanding the conflicts must originate in understanding religious differences.

When religious practice strayed too far from mainstream values, even in the West, with its mythic sympathy for individualism, the federal government forcefully imposed mainstream values. When President Buchanan sent the army to Utah Territory in 1857, he argued that the force was necessary to install federal officials. With federal authority restored and the Civil War re-solved, the government turned its attention to imposing mainstream family structures on the Saints. The issues that brought federal force to Utah can-not be understood apart from the tenets of the Church of Jesus Christ of Latter-day Saints that conflicted with the Judeo-Christian values of main-stream America. When Ghost Dance hysteria swept Lakota country in 1890, the army moved to protect white property and federal authority on Indian reservations. The "excitement" among Lakotas that prompted federal action cannot be understood apart from the Ghost Dance tenets that promised Lako-tas a better life and threatened white Americans and their vision of a West built on a Judeo-Christian foundation. Finally, the weapons activity that brought federal attention and violence to the Branch Davidians cannot be un-derstood apart from the religious beliefs taught by David Koresh, who re-ordered family structure and prepared his followers for an apocalyptic bat-tle with the government. The Branch Davidians, too, threatened law, order, and mainstream Judeo-Christian values.

In each case local authorities either lacked the resources to establish order or simply did not exist. In the Great Basin, authority took the form of the Nauvoo Legion until the army arrived to assert federal dominance. In the sparsely settled regions of western Nebraska and the Dakotas bordering Lakota country, local and state agencies could hardly have acted effectively against the feared large-scale Lakota insurgency. In rural Texas, local law-enforcement agencies lacked the personnel and weaponry to face down the Branch Davidians, if the allegations against them proved true. In Utah Ter-ritory, Lakota country, and rural Texas, then, the federal government en-forced U.S. law and culture, ensuring an American West.

The Heaven's Gate suicides and the anecdotes about their "alternative" neighbors in New Mexico show that exceptional religious—and other—groups continue to inhabit the West and will continue to shock mainstream Amer-ica. Perhaps an understanding of lessons such as those discussed here can help avoid future death and destruction. Mormons, Ghost Dancers, and Branch Davidians hoped to attain their millennial vision in the West but experienced a cultural collision with the "messianic nationalism" of the U.S. government expanding its boundaries and defending the republic and its values. If other groups collide with mainstream values to the threat of nonmembers, the gov-ernment should exercise its duty to protect citizens. In such a case, however, it is to be hoped that future "barbarians" perceived as threatening America's garden will receive a more civilized response than their predecessors received. Did religion make a difference in the West? Indeed it did—and does.

★

NOTES

Introduction

1. Frederick Jackson Turner, "The Significance of the Frontier in American History," in Turner, *The Frontier in American History* (New York: Holt, Rinehart and Winston, 1947; repr., Tucson: University of Arizona Press, 1986), 1–38.

2. Henry Nash Smith, *Virgin Land: The American West as Symbol and Myth* (Cambridge, Mass.: Harvard University Press, 1950), 4, 12. Robert G. Athearn argues that the myth endured, with modifications, into the twentieth century in *The Mythic West in Twentieth-Century America* (Lawrence: University Press of Kansas, 1986). See also the works by Richard Slotkin: *Regeneration through Violence: The Mythology of the American Frontier, 1600–1860* (Middletown, Conn.: Wesleyan University Press, 1973); *The Fatal Environment: The Myth of the Frontier in the Age of Industrialization, 1800–1890* (New York: Atheneum, 1985); and *Gunfighter Nation: The Myth of the Frontier in Twentieth-Century America* (New York: Maxwell Macmillan International, 1992).

3. Robert V. Hine, *The American West: An Interpretive History,* 2d ed. (New York: HarperCollins, 1984), 284–99.

4. Edwin Scott Gaustad, *Dissent in American Religion* (Chicago: University of Chicago Press, 1973), 5, 8–40.

5. See Patricia Nelson Limerick, *The Legacy of Conquest: The Unbroken History of the American West* (New York: Norton, 1987); Richard White, *"It's Your Misfortune and None of My Own": A New History of the American West* (Norman: University of Oklahoma Press, 1991).

6. Donald Worster, *Rivers of Empire: Water, Aridity, and the Growth of the American West* (New York: Oxford University Press, 1985), 4, 37, 50–52, 129–31.

7. Gerald D. Nash, *The American West Transformed: The Impact of the Second World War* (Bloomington: Indiana University Press, 1985), 3–14, 201–16; idem, *World War II and the West: Reshaping the Economy* (Lincoln: University of Nebraska Press, 1990), 1–17, 218–26.

8. White, *"It's Your Misfortune,"* 57–59 (quotation, 58).

9. William Deverell, "Fighting Words: The Significance of the American West in the History of the United States," *Western Historical Quarterly* 25 (Summer 1994): 187.

10. Ibid., 194.

11. Ibid., 197.

12. Timothy Dwight, *Greenfield Hill: A Poem* (New York, 1794), qtd. in Smith, *Virgin Land,* 10.

13. Ibid., 62.

14. U.S. Senate, *Congressional Globe,* 30th Cong., 1st sess., 7 February 1849 (Washington, D.C.: Blair and Rives, 1849), 473; Smith, *Virgin Land,* 27–28 (Benton material).

15. Clayton D. Laurie, "Filling the Breach: Military Aid to the Civil Power in the Trans-Mississippi West," *Western Historical Quarterly* 25 (Summer 1994): 149, 162.

16. David M. Emmons, "Constructed Province: History and the Making of the Last American West," *Western Historical Quarterly* 25 (Winter 1994): 442–43; Buchanan qtd. in Paul C. Nagle, *This Sacred Trust: American Nationality, 1798–1898* (New York: Oxford University Press, 1971), 147–48.

17. Emmons, "Constructed Province," 444–46, 450.

18. Whitman qtd. in Smith, *Virgin Land,* 124; Emmons, "Constructed Province," 451. For related material on myths of the West, see Leo Marx, *The Machine in the Garden: Technology and the Pastoral Ideal in America* (New York: Oxford University Press, 1964); Charles L. Sanford, *The Quest for Paradise: Europe and the American Moral Imagination* (Urbana: University of Illinois Press, 1961).

19. Darlis A. Miller, *Captain Jack Crawford: Buckskin Poet, Scout, and Showman* (Albuquerque: University of New Mexico Press, 1993), 259; Laurence M. Hauptman, "Mythologizing Westward Expansion: Schoolbooks and the Image of the American Frontier before Turner," *Western Historical Quarterly* 8 (July 1977): 271.

20. Martin E. Marty, *Righteous Empire: The Protestant Experience in America* (New York: Dial, 1970), 23, 48, 89.

21. Hauptman, "Mythologizing," 269–71 (quotation, 271).

22. Ibid., 272–82.

23. Sarah Barringer Gordon, *The Mormon Question: Polygamy and Constitutional Conflict in Nineteenth Century America* (Chapel Hill: University of North Carolina Press, 2002), 1–15; White, *"It's Your Misfortune,"* 103, 109–11; Gaustad, *Dissent,* 85–100.

24. Jon Butler, "Jack-in-the-Box Faith: The Religion Problem in Modern American History," *Journal of American History* 90 (Mar. 2004): 1358–60.

25. Ibid., 1362, 1370–71, 1378; Darren Barbee, "Faith Moving to Center Stage," *Fort Worth (Tx.) Star-Telegram,* 10 August 2004.

26. Carl Guarneri and David Alvarez, eds., *Religion and Society in the American West: Historical Essays* (New York: University Press of America, 1987), xii, xiv; Ferenc M. Szasz and Margaret Connell Szasz, "Religion and Spirituality," in *The Oxford History of the American West,* ed. Clyde A. Milner II, Carol A. O'Connor, and Martha Sandweiss, 359–91 (New York: Oxford University Press, 1994), 360; Ferenc Morton Szasz, *Religion in the Modern American West* (Tucson: University of Arizona Press, 2000), xv–xvi.

27. Hine, *The American West,* 244–45, 252–53.
28. Gaustad, *Dissent,* 100.

Chapter 1: God's Country

1. Patricia Nelson Limerick, *Something in the Soil: Legacies and Reckonings in the New West* (New York: Norton, 2000), 18–22.

2. J. Frederick Fausz, "Opechancanough: Indian Resistance Leader," in *Struggle and Survival in Colonial America,* ed. David G. Sweet and Gary B. Nash, 21–37 (Berkeley: University of California Press, 1981), 30–35.

3. See Andrew L. Knaut, *The Pueblo Revolt of 1680: Conquest and Resistance in Seventeenth-Century New Mexico* (Norman: University of Oklahoma Press, 1995).

4. Howard H. Peckham, *Pontiac and the Indian Uprising,* 2d ed. (New York: Russell and Russell, 1961), 98–101.

5. R. David Edmunds, *Tecumseh and the Quest for Indian Leadership* (Boston: Little, Brown, 1984), 75–86, 108–13, 120, 154–60. See also R. David Edmunds, *The Shawnee Prophet* (Lincoln: University of Nebraska Press, 1983).

6. Oliver Knight, *Following the Indian Wars: The Story of the Newspaper Correspondents among the Indian Campaigners* (Norman: University of Oklahoma Press, 1960), 305–6. See also U.S. House of Representatives, *Report of the Secretary of War,* 47th Cong., 1st sess., 1881, ex. doc. 1, pt. 2, serial 2010, 4 vols. (Washington, D.C.: GPO, 1881), 1:139–43, 153–55. Nokay Delklinne also appears in records as "Nickay Delklinne" and "Nocky-del-lin-ne."

7. Gary B. Nash, *Red, White, and Black: The Peoples of Early North America,* 3d ed. (Englewood Cliffs, N.J.: Prentice Hall, 1992), 66–73.

8. Leonard W. Levy, *Jefferson and Civil Liberties: The Darker Side* (Cambridge, Mass.: Harvard University Press, 1963), 3–24.

9. Thomas Jefferson, "An Act for Establishing Religious Freedom, 1786," in Jefferson, *Notes on the State of Virginia,* ed. William Peden, 223–25 (Chapel Hill: University of North Carolina Press, 1955), 224.

10. Levy, *Jefferson,* 3–24.

11. Ibid., 128.

12. Ruth H. Bloch, *Visionary Republic: Millennial Themes in American Thought, 1756–1800* (New York: Cambridge University Press, 1985), xii–xvi.

13. Nathan O. Hatch, *The Sacred Cause of Liberty: Republican Thought and the Millennium in Revolutionary New England* (New Haven, Conn.: Yale University Press, 1977), 16–19.

14. Ibid., 141, 156, 170–73.

15. James Madison, "Memorial and Remonstrance against Religious Assessments," in Madison, *The Writings of James Madison: Comprising His Public Papers and His Private Correspondence, Including Numerous Letters and Documents Now for the First Time Printed,* ed. Gaillard Hunt, 9 vols. (New York: Putnam's, 1901), 2:184–85, 189.

16. Nathan O. Hatch, *The Democratization of American Christianity* (New Haven, Conn.: Yale University Press, 1989), 3, 5, 9–11. Hatch describes the Mormons' organizational structure as a "virtual religious dictatorship."

17. Donald G. Matthews, "The Second Great Awakening as an Organizing Process, 1780–1830: An Hypothesis," *American Quarterly* 21 (Spring 1969): 27; Martin E. Marty, *Righteous Empire: The Protestant Experience in America* (New York: Dial, 1970), 93.

18. Matthews, "Second Great Awakening," 29, 33, 39–40. See also Warren Sweet, *Religion in the Development of American Culture, 1765–1840* (New York: Scribner's, 1952); idem, *Revivalism in America: Its Origin, Growth, and Decline* (New York: Scribner's, 1944); T. Scott Miyakawa, *Protestants and Pioneers: Individualism and Conformity on the American Frontier* (Chicago: University of Chicago Press, 1964); Marty, *Righteous Empire*, 121–24, 181–82. None of these authors recognizes efforts to effect religious change among Native Americans.

19. Paul E. Johnson and Sean Wilentz, *The Kingdom of Matthias* (New York: Oxford University Press, 1994), 105. Johnson and Wilentz provide a thorough overview of the Kingdom of Matthias. As they had done with Matthias, several eastern communities bounced John Humphrey Noyes, founder of the Oneida Community, out of their jurisdictions. They applied various legal and social inducements (perhaps *coercion* would be a better term) until, in the late 1840s, Noyes and his followers fled to land once part of the Oneida Indian Reservation. This land had reverted to New York and was then offered on easy terms to white settlers. The community itself survived only until 1880, but some of its businesses still function today. For an eminently readable survey of Oneida and John Humphrey Noyes's life and teachings, see Spencer Klaw, *Without Sin: The Life and Death of the Oneida Community* (New York: Penguin, 1994).

20. Johnson and Wilentz, *Kingdom of Matthias*, 172–73, 177.

21. John P. Marschall, "Jews in Nevada, 1850–1900," *Journal of the West* 23 (Jan. 1984): 62–72; Don W. Wilson, "Pioneer Jews in California and Arizona, 1849–1875," *Journal of the West* 6 (Apr. 1967): 226–36; Robert E. Levinson, "American Jews in the West," *Western Historical Quarterly* 5 (July 1974): 235–94. These generalizations receive support also in Moses Rischin and John Livingston, eds., *Jews of the American West* (Detroit: Wayne State University Press, 1991), and seem to apply to Jews who settled on the Great Plains, as discussed in Hal Rothman, "Same Horse, New Wagon: Tradition and Assimilation among the Jews of Wichita, 1865–1930," *Great Plains Quarterly* 15 (Spring 1995): 83–104. See also William Toll, "Judaism as a Civic Religion in the American West," in *Religion and Society in the American West: Historical Essays,* ed. Carl Guarneri and David Alvarez, 197–220 (New York: University Press of America, 1987).

22. Moses Rischin, "The Jewish Experience in America: A View from the West," in *Jews of the American West,* ed. Rischin and Livingston, 26–47 (36); Fred Rosenbaum, "Zionism versus Anti-Zionism: The State of Israel Comes to San Francisco," in *Jews of the American West,* ed. Rischin and Livingston, 119–35; and Earl Pomeroy, "On Becoming a Westerner," in *Jews of the American West,* ed. Rischin and Livingston, 194–212.

23. Robert A. Goldberg, "Zion in Utah," in *Jews of the American West,* ed. Rischin and Livingston, 69–87. Likewise, Jewish farmers in North Dakota tended not to fare well on the land and often remained only long enough to prove up their homestead claims before selling their farms to earn capital to pursue more traditionally Jewish occupations in towns (Janet E. Schulte, "'Proving Up and Moving Up': Jewish Homesteading Activity in North Dakota," *Great Plains Quarterly* 10 [Fall 1990]: 228–44).

24. Robert V. Hine, *California's Utopian Colonies* (New Haven, Conn.: Yale University Press, 1966), 12–32.

25. Ibid., 33–54.

26. Ferenc M. Szasz and Margaret Connell Szasz, "Religion and Spirituality," in *The Oxford History of the American West,* ed. Clyde A. Milner II, Carol A. O'Connor, and Martha Sandweiss, 359–91 (New York: Oxford University Press, 1994), 382–83.

27. Hine, *California's Utopian Colonies,* 154–57.

28. Szasz and Szasz, "Religion and Spirituality," 374.

29. Brian Masaru Hayashi, "The Japanese 'Invasion' of California: Major Kobayashi and the Japanese Salvation Army, 1919–1926," *Journal of the West* 23 (Jan. 1984): 73–82.

30. James McBride, "The Far East, the Far West, and the Second Coming: The Unification Church in America," in *Religion and Society,* ed. Guarneri and Alvarez, 449–76.

31. Lewis F. Carter, *Charisma and Control in Rajneeshpuram: The Role of Shared Values in the Creation of a Community* (New York: Cambridge University Press, 1990), 37.

32. Ibid., 41–72.

33. Ibid., xv, 122–27.

34. Ibid., 235–40.

35. See Ray Allen Billington, *The Protestant Crusade, 1800–1860: A Study of the Origins of American Nativism* (New York: Macmillan, 1938; repr., New York: Quadrangle, 1964), 2, 7, 17, 21, 41, 75–76, 88, 118–22, 157, 198, 239, 273, 284, 345, 351.

36. Jeffrey M. Burns, "The Mexican American Catholic Community in California, 1850–1980," in *Religion and Society,* ed. Guarneri and David Alvarez, 255–73 (258).

37. Edwin B. Almirol, "Church Life among Filipinos in Central California: Social Ties and Ethnic Identity," in *Religion and Society,* ed. Guarneri and Alvarez, 299–316 (306).

38. Norman F. Furniss, *The Mormon Conflict, 1850–1859* (New Haven, Conn.: Yale University Press, 1960), 176–89.

39. *Appendix to the History of the Dakota Presbytery, a List of Churches and White and Native Pastors from Its Organization to April 1890,* Oahe Mission Collection, box 1, folder 4B, Center for Western Studies, Augustana College, Sioux Falls, S.D.; "Wanagi Akdi Kta [Ghosts Will Come]," *Iapi Oaye* (Santee, Ne.), November 1890.

40. James D. Tabor and Eugene V. Gallagher, *Why Waco? Cults and the Battle for Religious Freedom in America* (Berkeley: University of California Press, 1995), 3, 6, 14–15, 18, 107, 254–55.

Chapter 2: Uncle Sam and the Saints

1. Paul Bailey, *The Armies of God* (Garden City, N.Y.: Doubleday, 1968), 196–98; B. H. Roberts, *A Comprehensive History of the Church of Jesus Christ of Latter-day Saints, Century I,* 7 vols. (Provo, Utah: Brigham Young University Press, 1965), 4:231.

2. David Brion Davis, "Some Themes of Counter-Subversion: An Analysis of Anti-Masonic, Anti-Catholic, and Anti-Mormon Literature," *Mississippi Valley Historical Review* 47 (Sept. 1960): 209.

3. The term *Saints* refers to members of the church, which does not assign special sanctity to the term and does not have a canonization process. Church members

are also known as Mormons, derived from the *Book of Mormon*, which is accepted as scripture by members (Davis Bitton, *Historical Dictionary of Mormonism* [Metuchen, N.J.: Scarecrow, 1994], 205).

4. Gustive O. Larson, *The "Americanization" of Utah for Statehood* (San Marino, Calif.: Huntington Library, 1971), ix. Monographs devoted to the Utah Expedition include Norman F. Furniss, *The Mormon Conflict, 1850–1859* (New Haven, Conn.: Yale University Press, 1960); and Donald R. Moorman with Gene A. Sessions, *Camp Floyd and the Mormons: The Utah War* (Salt Lake City: University of Utah Press, 1992).

5. Bitton, *Historical Dictionary*, 217; Nathan O. Hatch, *The Democratization of American Christianity* (New Haven, Conn.: Yale University Press, 1989), 115. For an account that ties Mormon beliefs to previous religious movements and examines its supernatural elements and some of the crimes with which the Mormons were charged, see John L. Brooke, *The Refiner's Fire: The Making of Mormon Cosmology, 1644–1844* (New York: Cambridge University Press, 1994). For a sympathetic biography of Joseph Smith, see Richard L. Bushman, *Joseph Smith and the Beginnings of Mormonism* (Urbana: University of Illinois Press, 1984); for a more critical account, see Fawn McKay Brodie, *No Man Knows My History: The Life Story of Joseph Smith, the Mormon Prophet* (New York: Knopf, 1957).

6. Bitton, *Historical Dictionary*, 149, 217.

7. *The Book of Mormon: Another Testament of Jesus Christ* (Salt Lake City, Utah: Corporation of the President of The Church of Jesus Christ of Latter-day Saints, 1981), ii.

8. Jan Shipps, *Mormonism: The Story of a New Religious Tradition* (Urbana: University of Illinois Press, 1985), 25–26; Leonard J. Arrington and Davis Bitton, *The Mormon Experience: A History of the Latter-day Saints* (New York: Knopf, 1979), 23–34 (quotation, 43).

9. Shipps, *Mormonism*, 26, 33, 36. For the development of ecclesiastical and theocratic powers in Mormonism during Smith's life and through 1847 under Brigham Young, see D. Michael Quinn, *The Mormon Hierarchy: Origins of Power* (Salt Lake City, Utah: Signature Books, 1994).

10. Edwin Brown Firmage and Richard Collin Mangrum, *Zion in the Courts: A Legal History of the Latter-day Saints, 1830–1900* (Urbana: University of Illinois Press, 1988), 5, 11. See also Reed D. Slack, "The Mormon Belief of an Inspired Constitution," *Journal of Church and State* 36 (Winter 1994): 35–56.

11. *The Doctrine and Covenants of the Church of Jesus Christ of Latter-day Saints, Containing Revelations Given to Joseph Smith, the Prophet, with Some Additions by His Successors in the Presidency of the Church* (Salt Lake City, Utah: Church of Jesus Christ of Latter-day Saints, 1981), 29:34–35. Hereinafter cited as Doctrine and Covenants.

12. Reba Lou Keele, "A Doctrinal Group Counterattacks: An Analysis of the Oral Rhetoric of the Mormons in the Utah War, 1855–1859" (Ph.D. diss., Purdue University, 1974), 25.

13. Arrington and Bitton, *Mormon Experience*, 46.

14. Ibid., 47.

15. Firmage and Mangrum, *Zion in the Courts*, 48, 50, 54–56, 58. For a different interpretation of the Kirtland banking scandal, see Brooke, *Refiner's Fire*.

16. Arrington and Bitton, *Mormon Experience*, 48, 145.

17. Ibid., 49.

18. Ibid., 49–53, 62.

19. M. Guy Bishop, "Waging Holy War: Mormon-Congregationalist Conflict in Mid-Nineteenth-Century Hawaii," *Journal of Mormon History* 17 (1991): 111.

20. T. Edgar Lyon, "Religious Activities and Development in Utah, 1847–1910," *Utah Historical Quarterly* 35 (Fall 1967): 294–98.

21. William G. Hartley, "'Almost Too Intolerable a Burthen': The Winter Exodus from Missouri, 1838–39," *Journal of Mormon History* 18 (Fall 1992): 9; Firmage and Mangrum, *Zion in the Courts,* 64.

22. James H. Hunt, *A History of the Mormon War* (St. Louis, Mo.: Ustick and Davies, 1844), iv. Hunt's work provides insight into mainstream American attitudes toward the Saints in the mid-1840s. First, despite his promise of objectivity, Hunt created an extraordinarily biased account that would become an often used source of information about the shocking events in Missouri. It added an anti-Mormon book to the voices of the anti-Mormon print media already established. Second, Hunt clearly states objections to Mormonism common among mainstream Americans. For instance, he referred to the Book of Mormon as a "novel." So, as early as 1844, America had established anti-Mormon media spreading clearly anti-Mormon prejudices.

23. Brooke, *Refiner's Fire,* 232–34; William Mulder and A. Russell Mortensen, eds., *Among the Mormons: Historic Accounts by Contemporary Observers* (New York: Knopf, 1958; repr., Lincoln: University of Nebraska Press, 1973), 102–3; Hartley, "Almost Too Intolerable," 9, 40; G. Homer Durham, "A Political Interpretation of Mormon History," *Pacific Historical Review* 13 (Mar. 1944): 138.

24. Firmage and Mangrum, *Zion in the Courts,* 83.

25. Arrington and Bitton, *Mormon Experience,* 69.

26. Roger D. Launius, "Anti-Mormonism in Illinois: Thomas C. Sharp's Unfinished History of the Mormon War, 1845," *Journal of Mormon History* 15 (Spring 1989): 29–30.

27. Durham, "Political Interpretation," 140; Brooke, *Refiner's Fire,* 268.

28. The split produced several groups beyond the one that followed Young to the Great Basin, the best known of which became the Community of Christ, formerly known as the Reorganized Church of Jesus Christ of Latter Day Saints, with its headquarters in Independence, Missouri. Key issues included succession to leadership and practices such as plural marriage and temple rites.

29. Bitton, *Historical Dictionary,* 268–72; T. B. H. Stenhouse, *The Rocky Mountain Saints: A Full and Complete History of the Mormons, from the First Vision of Joseph Smith to the Last Courtship of Brigham Young* . . . (New York: D. Appleton, 1873), 127–28. For an excellent biography of Young, see Leonard J. Arrington, *Brigham Young: American Moses* (New York: Knopf, 1985).

30. Arrington and Bitton, *Mormon Experience,* 94–95, 98; Brooke, *Refiner's Fire,* 270–71; Bitton, *Historical Dictionary,* 270.

31. Bitton, *Historical Dictionary,* 149–50.

32. Brigham Young, "A Series of Instructions and Remarks by President Brigham Young, at a Special Council, Tabernacle, March 21, 1858," Western Americana Collection, Beinecke Rare Book and Manuscript Library, Yale University (hereinafter cited as WAC).

33. Shipps, *Mormonism*, 122–23; Arrington and Bitton, *Mormon Experience*, 110.

34. Howard Roberts Lamar, *The Far Southwest, 1846–1912: A Territorial History* (New Haven, Conn.: Yale University Press, 1966), 320–21. For a concise overview of Mormon and local government organizations in 1850s Utah, see James B. Allen, "Ecclesiastical Influence on Local Government in the Territory of Utah," *Arizona and the West* 8 (Spring 1966): 35–48. See also Firmage and Mangrum, *Zion in the Courts*.

35. Lamar, *The Far Southwest*, 318–19.

36. Angus E. Crane, "Millard Fillmore and the Mormons," *Journal of the West* 34 (Jan. 1995): 73–74.

37. Firmage and Mangrum, *Zion in the Courts*, 13, 18, 20.

38. Allen, "Ecclesiastical Influence," 37–38.

39. Doctrine and Covenants, 98:5–6, 101:77, 80.

40. Ibid., 98:10, 101:86–89.

41. Lamar, *The Far Southwest*, 327–29.

42. Qtd. in Justin S. Morrill, "Speech of Hon. Justin S. Morrill, of Vermont, on Utah Territory and Its Laws—Polygamy and Its License; Delivered in the House of Representatives, February 23, 1857," *Appendix to the Congressional Globe: Containing Speeches, Important State Papers, Laws, Etc. of the Third Session, Thirty-fourth Congress* (Washington, D.C.: Congressional Globe, 1857), 287.

43. Lamar, *The Far Southwest*, 328–29.

44. U.S. House of Representatives, *Utah Expedition*, 35th Congress, 1st sess., 1858, ex. doc. 71, serial 956 (Washington, D.C.: Congressional Globe, 1858), 176.

45. Charles A. Cannon, "The Awesome Power of Sex: The Polemical Campaign against Mormon Polygamy," *Pacific Historical Review* 43 (February 1974): 61–66, 74, 76; Lamar, *The Far Southwest*, 329–30; Davis, "Some Themes," 216–17.

46. Lamar, *The Far Southwest*, 330.

47. Although he does not invoke "salutary neglect" to describe this era of Mormon history, Angus Crane argues that the Mormons enjoyed this period of relative independence, which led them to remain in Utah, where they thrived (Crane, "Millard Fillmore," 74–75).

48. Lamar, *The Far Southwest*, 331–32.

49. House of Representatives, *Utah Expedition*, 212.

50. Lamar, *The Far Southwest*, 335; Paul H. Peterson, "The Mormon Reformation of 1856–1857: The Rhetoric and the Reality," *Journal of Mormon History* 15 (Spring 1989): 60, 64.

51. Peterson, "Mormon Reformation," 66–67; M. Hamlin Cannon, "The Mormon War: A Study in Territorial Rebellion" (master's thesis, George Washington University, 1938), 14.

52. Peterson, 71; see also Stanley S. Ivins, "Notes on Mormon Polygamy," *Western Humanities Review* 10 (Summer 1956): 229–39 (repr., *Utah Historical Quarterly* 35 [Fall 1967]: 309–21).

53. "Letter from Utah," *New York Daily Tribune*, 1 March 1858.

54. Qtd. in Peterson, "Mormon Reformation," 73, 77.

55. Lamar, *The Far Southwest*, 331, 335–36.

56. Ibid., 336–37; Juanita Brooks, *The Mountain Meadows Massacre* (Norman: University of Oklahoma Press, 1962), 13.

57. Richard D. Poll, "The Mormon Question Enters National Politics, 1850–1856," *Utah Historical Quarterly* 25 (Apr. 1957): 123–24.

58. Ibid., 131.

59. "James Buchanan and the Political Crisis of the 1850s: A Panel Discussion," Michael J. Birkner, moderator, *Pennsylvania History* 60 (July 1993): 262; Will Bagley, *Blood of the Prophets: Brigham Young and the Massacre at Mountain Meadows* (Norman: University of Oklahoma Press, 2002), 73–74; Lamar, *The Far Southwest*, 338–41. See also William F. MacKinnon, "The Buchanan Spoils System and the Utah Expedition: Careers of W. M. F. Magraw and John M. Hockaday," *Utah Historical Quarterly* 31 (Spring 1963): 127–50.

60. Qtd. in MacKinnon, "Buchanan Spoils System," 129; Robert W. Coakley, *The Role of Federal Military Forces in Domestic Disorders, 1789–1878* (Washington, D.C.: Center of Military History, U.S. Army, 1988), 196.

61. Juanita Brooks, ed., *On the Mormon Frontier: The Diary of Hosea Stout, 1844–1861,* 2 vols. (Salt Lake City: University of Utah Press, 1964), 2:628; Bagley, *Blood of the Prophets,* 77.

62. Qtd. Poll, "Mormon Question," 118–19.

63. Birkner, "James Buchanan," 265–67; Lamar, *The Far Southwest*, 340–41; Bagley, *Blood of the Prophets,* 75–77.

64. U.S., President, 1857–1861 (Buchanan), A Proclamation, 6 April 1858, WAC.

65. Ibid.

66. U.S., President, Message of the President of the United States delivered to the Senate and House of Representatives, 6 December 1858 (Washington, D.C.: Congressional Globe, 1858), WAC.

67. A. Russell Mortensen, "A Local Paper Reports on the Utah War," *Utah Historical Quarterly* 25 (Oct. 1957): 297.

68. Qtd. in ibid., 303.

69. Doctrine and Covenants, 101:86–89; Nauvoo Legion, Record of Orders, Returns, and Courts Martial Etc. of 2d Brigade, 1st Division, Nauvoo Legion, Headquarters, 14th Ward G. S. L. City, July 1857, pp. 6–7, WAC; Col. T. W. Ellerbeck, chief of ordnance, Nauvoo Legion, report of 14 January 1858, Nauvoo Legion, general orders no. 1, MS L-1106 N226, WAC; Andrew Love, diary, September 1852–September 1875, MS 2737, box 1, folder 7, HDC.

70. Brigham Young, *Diary of Brigham Young, 1857,* ed. Everett L. Cooley (Salt Lake City: Tanner Trust Fund, University of Utah Library, 1980), 49–50, 58.

71. Keele, "Doctrinal Group," 99.

72. Lamar, *The Far Southwest,* 342–43; Utah Territory, Governor, 1850–58 (Brigham Young), proclamation by the governor, 5 August 1857, broadside, WAC.

73. Both quotations in Utah Territory, Governor, proclamation.

74. Susan Staker, ed., *Waiting for World's End: The Diaries of Wilford Woodruff* (Salt Lake City: Signature, 1993), 199, 206–7.

75. S. W. Richards to Thomas L. Kane, 16 September 1857, Kane Papers, box 1, folder, 3, WAC.

76. Asa Smith Hawley, "Autobiography" (n.d.), MS 7804, Historical Department of the Church of Jesus Christ of Latter-day Saints, Salt Lake City, Utah (hereinafter cited as HDC). The complete lyrics of the untitled song follow.

Come all you good people, I'll not keep you long,
About the Mormons I'll sing you a song,
The gentiles have tried it again and again,
To kill all the Mormons and blot out their name,
For to kill all the Mormons and blot out their name.

We've been hunted and driven, winter and storm,
They've plundered our houses, they thought it no harm,
They have murdered our Prophet, they have taken our rights,
They have called on our soldiers, their battles to fight,
And they have called on our soldiers, their battles to fight.

We have petitioned, remonstrated, but all was in vain,
For redress of wrongs that we have sustained,
Our petitions you slighted with disdain,
And drove us to wander again and again,
And drove us to wander again and again.

Oh land of Missouri, a renown not of fame,
A blot on your pages will ever remain,
Oh land of Missouri, now hark to the sound,
The blood of our people now cries from the ground,
The blood of our people now cries from the ground.

Illinois, Illinois, you will soon cease to bloom,
The deeds you committed it has sealed your doom,
You have drove the poor Mormons without restrain,
And caused them to wander far over the Plain,
And caused them to wander far over the Plain.

You people of Carthage you may well bewail,
Our Prophet and Patriarch was slain in your jail,
You have sealed yourself up to eternal damnation,
You spilt the best blood of this generation,
You have spilt the best blood of this generation.

We have traversed o'er hills, o'er deserts, o'er plains,
Till these peaceful valleys we did obtain,
Now if you pursue us to drive us again,
Your bones they shall molder and bleach on the Plains,
Your bones they shall molder and bleach on the Plains.

We will clean up our rifles, our pistols and swords,
And we will ever be ready to march at the word,
We will trust in the Lord and take good aim,
And the kingdom of Heaven we will it maintain,
And the kingdom of Heaven we will it maintain.

77. David Candland, journal, 17 September 1857, MS 1891, HDC; Esaias Edwards, autobiography and journal, 1855–82, 26 November 1857, photocopy of typescript, MS 1885, HDC.

78. Love, diary.

79. "The Utah Expedition," *New York Daily Tribune,* 10 Sept. 1857.

80. Utah, Legislative Assembly, Memorial of the Members and Officers of the Legislative Assembly of the Territory of Utah, 6 January 1858, WAC; Young, "A Series of Instructions."

81. Brooks, *On the Mormon Frontier,* 641; Albert Sydney Johnston to Major (unnamed), 4 January 1858, MS S-1245 J641, WAC.

82. Lamar, *The Far Southwest,* 345.

83. Captain John L. Ginn, "Mormon and Indian Wars: The Mountain Meadows Massacre, and Other Tragedies and Transactions Incident to the Mormon Rebellion of 1857. Together with the Personal Recollection of a Civilian who Witnessed Many of the Thrilling Scenes Described," bound typescript, n.d., 6–7, MS S-271, WAC.

84. Henry S. Hamilton, *Reminiscences of a Veteran* (Concord, N.H.: Republican Press Association, 1897), 80, 97.

85. Brooks, *Mountain Meadows Massacre,* 21, 31–33, 41, 58; Bitton, *Historical Dictionary,* 183.

86. In addition to Brooks's pioneering work on Mountain Meadows, recent interpretations include Bagley's previously cited work and Sally Denton, *American Massacre: The Tragedy at Mountain Meadows, September 1857* (New York: Knopf, 2003).

87. Bagley, *Blood of the Prophets,* 88–89, 92, 97.

88. Brooks, *Mountain Meadows Massacre,* 46, 53.

89. Bagley, *Blood of the Prophets,* 117–18.

90. Brooks, *Mountain Meadows Massacre,* 67, 109, 184–85, 191–210; Bagley, *Blood of the Prophets,* 10, 75.

91. Coakley, *Federal Military Forces,* 206.

92. John Pulsipher, journal (1827–91), typescript, MS A 928-1, Utah State Historical Society, Salt Lake City, Utah (hereinafter cited as USHS).

93. William Wallace Hammond, autobiography, n.d., 10–17, MS 4478, HDC.

94. Harold D. Langley, ed., *To Utah with the Dragoons and Glimpses of Life in Arizona and California, 1858–1859* (Salt Lake City: University of Utah Press, 1974), xiv–xv, 2, 9, 133 (quotation).

95. Ibid., 21.

96. Ibid., 22–23.

97. Ibid., 44, 65–66.

98. Ibid., 91, 102.

99. Ginn, "Mormon and Indian Wars," 13.

100. Ibid., 14–15.

101. Ibid., 18–19.

102. William Rufus Rogers Stowell, journal (ca. 1857), MS 4602, HDC.

103. Qtd. in Wilford Hill LeCheminant, "A Crisis Averted? General Harney and the Change in Command of the Utah Expedition," *Utah Historical Quarterly* 51 (Winter 1983): 30.

104. U.S. House of Representatives, *Special Report of the Mountain Meadow Massacre, by J. H. Carleton, Brevet Major, United States Army, Captain, First Dragoons, 10 May 1902,* 57th Cong., 1st sess., doc. no. 605, serial 4377 (Washington, D.C.: GPO, 1902), 16.

105. Ibid., 16.

106. Ibid., 17.

107. Ibid., 17.

108. LeRoy R. Hafen and Ann W. Hafen, eds., *The Utah Expedition, 1857–1858: A Documentary Account of the United States Military Movement under Colonel Albert Sidney Johnston, and the Resistance by Brigham Young and the Mormon Nauvoo Legion* (Glendale, Calif.: Arthur H. Clark, 1958), 89.

109. John Wolcott Phelps, diary, 2 October 1857, typescript, John Wolcott Phelps Collection, USHS.

110. Phelps to Hickman, 11 December 1857, typescript, Phelps letters, B120-1, book 1, USHS.

111. Phelps to Charles Phelps, 29 December 1857, Phelps letters, B120-1, book 1, USHS.

112. Ibid.

113. Phelps to his sister Eunice, May 30, 1858, typescript, Phelps letters, B120-1, book 1, USHS.

114. Ibid.

115. Phelps, diary, 6 June 1858, typescript, Phelps Collection, USHS; Phelps to General Sylvester Churchill, 6 June 1858, typescript, Phelps letters, B120-1, book 2, USHS; Phelps to Frederic (surname unknown), 30 July 1858, Phelps letters, B120-1, book 2, USHS.

116. Phelps to Lily (surname unknown), 27 June 1858, Phelps letters, B120-1, book 2, USHS.

117. Phelps to Lily (surname unknown), 5 July 1858, Phelps letters, B120-1, book 2, USHS.

118. Ibid.

119. Hatch, *Democratization,* 116, 121.

120. Phelps to Lily (surname unknown), 5 July 1858.

121. Phelps to General (surname unknown), 11 October 1858, Phelps letters, B120-1, book 2, USHS.

122. Phelps, diary, 3 July 1859; Phelps to General (surname unknown), 29 July 1858, typescript, Phelps letters, B120-1, book 2, USHS; Phelps to his sister Helen, 4 August 1858, Phelps letters, B120-1, book 2, USHS.

123. Phelps, diary, 22 October 1859; Phelps to Charles Phelps, 21 March 1859, typescript, Phelps letters, B120-1, book 3, USHS.

124. Phelps to Levine (first name unknown), 13 April 1859, Phelps letters, B120-1, book 3, USHS.

125. U.S. House of Representatives, *Report of the Secretary of War,* 35th Cong., 1st sess., ex. doc. 2, serial 943 (Washington, D.C.: Cornelius Wendell, 1857), 6, 7.

126. Ibid., 7–8 (quotation on 8).

127. Lamar, *The Far Southwest,* 345–46.

128. Hon. C. J. Faulkner, "In Favor of an Increase of the Army, and in Opposition to the Employment of Volunteers in Utah," 9 March 1858, p. 10, Marriott Library, University of Utah (hereinafter cited as UU).

129. Samuel R. Curtis, "Speech of Hon. Samuel R. Curtis of Iowa," 10 March 1858, UU.

130. John Thompson, "Speech of Hon. John Thompson, of New York," 27 January 1858, UU.

131. Lamar, *The Far Southwest,* 347–50.

132. George D. Smith to Brother T. B. H. Stenhouse, 23 June 23, 1858, Church Historian's Office letterpress copybooks, 1854–79, microfilm CR 100 38, reel 1, p. 529, HDC; U.S. House of Representatives, *Cessation of Difficulties in Utah,* 35th Cong., 1st sess., 1858, ex. doc. no. 138, serial 959 (Washington, D.C.: n.p., 1858), 2, 5.

133. See Leonard J. Arrington, "'In Honorable Remembrance': Thomas L. Kane's Services to the Mormons," *Brigham Young University Studies* 21 (Summer 1981): 389–402; Richard D. Poll, *Quixotic Mediator: Thomas L. Kane and the Utah War* (Ogden, Utah: Weber State Press, 1985); idem, "Thomas L. Kane and the Utah War," *Utah Historical Quarterly* 61 (Spring 1993): 112–35; Woodruff to Kane, 8 March 1859, Kane Papers, box 1, folder 6, WAC.

134. Lamar, *The Far Southwest,* 347–50, 352; Coakley, *Federal Military Forces,* 214–15, 218, 221, 225.

135. G. D. Smith (Historian's Office, Salt Lake City) to Col. Kane, 11 September 1858, Kane Papers, box 1, folder 4, WAC; William Wallace Hammond, autobiography, [n.d.], MS 4478, pp. 6–7, HDC; Candland, journal, November 1858, HDC.

136. Qtd. in Mulder and Mortensen, *Among the Mormons,* 307. See also Audrey M. Godfrey, "Housewives, Hussies, and Heroines, or the Women of Johnston's Army," *Utah Historical Quarterly* 54 (Spring 1986): 157–78; Mulder and Mortensen, *Among the Mormons,* 310, 314.

137. Edwards, autobiography and journal, 8 August 1858, MS 1885, HDC.

138. Ibid.

139. Philip A. M. Taylor, "Why Did British Mormons Emigrate?" *Utah Historical Quarterly* 22 (July 1954): 249–50, 261.

140. Qtd. in Mortensen, "Local Paper Reports," 316.

141. Brigham Young to Horace S. Eldridge, 20 November 1858, MS S-1639, box 1, folder 2, WAC; John Taylor to George, 12 January 1859, MS 279, folder 6, WAC.

142. Coakley, *Federal Military Forces,* 217, 225.

143. Young to Eldridge, 20 October 1858.

144. Lamar, *The Far Southwest,* 352–53.

145. Ibid., 357.

146. Ibid., 357–58.

147. Ibid., 364.

148. Morrill, "Speech."

149. Ibid.

150. Ibid.

151. Firmage and Mangrum, *Zion in the Courts,* 131; Lamar, *The Far Southwest,* 365–67; Gordon, *The Mormon Question,* 81–83.

152. Robert Joseph Dwyer, "The Gentile Comes to Utah: A Study in Religious and Social Conflict, 1862–1890" (Ph.D. diss., Catholic University of America, 1941), 74, 80 (quotation).

153. Ibid., 80–86; *Clinton v. Engelbrecht,* 80 U.S. 434 (1872).

154. Bitton, *Historical Dictionary,* 240.

155. *Reynolds v. United States,* 98 U.S. 145 (1878); Firmage and Mangrum, *Zion in the Courts,* 151–56; Gordon, *The Mormon Question,* 135.

156. Lamar, *The Far Southwest,* 389.

157. Qtd. in Sarah Barringer Gordon, "'The Liberty of Self-Degradation': Polyg-

amy, Woman Suffrage, and Consent in Nineteenth-Century America," *Journal of American History* 83 (Dec. 1996): 815.

158. Lamar, *The Far Southwest,* 389–91.

159. Firmage and Mangrum, *Zion in the Courts,* 161–62. See also U.S. Congress and Secretary of State, "Chapter 47," *The Statutes at Large of the United States of America from December, 1881, to March, 1883* . . . (Washington, D.C.: GPO, 1883), vol. 22, pp. 30–32.

160. For details of the Edmunds Act's effectiveness, see Lamar, *The Far Southwest,* 393–94.

161. Lamar, *The Far Southwest,* 397–98; Firmage and Mangrum, *Zion in the Courts,* 198–204.

162. Lamar, *The Far Southwest,* 399–400; Bitton, *Historical Dictionary,* 240; Firmage and Mangrum, *Zion in the Courts,* 168.

163. Mulder and Mortensen, *Among the Mormons,* 411.

164. Lamar, *The Far Southwest,* 402–3; William C. Ringenberg, "Benjamin Harrison: The Religious Thought and Practice of a Presbyterian President," *American Presbyterians* 64 (Fall 1986): 175, 177, 182.

165. Ringenberg, "Benjamin Harrison," 183.

166. Lamar, *The Far Southwest,* 403–5; Durham, "Political Interpretation," 147–48; Shipps, *Mormonism,* 126–29.

167. Martha Sonntag Bradley, *Kidnapped from That Land: The Government Raids on the Short Creek Polygamists* (Salt Lake City: University of Utah Press, 1993), 6–7; Gordon, *The Mormon Question,* 220.

168. Ibid., 16–17, 182–83, 192–93.

169. Howard R. Lamar, "Statehood for Utah: A Different Path," *Utah Historical Quarterly* 39 (Fall 1971): 308; Gordon, *The Mormon Question,* 238.

Chapter 3: Uncle Sam and the Lying Messiah

1. Colin G. Calloway, ed., *Our Hearts Fell to the Ground: Plains Indian Views of How the West Was Lost* (Boston: Bedford Books, 1996), 191–95; Robert M. Utley, *The Lance and the Shield: The Life and Times of Sitting Bull* (New York: Henry Holt, 1993), 291–307.

2. L. G. Moses, "'The Father Tells Me So!' Wovoka: The Ghost Dance Prophet," *American Indian Quarterly* 9 (Summer 1985): 335–36.

3. James Mooney, *The Ghost Dance Religion and the Sioux Outbreak of 1890* (Washington, D.C.: GPO, 1896; repr., Lincoln: University of Nebraska Press, 1991), 773, 774, 777, 781; Raymond J. DeMallie, "The Lakota Ghost Dance: An Ethnohistorical Account," *Pacific Historical Review* 51 (Nov. 1982): 387–88.

4. DeMallie, "Lakota Ghost Dance," 388. DeMallie offers a convincing argument for the inadequacy of most studies of the Ghost Dance, nearly all of which focus on the religion as merely a response to land loss and hunger or an attempt to revitalize a dying culture. To remedy this, he argues, "the ghost dance needs to be seen as part of the integral, ongoing whole of Lakota culture and its suppression as part of the historical process of religious persecution led by Indian agents and missionaries against the Lakotas living on the Great Sioux Reservation" (392–93).

5. DeMallie argues less convincingly that the Ghost Dance had nothing to do with Sitting Bull's assassination per se but merely provided an opportunity for his old nemesis, Standing Rock Indian agent James McLaughlin, to rid himself of the Hunkpapa leader (DeMallie, "Lakota Ghost Dance," 394).

Estimates of the number of Lakotas killed at Wounded Knee differ. An army-escorted burial party interred 146 Lakotas on 3 January 1891, but families of victims almost certainly removed some bodies for burial prior to that. Also, many wounded died in the days and weeks following the massacre. All told, the number of Lakotas killed could easily exceed 250, according to Richard E. Jensen, R. Eli Paul, and John Carter, *Eyewitness at Wounded Knee* (Lincoln: University of Nebraska Press, 1991), 20.

James Mooney's work on the Ghost Dance is the standard text on the subject.

6. Commissioner of Indian Affairs, *Fifty-ninth Annual Report* (Washington, D.C.: GPO, 1890), vii, xxxv, cli.

7. Eli Ricker made these speculations based on his interviews with participants in the massacre; see Ricker Collection, reel 2, tablet 5, pp. 141–42, Nebraska State Historical Society, Lincoln (hereinafter cited as Ricker).

8. Ricker, reel 2, tablet 8, pp. 23–24.

9. Commissioner of Indian Affairs, *Fifty-ninth Report,* vii (quotation), xxxv, cli.

10. Commissioner of Indian Affairs, *Sixtieth Annual Report* (Washington, D.C.: GPO, 1891), 490–91. Hereinafter cited as CIA, *Sixtieth Report.*

11. From its founding in 1871 until January 1873, the paper went by *Iapi Oaye.* From January 1873 until March 1884, the paper carried a bilingual masthead, with *Iapi Oaye* appearing above *The Word Carrier.* Beginning in March 1884 the school printed two separate papers, *Iapi Oaye* in Dakota and *The Word Carrier* in English; both papers folded in March 1939. Altogether the publication ran longer than any other native-language periodical in America (Daniel F. Littlefield Jr. and James W. Parins, *American Indian and Alaska Native Newspapers and Periodicals, 1826–1924* [Westport, Conn.: Greenwood, 1984], 151–56). For a more detailed discussion of these papers and how they reported events related to the Ghost Dance and Wounded Knee massacre, see Todd Kerstetter, "Spin Doctors at Santee: Missionaries and the Dakota-language Reporting of the Ghost Dance and Wounded Knee," *Western Historical Quarterly* 28 (Spring 1997): 45–67.

12. "The Sioux War," *Iapi Oaye/The Word Carrier,* September 1876.

13. Utley, *Lance and Shield,* 137–39, 161.

14. "The Sioux War," *Iapi Oaye/The Word Carrier,* September 1876. The editors did not discriminate in their use of the terms *Dakota* and *Lakota.* Here they refer to Sitting Bull, Red Cloud, and their followers, all of whom were Lakotas.

15. Ibid.

16. Qtd. in Littlefield and Parins, *American Indian Newspapers,* 153.

17. "The Sioux War."

18. Littlefield and Parins, *American Indian Newspapers,* 153.

19. "Raise No More Indians," *Iapi Oaye/The Word Carrier,* October 1876.

20. William T. Hagan, *Indian Police and Judges: Experiments in Acculturation and Control* (New Haven, Conn.: Yale University Press, 1966), 26–27, 42–43.

21. Ibid., 48.

22. Ibid., 69–70, 73.

23. Ibid., 104, 107–9, 123; John R. Wunder, *"Retained by The People": A History of American Indians and the Bill of Rights* (New York: Oxford University Press, 1994), 35–36; Joel W. Martin, *The Land Looks after Us: A History of Native American Religion* (New York: Oxford, 1999), 91–92.

24. Ibid., 11.

25. CIA, *Sixtieth Report*, 389–90.

26. Ricker, reel 1, tablet 4, pp. 135–36; Ricker, reel 2, tablet 5, pp. 120–22.

27. "Capt. Bourke's Suggestion," *Omaha Morning World-Herald* (hereinafter *OMW-H*), 14 December 1890.

28. Ibid.

29. Mooney, *Ghost Dance Religion*, 894–95, 902.

30. Ibid., 802–5, 897–98.

31. Every effort has been made to identify Indian peoples. Despite its derogatory connotations, *Sioux* is retained as an umbrella term to refer to all three groups or when precise identity is unclear. See Royal B. Hassrick, *The Sioux: Life and Customs of a Warrior Society* (Norman: University of Oklahoma Press, 1964), ix, 3–6; Elizabeth S. Grobsmith, *Lakota of the Rosebud: A Contemporary Ethnography* (New York: Holt, Rinehart, and Winston, 1981), 6–8.

32. Roy W. Meyer, *History of the Santee Sioux: United States Indian Policy on Trial*, rev. ed. (Lincoln: University of Nebraska Press, 1993), 1, 24, 139–41, 154–58; Richard L. Guenther, "The Santee Normal Training School," *Nebraska History* 51 (Fall 1970): 359–78.

33. Alan R. Woolworth, "Ethnohistorical Report on the Yankton Sioux," in *Sioux Indians III*, ed. and comp. David Agee Horr, 9–245 (New York: Garland, 1974), 52–54, 178–82. See also Herbert T. Hoover in collaboration with Leonard R. Bruguier, *The Yankton Sioux* (New York: Chelsea House, 1988).

34. Hassrick (*The Sioux*, ix) writes that Sioux life achieved its "era of greatest vigor and renown" during the years between 1830 and 1870. See also Richard White, "The Winning of the West: The Expansion of the Western Sioux in the Eighteenth and Nineteenth Centuries," *Journal of American History* 65 (Sept. 1978): 319–43; Grobsmith, *Lakota of the Rosebud*, 6–8.

35. In analyzing the causes of the Ghost Dance and related disturbances at the Sioux agencies, the U.S. government cited twelve factors, including the "calamity" of the buffalo's disappearance, which forced the Sioux to depend on government handouts and to assume, without experience, an agricultural lifestyle (CIA, *Sixtieth Report*, 132). Dan Flores offers the thought-provoking suggestion that the buffalo's demise can ultimately be traced to Indian hunting practices, which began thinning the herds considerably in the early nineteenth century. "The more familiar events of the 1870s," Flores writes, "only delivered the *coup de grace* to the free Indian life on the Great Plains" ("Bison Ecology and Bison Diplomacy: The Southern Plains from 1800 to 1850," *Journal of American History* 78 [Sept. 1991]: 465–85).

36. CIA, *Sixtieth Report*, 126.

37. Robert M. Utley, *The Last Days of the Sioux Nation* (New Haven, Conn.: Yale University Press, 1963), 60–62, 68, 71.

38. Ibid., 72–73.

39. Ibid., 76, 86–87, 135, 163.

40. Ricker, reel 5, tablet 25, pp. 125–26.

41. William McKusick, U.S. Indian Agent, Sisseton Agency, to Commissioner of Indian Affairs, 26 November 1890, Ricker, box 28, folder 82.

42. Ricker, reel 2, tablet 5, 115–16.

43. Ibid., 118–20.

44. Although the AMA had missions to tribes outside Nebraska and the Dakota Territory, the overwhelming majority of their missionary work took place in those two regions. For 1885–88 the AMA's missions included the following: Santee Agency, Nebraska; Ponca Agency, Nebraska; Oahe, Dakota; Cheyenne River Agency, Dakota; Rosebud Agency, Dakota; Standing Rock Agency, Dakota; Fort Berthold Agency, Dakota; S'Kokomish Agency, Washington Territory; and Santa Fe, New Mexico Territory. For 1890 and 1891 the AMA no longer included the Santa Fe mission but added a mission at Cape Prince of Wales, Alaska. Although the existence of missions to non-Sioux tribes raises questions about the validity of these figures as indicators of the Ghost Dance, the small staffs at the New Mexico, Washington, and Alaska missions indicate they were but minor concerns relative to the missions in Nebraska and Dakota. The Washington staff consisted of one missionary; the New Mexico staff included a principal, two matrons, and a teacher; and the Alaska staff consisted of two men whose jobs the AMA did not describe in its annual reports. The Santee Agency alone had a staff of thirty for 1891 (collectively, the Nebraska and Dakota missions had eighty-six staff members that year), indicating the relative numerical significance of the Nebraska and Dakota agencies to the AMA's overall commitments to Indian missions. It seems safe to assume, then, that institution and enrollment figures for the AMA's Indian missions reflect predominately Nebraska and Dakota events for the period 1885 through 1891.

Information for both the text and this note is drawn from American Missionary Association Executive Committee, "Thirty-ninth Annual Report of the Executive Committee, for the Year Ending September 30, 1885," *The American Missionary* 39 (November 1885): 311; "Fortieth Annual Report of the Executive Committee, for the Year Ending September 30, 1886," *The American Missionary* 40 (November 1886): 314; "Forty-first Annual Report of the Executive Committee, for the Year Ending September 30, 1887," *The American Missionary* 41 (November 1887): 322; "Forty-second Annual Report of the Executive Committee, for the Year Ending September 30, 1888," *The American Missionary* 42 (November 1888): 308; "Forty-third Annual Report of the Executive Committee, for the Year Ending September 30, 1889," *The American Missionary* 43 (November 1889): 313; "Forty-fourth Annual Report of the Executive Committee, for the Year Ending September 30, 1890," *The American Missionary* 44 (November 1890): 345; "Forty-fifth Annual Report of the Executive Committee, for the Year Ending September 30, 1891," *The American Missionary* 45 (November 1891): 391; Ricker, reel 2, tablet 5, pp. 118–20.

45. Utley, *Last Days*, 74–5.

46. CIA, *Sixtieth Report*, 124.

47. Ibid., 125.

48. James McLaughlin, *My Friend the Indian* (Boston: Houghton Mifflin, 1926), 21, 65.

49. CIA, *Sixtieth Report*, 126, 330.

50. Ibid., 125, 329.

51. Ibid., 126, 330.

52. Ibid., 411–12.

53. Ibid.

54. "Let Them Alone," *OMW-H*, 8 November 1890.

55. "Apprehensions of Indian Trouble," *Omaha Bee* (hereinafter *OB*), 12 November 1890.

56. "The Indian Religious Craze," *OB*, 13 November 1890.

57. "New Christ of the Indians," "The Settlers Alarmed," "No Troops Ordered Out," and "The Sioux Uneasy," *OB*, 18 November 1890.

58. "The Agitated Indians," *OB*, 19 November 1890.

59. "Bishop Hare's View," *OB*, 20 November 1890.

60. "Causes of the Indian Outbreak," *The Word Carrier*, December 1890.

61. "Southern Indians Excited," *The Word Carrier*, 26 November 1890; "Oklahoma Indians Peaceful," *The Word Carrier*, 11 December 1890.

62. "Messiya Itonśni," *Iapi Oaye*, November 1890.

63. Ibid. White Bird quotes from Matthew 24:3, 4, 11–13, 23.

64. Qtd. in "Wanagi Akdi Kta [Ghosts Will Come]," *Iapi Oaye*, November 1890. Mazawakinyanna's native-language name has been retained because he wrote under it.

65. Ibid.

66. *Ikewiaśta* means "common man," but the Sioux used the term to refer to themselves as a group and, perhaps, to Indians generically.

67. Qtd. in "Wanagi Akdi Kta."

68. Ibid.

69. "Hounded On by Hunger," *OB*, 25 November 1890.

70. CIA, *Sixtieth Report*, 330; "Settlers Feeling Safer," *OB*, 16 November 1890.

71. "Will Make Good Indians," *OB*, 19 November 1890; CIA, *Sixtieth Report*, 331.

72. "On to the Front," *OB*, 20 November 1890.

73. "In Wounded Knee," *OMW-H*, 20 November 1890.

74. "Soldiers Take the Field" and "Causes of the Trouble," *OB*, 19 November 1890.

75. "They Are Wild," *OB*, 21 November 1890.

76. "A Crisis Imminent," *OB*, 23 November 1890.

77. "At Rosebud," *OMW-H*, 22 November 1890.

78. "The Craze Still Spreads," *OMW-H*, 22 December 1890.

79. "Sitting Bull in Irons," *OMW-H*, 20 November 1890.

80. "The Story of Plenty Bear," *OB*, 29 November 1890.

81. "Letters from Settlers," *OMW-H*, 25 November 1890; "Tangled Rumors," *OB*, 20 November 1890 (quotations).

82. "The Millennium Craze," *Rushville (Neb.) Standard*, 7 November 1890.

83. "Little Wound's Letter," *OB*, 23 November 1890.

84. "More Ghost Dancers," *OMW-H*, 23 November 1890; "No Excitement in Santee," *OMW-H*, 26 November 1890; "Red Men Bite the [?]" and "General Miles' Opinion," *OMW-H*, 28 November 1890; "Probable Uprising of the Navajos," *OB*, 30 November 1890; "Comanches and Kiowas Dancing," *OB*, 30 November 1890; "California Indians Dancing," *OB*, 17 December 1890.

85. "The Messiah Craze in Montana," *Ainsworth (Neb.) Star*, 27 November 1890.

86. "With Rifle on Back," *OB*, 21 November 1890.

87. "No Good Prospect for War," *OMW-H*, 22 November 1890.

88. "The Turbulent Reds," *OB*, 22 November 1890.

89. "Sanders on the Situation," *OMW-H*, 7 December 1890.

90. Mooney, *Ghost Dance Religion*, 798–99.

91. "More Troops Ordered Out," *OB*, 3 December 1890.

92. Maj. Gen. Nelson A. Miles to Maj. G.W. Baird, 20 November 1891, Western Americana Collection, Beinecke Rare Book and Manuscript Library (hereinafter cited as WAC).

93. "Saw the Ghost Dance," *OMW-H*, 22 November 1890.

94. "No War Yet at Pine Ridge," *OMW-H*, 23 November 1890.

95. Newspapers reporting on Wounded Knee, particularly the *Omaha Morning World-Herald,* earned a reputation for basing their stories on poor sources and for distorting the truth. See Oliver Knight, *Following the Indian Wars: The Story of the Newspaper Correspondents among the Indian Campaigners* (Norman: University of Oklahoma Press, 1960; repr., 1993), 314.

96. "Marching on the Raiders," *OMW-H*, 9 December 1890.

97. "Short Bull Starts a Scare," *OMW-H*, 27 November 1890.

98. "General Miles Appealed To," *OMW-H*, 27 November 1890.

99. "A Vigorous Kick," *OMW-H*, 28 November 1890.

100. "Lower Brules Dancing" and "Broke Up the Dance," *OB*, 29 November 1890. "Broke Up the Dance" says eight dancers were arrested. This conflicts with the agent's report, cited in the next portion of the paragraph, which indicates that Indian police arrested twenty-two Ghost Dancers—although he may be referring to a different incident.

101. CIA, *Sixtieth Report*, 403.

102. "A Battle with the Sioux," *OMW-H*, 8 December 1890.

103. "Marching on the Raiders," *OMW-H*, 8 December 1890.

104. "Rounding Up the Sioux," *OMW-H*, 13 December 1890.

105. "A Scare at Rockford," *OMW-H*, 13 December 1890.

106. "Plan of the Campaign," *OB*, 11 December 1890; "Choose Partners for the Ghost Dance," *Rushville (Neb.) Standard*, 5 December 1890.

107. "General Miles' Advices," *OB*, 24 November 1890; "At Standing Rock," *OMW-H*, 26 November 1890.

108. "Moving against Hostiles," *OMW-H*, 15 December 1890.

109. McLaughlin, *My Friend the Indian*, 205.

110. Ibid., 208–10.

111. "Stopped at Standing Rock," *OMW-H*, 23 November 1890; "Quiet at Standing Rock," *OMW-H*, 25 November 1890.

112. Inyanbosdata Etanhan [From Standing Rock]," *Iapi Oaye*, January 1891.

113. "Last Visit to Sitting Bull," *OB*, 16 December 1890.

114. Calloway, *Our Hearts Fell*, 193; Utley, *Lance and Shield*, 298, 300–301. V. T. McGillicuddy, former agent at Pine Ridge, agreed with this strategy, having recommended in a November interview that Sitting Bull be confined ("They Don't Know the Injun," *OMW-H*, 28 November 1890).

115. Calloway, *Our Hearts Fell*, 191–95.

116. Hagan, *Indian Police*, 86.

117. Calloway, *Our Hearts Fell*, 191–93; Utley, *Lance and Shield*, 300.

118. Calloway, *Our Hearts Fell*, 193; Utley, *Lance and Shield*, 298, 300–301.

119. Calloway, *Our Hearts Fell*, 194; Utley, *Lance and Shield*, 302.

120. Calloway, *Our Hearts Fell*, 195.

121. "Bull's Warriors Surrender," *OB*, 23 December 1890; "What General Miles Says," *OMW-H*, 3 December 1890; "Buffalo Bill's Opinions," *OMW-H*, 3 December 1890; "Causes of the Indian Outbreak," *The Word Carrier*, December 1890.

122. McLaughlin, *My Friend the Indian*, 221.

123. "Sitting Bull's Ghost Appears," *OB*, 21 December 1890.

124. "The Craze Still Spreads," *OMW-H*, 22 December 1890.

125. "The Christ, Hopkins," *OB*, 23 December 1890; "The Imposter Hopkins," ibid., 24 December 1890; Utley, *Last Days*, 172–73.

126. "Short Bull's Prophecy," *OB*, 28 December 1890.

127. "Making Their Last Appeal," *OMW-H*, 20 December 1890. The reporter filed this story from Pine Ridge, leading to the speculation that the emissaries were Oglalas.

128. Jensen, Paul, and Carter, *Eyewitness*, 12.

129. Ibid., 17.

130. Ibid., 17–19.

131. Ricker, reel 3, tablet 12, pp. 62–63.

132. Ibid., reel 2, tablet 5, pp. 27–44.

133. Ibid., 44–52.

134. Ibid., 53–55, 67–70.

135. Ibid., tablet 11, pp. 31–32.

136. "The Beginning of the End," *OB*, 2 January 1891.

137. "Another Account," *OMW-H*, 30 December 1890.

138. Ricker, reel 1, tablet 3, pp. 16–18; ibid., reel 5, tablet 27, 94–95.

139. Ibid., reel 3, tablet 12, pp. 91–93.

140. Ibid., reel 7, tablet 48, 18–19.

141. "All Ready to Fight," *OB*, 3 January 1891; "Sang War Songs," *OMW-H*, 1 January 1891.

142. Maj. Gen. Nelson A. Miles to Adj. Gen. J. C. Kelton, 2 March 1891, WAC.

143. "Wowapi Maqupi" and "Mahpiyaduta Ti Etanhan [From Red Cloud's Home]," *Iapi Oaye*, February 1891.

144. Letter from Paul Crow Eagle (Kangiwabli), *Iapi Oaye*, February 1891.

145. Untitled article, *The Word Carrier*, January 1891.

146. Ricker, reel 5, tablet 27, 105. The report of Ghost Dance leaders being exiled to Europe as part of Wild West show is confirmed in Don Russell, *The Lives and Legends of Buffalo Bill* (Norman: University of Oklahoma Press, 1960), 369; Utley, *Last Days*, 271–72; Raymond J. DeMallie, ed., *The Sixth Grandfather: Black Elk's Teachings Given to John G. Neihardt* (Lincoln: University of Nebraska Press, 1984), 10 (Wild West Show contracts).

147. Miles to Baird, WAC; "General Miles' Address," *OB*, 19 January 1891.

148. "Simply More or Less Beef," *OB*, 24 January 1891.

149. "Forsythe's Case," *OB*, 7 January 1891.

150. "First Scalp Taken," *OB*, 8 January 1891; CIA, *Sixtieth Report,* 410, 412.

151. "Kansas Indians Dancing," *OB*, 2 January 1891; "The Kickapoos Slandered," *OMW-H*, 22 December 1890; "A Bannock Outbreak in Idaho," "Snakes and Shoshones Will Dance," and "Ghost Dances in Iowa," *OB*, 9 January 1891; Brigham D. Madsen, *The Bannock of Idaho* (Caldwell, Id.: Caxton, 1958), 319–20. For information on the Ghost Dance among the western Shoshones, see Steven J. Crum, *Po'i Pentun Tammen Kimmappeh (The Road on Which We Came): A History of the Western Shoshone* (Salt Lake City: University of Utah Press, 1994), 56, 62–63. Joseph G. Jorgensen theorizes that the Ghost Dance continued among the Utes and Shoshones from 1890 to 1895, although it declined during those years as the tribes underwent an ideological transformation (Jorgensen, *The Sun Dance Religion: Power for the Powerless* [Chicago: University of Chicago Press, 1972]), 77.

152. Ricker, reel 5, tablet 26, 63–64. Richmond L. Clow also shows evidence that Lakotas practiced the Ghost Dance at least through 1892, that Kicking Bear taught the ceremony as late as 1902, and that a Ghost Dance congregation existed in the 1960s ("The Lakota Ghost Dance after 1890," *South Dakota History* 20 [Winter 1990]: 323–33).

153. Commissioner of Indian Affairs, *Sixty-first Annual Report* (Washington, D.C.: GPO, 1892), 395; Mooney, *Ghost Dance Religion,* 902.

154. Alexander Lesser, *The Pawnee Ghost Dance Hand Game* (New York: Columbia University Press, 1933), 60–61, 64–67; Commissioner of Indian Affairs, *Sixty-first Report,* 395.

155. Lesser, *Pawnee Ghost Dance,* 67–68; Gene Weltfish, *The Lost Universe* (New York: Basic Books, 1965), 446–47; Von Del Chamberlain, *When Stars Came Down to Earth: Cosmology of the Skidi Pawnee Indians of North America* (Los Altos, Calif.: Ballena, 1982), 33–34.

156. Maurice Boyd, *Kiowa Voices: Ceremonial Dance, Ritual and Song,* 2 vols. (Fort Worth: Texas Christian University Press, 1981), 1:89–90.

157. Mooney, *Ghost Dance Religion,* 908–14.

158. Ibid.

159. CIA, *Sixtieth Report,* 412.

160. Boyd, *Kiowa Voices,* 91–93.

161. Ibid., 98; Mooney, *Ghost Dance Religion,* 908–14; CIA, *Sixtieth Report,* 412.

162. Martin, *Land Looks after Us,* 99–107.

163. Mooney, *Ghost Dance Religion,* 828.

Chapter 4: Uncle Sam and the Sinful Messiah

1. U.S. Department of Justice, *Report to the Deputy Attorney General on the Events at Waco, Texas, February 28 to April 19, 1993,* redacted version (Washington, D.C.: GPO, 1993), 110, 289. Hereinafter cited as *Justice Report.* A number of monographs on the Branch Davidian tragedy appeared in the years following. Journalists who wrote about the tragedy include Brad Bailey and Bob Darden (*Mad Man in Waco: The Complete Story of the Davidian Cult, David Koresh and the Waco Massacre* [Waco, Texas: WRS, 1993]) and Dick J. Reavis (*The Ashes of Waco: An Investigation* [New York: Simon and Schuster, 1995]). A former Branch Davidian tells his version of Branch

Davidian life in a book by Marc Breault and Martin King, *Inside the Cult: A Member's Chilling, Exclusive Account of Madness and Depravity in David Koresh's Compound* (New York: Signet Books, 1993). Treatments by academicians include James R. Lewis, ed., *From the Ashes: Making Sense of Waco* (Lanham, Md.: Rowman and Littlefield, 1994); James D. Tabor and Eugene V. Gallagher, *Why Waco? Cults and the Battle for Religious Freedom in America* (Berkeley: University of California Press, 1995); Stuart A. Wright, ed., *Armageddon in Waco: Critical Perspectives on the Branch Davidian Conflict* (Chicago: University of Chicago Press, 1995).

2. "Expert: FBI Tanks Cut Off Escape Route," *Waco Tribune-Herald* (hereinafter *WTH*), 27 August 1993.

3. *Justice Report*, 6, 111–12; Tabor and Gallagher, *Why Waco?* 21–22, 254–55; James M. Wall, "Eager for the End," *Christian Century* 110 (5 May 1993): 475. According to the FBI, the Davidians started the fires; surviving Davidians vehemently deny this.

4. Tabor and Gallagher, *Why Waco?* 33–35, 37–41; "Howell Said to Have Lived Double Life," *WTH*, 2 May 1993.

5. "Howell Lived Double Life."

6. Ibid.

7. Tabor and Gallagher, *Why Waco?* 8, 42–43, 58; U.S. Department of the Treasury, *Report of the Department of the Treasury on the Bureau of Alcohol, Tobacco, and Firearms Investigation of Vernon Wayne Howell also known as David Koresh* (Washington, D.C.: GPO, 1993), 125 (herineafter cited as *Treasury Report*).

8. "The Sinful Messiah," pt. 1, *WTH*, 27 February 1993.

9. "The Sinful Messiah," pt. 2, *WTH*, 28 February 1993.

10. U.S. House of Representatives, Committee on the Judiciary, *Activities of Federal Law Enforcement Agencies toward the Branch Davidians: Joint Hearings before the Subcommittee on Crime of the Committee on the Judiciary and the Subcommittee on National Security, International Affairs, and Criminal Justice of the Committee on Government Reform and Oversight (Part 2)*, 104th Cong., 1st sess., 25, 26, and 27 July 1995 (Washington, D.C.: GPO, 1996), 243–44. Hereinafter cited as *Hearings Part 2*.

11. "Revelation Finds Many Interpretations," *WTH*, 1 April 1993.

12. Paul Boyer, *When Time Shall Be No More: Prophecy Belief in Modern American Culture* (Cambridge, Mass.: Harvard University Press, 1992), 2–3.

13. Ibid., 2–3, 13.

14. Qtd. in Wall, "Eager for the End," 476.

15. "Seven Seals Key to Vernon Howell's Power," *WTH*, 28 February 1993.

16. Paul Boyer, "A Brief History of the End of Time," *New Republic* 208 (17 May 1993): 30, 32.

17. Ibid., 33.

18. "End Was Focus of Teaching" and "Margins of Bible Eerily Foretell of Cult's Apocalypse," *WTH*, 1 May 1993.

19. "Sinful Messiah," pt. 1.

20. Ibid., pts. 5–6, *WTH*, 1 March 1993; "Cult Planned Sham Marriages for Members," *WTH*, 6 March 1993.

21. "The Sinful Messiah," pt. 3, *WTH*, 1 March 1993; "A Prophet for Profit?" *WTH*, 6 March 1993; Catherine Collins and Douglas Frantz, "Tales from the Cult," *Modern Maturity* 37 (June 1994): 25–26.

22. "Raised in Fear: Life as Cult Kids," *WTH*, 5 May 1993.

23. "Girl Tells Harrowing Stories of Cult Life," *WTH*, 12 March 1993.

24. "Self-Proclaimed Messiahs Have Long Roamed the Earth," *WTH*, 7 March 1993.

25. "Is Jerusalem Syndrome at Work?" *WTH*, 11 March 1993.

26. "Sinful Messiah," pt. 1.

27. "Reporter Named in Lawsuit," *WTH*, 7 April 1993.

28. Michael Barkun, "Reflections after Waco: Millennialists and the State," *Christian Century* 110 (2 June 1993): 597.

29. "Sinful Messiah," pt. 1.

30. "Experts: Branch Davidians Dangerous, Destructive Cult," *WTH*, 1 March 1993; "Expert on Cults Charged," *WTH*, 10 June 1993.

31. "Sinful Messiah," pt. 3.

32. "FBI: Howell Cares Only for His Own Life," *WTH*, 28 March 1993; "Making Koresh a Kind of Hero," *WTH*, 4 April 1993; "'Visitor' Leaves Cult Compound," *WTH*, 18 April 1993; "Family Uneasy about 'Flea Market,'" *WTH*, 1 August 1993; Wall, "Eager for the End," 476; Sophronia Scott Gregory, "Children of a Lesser God," *Time*, 17 May 1993, p. 54.

33. "Guitar God or Son of God?" *WTH*, 6 March 1993.

34. Ibid.

35. Livingstone Fagan, "Mt. Carmel: The Unseen Reality," Internet document, http://www.giwersworld.org/mgiwer/mgiwer3/fagan1.html, accessed 20 July 2005; Jaime Castillo, "Is Not This the Christ?" Internet document, http://www.fountain .btinternet.co.uk/koresh/writings/CASTILL1.TXT, accessed 20 July 2005.

36. "Residents, Businessmen Say Howell Not a Recluse," *WTH*, 4 March 1993.

37. *Justice Report*, 51, 173, 208–9; "Davidian: Holy War a Cult Intent," *WTH*, 3 February 1994; *Treasury Report*, D-3.

38. "Sinful Messiah," pt. 1; George Witkin, "How David Koresh Got All Those Guns," *U.S. News and World Report* 114 (7 June 1993): 42.

39. "Bloodiest Day for Agency," *WTH*, 1 March 1993; *Treasury Report*, 17, 24, D-4.

40. "Lawyer: ATF Declined Chance to Inspect Guns," *WTH*, 11 September 1993; James L. Pate, "Waco: Behind the Cover-up," *Soldier of Fortune*, November 1993, p. 37; U.S. House of Representatives, Committee on the Judiciary, *Activities of Federal Law Enforcement Agencies toward the Branch Davidians: Joint Hearings before the Subcommittee on Crime of the Committee on the Judiciary and the Subcommittee on National Security, International Affairs, and Criminal Justice of the Committee on Government Reform and Oversight (Part 1)*, 104th Cong., 1st sess., 19, 20, 21, and 24 July 1995 (Washington, D.C.: GPO, 1996), 163 (hereinafter cited as *Hearings Part 1*).

41. *Treasury Report*, 38, D-11; "Undercover ATF Agent Haunted by Bullet That Never Came," *WTH*, 14 May 1993.

42. *Treasury Report*, 12, 27 (emphasis added in first quotation).

43. Ibid., 53; "Howell Not a Recluse."

44. *Treasury Report*, 53, 59, 65, 125, 127.

45. Ibid., 85, 90, 215; "6 Dead, 18 Hurt," *WTH*, 1 March, 1993; "Agents Say Raid Like a War Zone," *WTH*, 2 May 1993; "Lawyer Releases Howell Tape," *WTH*, 28 May 1993 (Koresh quotation). The Branch Davidian who gave directions to the camera oper-

ator reported the raid to Koresh, who in turn told the undercover agent Robert Rodriguez that he knew a raid was in the works. Rodriguez reported this, but the agents in charge proceeded with the raid.

46. *Justice Report,* 2, 10, app. B; *Treasury Report,* 115, 117.

47. "9-1-1 Records Panic, Horror," *WTH,* 10 June 1993; *Justice Report,* 209; "Fagan Still Irritant for ATF," *WTH,* 27 January 1994.

48. "Officers Watch and Wait," *WTH,* 4 March 1993; "Feds Vow to Give Cult Fair Shake," *WTH,* 7 March 1993.

49. *Justice Report,* 9, 160–65.

50. Ibid., 179–84. Alan A. Stone, a professor of psychiatry and law at Harvard University, concurred with the Smerick-Young approach. In a report written after the final debacle, Stone criticized the FBI tactical organizers for ignoring this advice and pursuing a strategy that ultimately led the Branch Davidians to set the fires and to kill themselves (Stone, "How the FBI Helped Fuel the Waco Fire," *Harper's,* February 1994, pp. 15–18).

51. "Talks with Cult Falter, Agents Say," *WTH,* 8 March 1993; *Justice Report,* 41–42, 49, 54–55; "The Book of Koresh," *Newsweek,* 11 October 1993, p. 27.

52. "Negotiators Taking Course in Revelation," *WTH,* 14 March 1993; *Hearings Part 2,* 362.

53. *Justice Report,* 68, 87.

54. "FBI Playing Mind Games on Cultists," *WTH,* 16 March 1993.

55. "High-Rank Man in Cult Walks Out," *WTH,* 24 March 1993; "Howell Called Coward," *WTH,* 25 March 1993.

56. "Howell Keeps Control over Those Who Leave," *WTH,* 26 March 1993; "Cultists Wait for the End," *WTH,* 27 March 1993.

57. "Cultists Wait for the End."

58. U.S. House of Representatives, Committee on the Judiciary, *Activities of Federal Law Enforcement Agencies toward the Branch Davidians: Joint Hearings before the Subcommittee on Crime of the Committee on the Judiciary and the Subcommittee on National Security, International Affairs, and Criminal Justice of the Committee on Government Reform and Oversight (Part 3),* 104th Cong., 1st sess., 28 and 31 July, 1 August 1995 (Washington, D.C.: GPO, 1996), 107, 110. Hereinafter cited as *Hearings Part 3.*

59. "FBI: Howell Cares Only for Own Life."

60. "'Yahweh' Contacts Howell," *WTH,* 11 April 1993; see Jeremiah 50:22–25 (quotation at 50:24). Photocopies of this and the three subsequent letters Koresh sent out can be found in *Justice Report,* app. E; *Justice Report,* 100.

61. "2nd Letter Promises No Peace," *WTH,* 13 April 1993.

62. "FBI Likens Howell's Offer to Cartoon," *WTH,* 17 April 1993.

63. Tabor and Gallagher, *Why Waco?* 3, 6, 14–15, 18, 107, 254–55; "New Talks Lend Hope of No Fight," *WTH,* 31 March 1993; "Feds Let Lawyer Run Ball," *WTH,* 1 April 1993.

64. *Justice Report,* 105.

65. Nancy Gibbs, "Firestorm in Waco," *Time,* 3 May 1993, pp. 33–40; Paul Anderson, *Janet Reno: Doing the Right Thing* (New York: Wiley, 1994), 191.

66. *Justice Report,* 109.

67. "Spotlight on Waco," *WTH,* 9 March 1993. As of 9 March 1993, the Waco Cham-

ber of Commerce and Salvation Army counted approximately four hundred media representatives from around the United States, Canada, Mexico, Great Britain, France, Germany, South Africa, and Australia.

68. Robert V. Hine, *The American West: An Interpretive History*, 2d ed. (New York: HarperCollins, 1984), 86–89.

69. Mordecai Podet, "Pioneer Jews of Waco," *Western States Jewish History* 21, no. 3 (1989): 195, 197, 199–201.

70. "Religious Controversy Nothing New to Waco," *WTH*, 7 March 1993.

71. "Elk Neighbors at Center of Sudden Notoriety," *WTH*, 3 March 1993; William Murray, letter to the editor, *WTH*, 4 March 1993.

72. "Libertarian Leaders Say ATF Picking on Cult," *WTH*, 8 March 1993.

73. "Tragedy Nearby Stuns Citizens," *WTH*, 2 March 1993.

74. "Prayer Vigils Planned," *WTH*, 8 March 1993; "Area Prayer Vigils," *WTH*, 15 March 1993.

75. "Prayers for Peace," *WTH*, 14 March 1993.

76. "Area Churches Pray for End to Siege," *WTH*, 8 March 1993.

77. "Food Donations Sought," *WTH*, 6 March 1993.

78. "A Taste of Central Texas," *WTH*, 1 April 1993; "ATF Departs with Signs of Gratitude," *WTH*, 12 June 1993.

79. "For Salvation Army Helpers, Current Mission Full of Irony," *WTH*, 13 March 1993.

80. "Weighing Use of Language of Faith," *WTH*, 21 March 1993.

81. Letter to the editor, *WTH*, 14 March 1993; photograph, *WTH*, 15 March 1993.

82. "Perhaps a Gun Cult?" *WTH*, 6 March 1993; "From Out of the Woodwork," *WTH*, 17 March 1993.

83. "It Concerns Our Liberty," *WTH*, 9 April 1993.

84. Ibid.

85. "Cult Standoff Expands Violent Texas Myth," *WTH*, 8 March 1993. See also Jan Jarboe, "David Koresh and the Myth of the Alamo," *Texas Monthly*, June 1993, pp. 136–38, 151.

86. Leon Wieseltier, "The True Fire," *New Republic*, 17 May 1993, p. 25.

87. Qtd. in *Treasury Report*, 120.

88. "The Messiah's Book," *WTH*, 16 April 1993.

89. "Emerging from Cult Command," *WTH*, 3 March 1993.

90. "Negotiators Taking Course."

91. "JPs Find Search 'Beyond Horror,'" *WTH*, 24 April 1993.

92. "Howell Died of Gunshot, Officials Say," *WTH*, 3 May 1993.

93. "FBI: 'My God, They're Killing Themselves,'" *WTH*, 20 April 1993; "Experts Sift Ashes For Answers on Cult," *WTH*, 14 May 1993.

94. *Hearings Part 3*, 111.

95. Ibid., 113; *Hearings Part 2*, 385–86; U.S. House of Representatives, Committee on Government Reform and Oversight, *Investigation into the Activities of Federal Law Enforcement Agencies Toward the Branch Davidians*, 104th Cong., 2d sess., 2 August 1996, report 104-749 (Washington, D.C.: GPO, 1996), 70.

96. *Justice Report*, 6; "Attorneys Describe Final Hours in Compound," *WTH*, 23 April 1993.

97. *Hearings Part 3*, 288–89.

98. "Not All Presidential Advisers Talk Politics," *New York Times*, national ed., 18 March 1997.

99. Bill Clinton, *My Life* (New York: Knopf, 2004), 498–99, 530.

100. "Reno's Darkest Hour," *Newsweek*, 31 July 1995, pp. 28–29.

101. *Hearings Part 2*, 353–54, 360, 406, 439; "The End Is Near?" *Time*, 26 April 1993, p. 32.

102. *Hearings Part 2*, 477; "The Contrary Voice of Janet Reno," *Newsweek*, 11 October 1993, p. 30.

103. "A Fiery End," special report, *WTH*, 19 April 1993; "Follower Awaits Howell's Return," *WTH*, 22 April 1993.

104. "Surviving Branch Davidians Await Howell's 2d Coming," *Waco Tribune-Herald* 23 May 1993.

105. "Awaiting Koresh's Resurrection," *WTH*, 28 February 1994.

106. Fagan, "Mt. Carmel"; Castillo, "Is Not This the Christ?" A significant collection of documents related to the Branch Davidians can be found on the Internet. As of July 2005 the Web page "The Waco Massacre," at www.serendipity.li/waco.html, contained numerous links to other relevant sites.

107. "Lawyers Condemn Tactics," *WTH*, 20 April 1993; "Authorities Mum about Cult Disk," *WTH*, 22 August 1993; "Howell's Writings on Disk," *WTH*, 25 September 1993; "Document Said to Be Howell's Text Released," *WTH*, 5 October 1993.

108. "Custody Tied to 'Reality,'" *WTH*, 11 June 1993.

109. "Howell Lived Double Life"; "Raid Like a War Zone."

110. "Trib Writers Honored for Series," *WTH*, 24 September 1993.

111. "Prayer Service to Start Healing," *WTH*, 20 April 1993; "Pastors Dedicate Service to Fallen Cult Members," *WTH*, 21 April 1993; "Unavoidable Sense of Guilt Causes Peace to Elude Us," *WTH*, 8 May 1993.

112. "Papers Show Howell Tipped," *WTH*, 22 April 1993; Wright, *Armageddon in Waco*, ix.

113. "12 Davidians Charged in New Indictment," *WTH*, 7 August 1993.

114. "Trial of Cultists to Begin," *WTH*, 9 January 1994.

115. Ibid.

116. Ibid.

117. "Children of the Cult," *Newsweek*, 17 May 1993, p. 49.

118. "'Sarge' Strikes a Bargain, *WTH*, 10 September 1993; "4 Cultists Walk Free; 7 Guilty on Lesser Counts," *WTH*, 27 February 1994; "Trial Was Grueling, Juror Says," *WTH*, 3 March 1994.

119. "Davidians' Gun Charge Reinstated," *WTH*, 10 March 1994; "Juror Seeks Davidian Leniency," *WTH*, 15 June 1994; "Judge Hard on Cultists," *WTH*, 18 June 1994; "Davidian Schroeder Sentenced," *WTH*, 9 July 1994.

120. "Out of the Ashes," *WTH*, 1 March 1994; "As Millions Cheer," *The Progressive*, June 1993, p. 8.

121. *Hearings Part 3*, 107.

122. "Teen's Words Bring Cult's Sins to Light," *WTH*, 20 July 1995; "Girl's Testimony Source of Pride, Relief," *WTH*, 21 July 1995; *Hearings Part 1*, 147–50; "Kiri Jewell Does 'What Feels Right,'" *WTH*, 30 July 1995.

123. "Oklahoma Prison Transfers Davidians," *WTH,* 5 May 1995; Mark S. Hamm, *Apocalypse in Oklahoma: Waco and Ruby Ridge Revenged* (Boston: Northeastern University Press, 1997), 103–5.

124. "Fighting a Cowboy Mentality," *WTH,* 7 May 1993.

125. Christopher Whitcomb, *Cold Zero: Inside the FBI Hostage Rescue Team* (Boston: Little, Brown, 2001), 201, 281–82, 286, 302.

126. Barkun, "Reflections after Waco," 596, 600. Boyer concurs, citing economic and spiritual insecurity in contemporary America as likely catalysts for continued fascination with prophecy interpretation (Boyer, "Brief History," 33).

127. Boyer, *When Time Shall Be No More,* 312–14.

128. David Corn, "Koresh's Children," *The Nation* 258 (23 May 1994): 690.

Chapter 5: Uncle Sam's Land

1. "39 Dead in Mass Suicide," *USA Today,* 27 March 1997; "Leader Believed in Space Aliens and Apocalypse," *New York Times,* national ed., 28 March 1997.

2. "Heaven's Gate Fit In with New Mexico's Offbeat Style," *New York Times,* national ed., 31 March 1997.

3. "Tapes Left by 39 in Cult Suicide Suggest Comet Was Sign to Die," *New York Times,* national ed., 28 March 1997; "On the Furthest Fringes of Millenialism," *New York Times,* national ed., 28 March 1997.

4. Carol Weisbrod, "*Reynolds v. United States* 98 U.S. (8 Otto) 145 (1879)," in *Religion and American Law: An Encyclopedia,* ed. Paul Finkelman, 417–21 (New York: Garland, 2000), 421.

5. Sydney E. Ahlstrom, *A Religious History of the American People* (New Haven, Conn.: Yale University Press, 1972), 508.

6. "Multiple Wives—and Fears," *Dallas Morning News,* 15 August 2004.

7. Ibid.

8. Ahlstrom, *Religious History,* 4–5, 13; Catherine L. Albanese, *America: Religions and Religion,* 2d ed. (Belmont, Calif.: Wadsworth, 1992), 9; Alexis de Tocqueville, *Democracy in America,* trans. Henry Reeve, ed. Phillips Bradley, 2 vols. (New York: Knopf, 1945), 1:303.

9. Weisbrod, "*Reynolds v. United States,*" 418.

★

INDEX

TODD M. KERSTETTER is an associate professor of history at Texas Christian University. His work has appeared in *Duke Magazine, Western Historical Quarterly, American Journalism, Great Plains Quarterly,* and *Nebraska History.*